BAKE ANIME

BAKE

75 SWEET RECIPES
Spotted in—and Inspired by—
Your Favorite Anime

ANIME

EMILY J. BUSHMAN

SIMON ELEMENT

NEW YORK   LONDON   TORONTO   SYDNEY   NEW DELHI

SIMON
ELEMENT

An Imprint of Simon & Schuster, Inc.
1230 Avenue of the Americas
New York, NY 10020

First Simon Element hardcover edition November 2022

SIMON ELEMENT is a trademark of Simon & Schuster, Inc.

For information about special discounts for bulk purchases, please contact Simon & Schuster Special Sales at 1-866-506-1949 or business@simonandschuster.com.

The Simon & Schuster Speakers Bureau can bring authors to your live event. For more information or to book an event, contact the Simon & Schuster Speakers Bureau at 1-866-248-3049 or visit our website at www.simonspeakers.com.

Interior design by Matt Ryan
Illustrations by Nero Hamaoui

Manufactured in China

10 9 8 7 6 5 4 3 2 1

Library of Congress Cataloging-in-Publication Data

Names: Bushman, Emily J., author.
Title: Bake anime : 75 sweet recipes inspired by—and spotted in—your favorite anime / Emily J. Bushman.
Description: First Simon Element hardcover edition. | New York : Simon Element, [2022] | Includes index.
Identifiers: LCCN 2021053264 (print) | LCCN 2021053265 (ebook) | ISBN 9781982186647 (hardcover) | ISBN 9781982186661 (ebook)
Subjects: LCSH: Baking—Japan. | Baking—Japan—Western influences. | Animated films—Japan | LCGFT: Cookbooks.
Classification: LCC TX765 .B945 2022 (print) | LCC TX765 (ebook) | DDC 641.81/5—dc23/eng/20211028
LC record available at https://lccn.loc.gov/2021053264
LC ebook record available at https://lccn.loc.gov/2021053265

ISBN 978-1-9821-8664-7
ISBN 978-1-9821-8666-1 (ebook)

To the amazing food illustrators
and animators in the industry,
for always inspiring me.

To Mom, Dad, Lizzy, Bex,
Sarah, and Hannah, for always
believing in me.

And finally, to all my
anime-loving friends, for giving
me someone to cook for.

CONTEN

TS

Silky-smooth whipped cream, luscious strawberries, and moist sponge cake. For me, this was my gateway drug into the enchanting world of anime desserts.

The first time I saw this perfect, delectable cake was during an episode of *Ouran High School Host Club.* In the scene, a character joyously munches his way through an entire picture-perfect strawberry shortcake.

Having grown up in America, the only strawberry shortcake I'd ever known consisted of jammy strawberries on a stout, close-crumbed biscuit with a dollop of whipped cream. Perfectly acceptable. But *anime strawberry shortcake*, that was something else. The cute, layered symmetry promised perfection. The thick, fluffy whipped cream promised to melt on my tongue. The perfectly ripe strawberries promised a sweet bite with every forkful of cake. It was a visual masterpiece—one I desperately longed to taste.

As a child, I was obsessed with anime. It offered a fun entry point into Japanese culture at large, a culture I loved and admired early on. I read manga religiously and watched whatever popped up on Toonami in sixth and seventh grades. It wasn't long before I asked my hairstylist to give me an "anime haircut" and begged my parents to take me out for Japanese food every night.

My father had lived in Japan for six months and left with a general disapproval of the food (he felt it was too bland), so he always vetoed my needy restaurant requests. My mother had lived in Japan for about a year, as well. She was concerned about my sudden and all-encompassing devotion to anime (she felt it was too risqué) and Japanese food, so she tried to distract me with bowls of Cinnamon Toast Crunch whenever I begged for sushi or teriyaki (it wasn't a *bad* trade-off). Of course, nothing really swayed me. For one of my birthdays, which fell during a holiday to Mexico that year, I insisted we had Japanese food for dinner. My parents commented on the absurdity of demanding Japanese food in Mexico City, but in the end, I got my gyoza.

As I grew older, my interests shifted from sampling food to making it. After a suggestion from the president of my college anime club, I started an anime food blog where I applied the cooking skills my mom and grandma taught me to learning Japanese cuisine. I threw myself into researching recipes. I wanted to know where dishes came from and what purpose they served in the anime they appeared in. I learned why Naruto ate so much ramen and why L from *Death Note* was obsessed with sweets. As I researched and tested recipes, I realized how food in anime was another way for audiences to understand Japanese culture (and these Japanese characters) more fully.

Desserts in particular show how Japanese history mingles with Japanese pop culture, so that's what I wanted to focus on in this book. I'd like to take you on a journey to explore what desserts look and taste like in Japan, how they give nuance to the country's culture, and, most important, how to make them yourself!

Before diving in, there are a few key things to know about Japanese sweets. Unlike American desserts, which can be decadent, rich, and sometimes over-the-top in their sweetness, Japanese desserts tend to be more refined, restrained, and, above all, aesthetically perfect. In order to learn more about why this is, I researched. There are only a few English-speaking sociologists and anthropologists who study the cultural whims of Japan, but you'd better believe I tracked them down. Something I learned from these scholars was that Japanese food and its ingredients are intrinsically tied with Japanese history.

"But wait," I can hear you saying, "isn't all food tied with the history of its home country?"

Good question, dear reader. If we're going to be obvious, yes. But allow me to dig deeper before you roll your eyes! While the islands of Japan have many natural resources, the popular sugarcane plant is not one of them. As a result, most traditional Japanese sweets rely on alternative sweetening ingredients, like beans and sweet potatoes. This remained the status quo until sugar imports became common enough that more people could afford them. When this happened, Japanese sweets changed forever, as did the social significance of sugar. You see, even with increased imports, you had to be pretty well-off to afford imported sugar on the regular, so this placed nontraditional desserts on a bit of a pedestal for the average citizen for some time. This dynamic *directly* translates into anime. Desserts in anime can be symbolic of the economic circumstances of the characters who are (or aren't) enjoying them.

One example is Setsuko from *Grave of the Fireflies*. The film follows the lives of two orphans, Setsuko and Seita, as they try to survive during World War II. Setsuko treasures a tin of <u>Sakuma Drops</u>, a popular candy of the time.

In the film, Setsuko's tin of Sakuma Drops becomes both a symbol of her hope for a return to normalcy and a reminder of what was lost to the war. The candy is also representative of the children's economic status: Before the war, they could afford small luxuries. As the war progressed, they began to starve because they couldn't afford a cup of rice, let alone candy. Setsuko clings to the tin long after the drops are gone, prizing it above her other belongings. To see her cherish it casts the poverty the children experience and the loss of their childhood into sharp focus. In the end, the various ways in which the tin is interwoven throughout the film's narrative show that the people who were hurt most by the war were those who were most innocent—everyday citizens who only wanted to enjoy the simple pleasures in life.

Sakuma Drops are a kind of dagashi, cheap multicolored hard candies comparable to penny candy in the US. Still available today, Sakuma Drops are sold in tin containers, partly to create an air of mystery regarding the treats inside.

Sweets are also *culturally* symbolic in anime, either due to the time period in which the anime takes place, or because they appear *outside* their time period. For example, a modern character who's eating a traditional Japanese sweet like ohagi (sticky-sweet rice balls covered in bean paste) or manju (a soft dough exterior filled with sweet bean paste) might be doing so because that character indulges in old-fashioned food to represent a fondness for tradition.

My favorite example of this is from *The Eccentric Family*, an anime that follows the lives of a tanuki family living in modern Kyoto, with special attention to the adventures of third son Yasaburo.

Tanuki are animals that have a larger-than-life role in Japanese folktales. In folklore, their predominant skill involves transforming themselves (and plant leaves) into different people or objects for the purpose of mischief. However, as time has passed and people, places, and ideas modernized, belief in tanuki and their magical properties, as well as other folktales, has dwindled.

Though the family lives in modern Kyoto and assumes human guises most of the time, they live in a shrine and often eat traditional foods. In particular, Yasaburo's mother, Tousen, snacks on yokan, a dessert made of red bean paste, agar, and sugar (you'll find a recipe for yokan on page 39). Red bean paste was traditionally eaten by Japanese monks as a replacement for meat, since meat was outlawed for much of Japan's history. As a result, quite a few desserts made to commemorate and celebrate important religious events contain red bean paste, which has a mild sweetness. Tousen snacking on yokan is a small nod to tradition, to a time when tanuki were regarded as having mythical properties. The juxtaposition of her eating yokan while instructing Yasaburo on how to navigate the modern world (and its modern problems) makes her choice of snack all the more impactful.

Another interesting fact I learned is that desserts in Japan tend to be more closely associated with women than with men, so when we see dessert in anime, it sometimes informs us about the social status and social view of the characters. If a male character is overindulging in sweets, he's defying cultural and societal expectations. This can be purposeful—in some cases, the character has no problem flaunting these unwritten rules of society, and in doing so, sets themselves up to be formidable in their own right. Honey from *Ouran High School Host Club* is a great representation of this. He purposely indulges in sweets because he made a decision to make himself happy rather than try to live up to the impossible expectations of his family. It's empowering for him to acknowledge the importance of his own preferences, and this lets audiences know that they, too, shouldn't hurt themselves to try to make others happy. In other cases, a male character's association with dessert exposes a "weakness"—a longing for sweets can be seen as quirky or a little off-putting, indicative of someone being a mushy romantic or embarrassingly undisciplined and overemotional.

It's important to remember that *anyone* can enjoy sweets, no matter what others may think of them. After all, almost everyone can appreciate good food (my condolences to anyone who suffers from loss in taste, truly), and it shouldn't be a sin to have excellent taste. Nonetheless, the stereotype occasionally persists in Japan. "Manly" foods tend toward the savory or the spicy, while "girly" foods tend toward the sweet. Luckily for me, I don't care what anyone thinks about my eating habits (in

America or Japan), so I've never held back when it comes to trying new things. We could get into the gender politics of this, but let's just . . . stick to the desserts.

Anyway, many years after I first dreamed of eating Japanese strawberry shortcake, I finally got the chance to have a real bite. I was twenty and in Japan for what would be the first of many visits. Underneath the train station next to my hotel was a food store that had a cake shop, each slice beautifully coiffed with swirls of cream, perfect globules of fruit, and delicate chocolate shavings. The thin layers of acetate that carefully sealed the moisture into each slice shone beautifully under the lights. The cakes gleamed like jewels in a case.

I couldn't wait. My plastic fork cut through the airy sponge cake easily, taking a chunk of strawberry with it. I felt shivers down my spine. I was finally tasting the cake I'd enviously watched my favorite characters gobble down for years: this was it! I was ready for my world to be rocked. As I chewed and chewed, I realized something truly soul wrenching.

It wasn't very good.

While it was clear that this was visually the same perfect-looking cake I'd admired for so long, it just didn't live up to my expectations at all. The cream was bland, the strawberry was a little too tart, and the sponge cake was a smidge too dry. To be honest, I was devastated. It wasn't that the cake was made incorrectly— it was just that Japanese desserts are usually lighter and less sweet than the American desserts I was accustomed to.

This disappointment would influence my methodology around cooking anime food. I decided that I cared less about making just visually perfect replicas of recipes: it was now my goal to, yes, try to make the food look as gorgeous as in the anime, but *also* make it absolutely scrumptious. I moved to Tokyo to get my hands on the best and most authentic ingredients and learned from locals how to re-create and honor some of these famous desserts. I also allowed myself to make occasional alterations to ingredients so I could get the sweetness I longed for.

This book is a collection of my favorite recipes, all based on animated renderings. Where my adaptation won't interfere with traditional flavors or techniques, I've changed a few ingredients to suit my American-influenced kitchen and tastes. I've organized the book so that our foray into the vast world of Japanese sweets is separated by influence. The first section covers traditional Japanese sweets, while the second covers non-Japanese and Western sweets popular in Japan. The third offers my own creative, whimsical melding of Japanese animation with Western-style desserts; this results in treats that aren't necessarily found *in* anime but are inspired by many popular animes' colors, patterns, characters, and themes.

Along with the recipes, I'll share some of my favorite facts about Japan's long and rich history with sugar and desserts, offer insights on what certain dishes might represent, and investigate how these representations impact the anime itself and the characters who eat them.

A Sugar Lover's Pantry

There's no enterprise more enjoyable than discovering the foods of another culture, especially when you can go to a store dedicated to that cuisine. Whether it's the meat and cheese section of an Italian neighborhood market or the fish section of my local Japanese grocery store, I've always been thrilled by the exploratory opportunity of it all. Visit your nearest Asian or Japanese grocery store and walk through the aisles to see if there are items you'd like to sample. Look up ingredients to learn what they're used for. At the very best, you'll have some kind of meet-cute, find your soul mate, and fall in love. But more likely, you'll walk out with a few new ingredients you can experiment with at home, as well as (hopefully) a deepened appreciation for a novel cuisine and its ingredients.

I've put together a handy list of the diverse ingredients that crop up in this book. If, however, you're looking to embark on a dessert journey and go all in with this book, scan this list to learn more about some of the special, recurring items needed for many of the recipes in the book. If your heart is set on making a particular recipe, remember to look over the ingredient list beforehand to see what you'll need.

ACTIVATED CHARCOAL POWDER: If you want to tint your food black naturally, this is the stuff to use. It's safe to eat and nontoxic.

AGAR POWDER: A vegetarian substitute for powdered gelatin, derived from red algae. It causes liquid to gel, producing a jiggly effect.

ANKO: Red bean paste. There are different types, all of them sweet and used in sweet recipes. Tsubuan is whole red bean paste, tsubushian is crushed red bean paste, and koshian is smooth red bean paste.

BUTTERFLY PEA EXTRACT: A natural blue colorant derived from the butterfly pea plant that turns purple when exposed to an acid (like lemon juice).

CANDY MELTS CANDY: A vegetable oil–based candy that melts easily for coating desserts and other applications, ideal for the baker who doesn't want to bother with tempering chocolate.

CHESTNUT PASTE: A sweet paste made from chestnuts. This can be purchased online if you can't find it in local stores.

COCOA POWDER: Unsweetened cocoa powder is a common baking ingredient. Dutch-process cocoa powder is a bit more unusual; this alkalized cocoa powder produces a darker chocolate product with a slightly more mellow flavor.

DAIKON: A type of mild radish that's long, thick, cylindrical, and white.

DANGOKO: Japanese rice dumpling flour blend (non-glutinous rice flour plus glutinous rice flour) specifically packaged to be used for dumplings like dango.

GEL FOOD COLORING: Similar to liquid food dye, gel food coloring produces vivid colors.

GOLD LEAF: Safe to ingest, this is gold that has been finely pounded to be thinner than paper-thin.

MATCHA: Green tea powder. This powdered tea is used often, both as a beverage and as an ingredient to flavor desserts.

JOSHINKO: Non-glutinous rice flour made from milled Japanese short-grain rice. Products made with joshinko tend to be chewy and doughy.

KINAKO: Roasted soybean flour. Golden tan in color, with a nutty taste.

KIRIMOCHI: A shelf-stable, precut rice cake that puffs up when toasted.

KUROMITSU: Black sugar syrup (literally "black honey"), similar in taste to molasses but a bit thinner and milder.

KURI KANRONI: Chestnuts in heavy syrup.

LADYFINGERS: Sweet biscuits roughly shaped like fingers. These are dry cookies that are good for absorbing liquids in desserts.

LOQUATS: A sweet and slightly tart fruit with citrusy notes.

MERINGUE POWDER: Often used to make royal icing, this is a powder made from egg whites (and other things) that acts as a stabilizer and thickener.

MIKAN ORANGES: Also called satsumas, mikan oranges are a type of mandarin orange.

MIRIN: Rice wine with a low alcohol content and high sugar content.

MOCHI GOME: Sticky glutinous rice used in sweets.

MONAKA SHELLS: Rice wafers pressed into pleasing shapes that, when paired together, make little 3D forms.

PERILLA LEAVES: A popular herb that tastes faintly of grass and anise. Sometimes referred to as sesame leaves, though they aren't actually from the same plant.

POCKY: Cookie sticks coated with chocolate; a popular Japanese snack food.

ROSE WATER: Flavoring made by steeping rose petals in water.

SAKE: Japanese alcohol made from fermented rice. Avoid any sake labeled "cooking sake," to which salt has been added to make it unpalatable on its own.

SATSUMAIMO: Japanese sweet potato.

SHIRATAMAKO: A type of glutinous rice flour (sweet rice flour) made from Japanese glutinous short-grain rice. It's rather chunky in the package but results in an elastic, chewy texture. Despite the term "glutinous," it's gluten-free.

SHIROAN: White bean paste. Similar to anko, but with a milder taste; especially pleasant for anyone who doesn't like the strong flavor of anko.

UMEBOSHI: Often translated as "salted Japanese plums," umeboshi are a popular Japanese pickle that is both very sour and sweet.

UME PLUM VINEGAR/UMEBOSHI VINEGAR: The brine from pickling Japanese plums (ume), mixed with salt and beefsteak (red shiso) leaves, the latter of which gives the vinegar its distinctive red appearance. It adds a vinegary, fruity punch to salads, meats, grains, and other dishes.

WARABI MOCHIKO: Bracken flour, also known as bracken starch. Produces a chewy confection. Can be replaced with tapioca starch or potato starch, but the resulting texture won't be quite the same.

Tools of the Trade

When it comes to tools for the kitchen, I've always regarded new purchases with skepticism. After all, I'm on a budget—the last thing I need is a new piece of equipment that turns out to be useful only once in a blue moon. While these kinds of tools can sometimes add ease to a recipe, if a kitchen device only has one use, I normally avoid buying it because my teeny-tiny Japanese kitchen doesn't have much storage for such equipment. However, for some of the recipes in this book, there *are* single-use tools that absolutely cannot be avoided. Review the list of items here for the ones I think will serve you well for most recipes and purchase what you like. Then check the list of items that have much more specific uses in the kitchen and buy what you need to make that recipe you're dying to try.

Good, All-Around Useful Tools

BENCH SCRAPER: A handheld tool useful for scraping up dough or flour that's stuck to your counter.

CHEF'S KNIFE: Usually 8 to 10 inches long, this knife is perfect for most kitchen cutting tasks.

CLOTH DISH TOWELS: These make cleaning up quick, easy, and environmentally friendly. Any dish towel will be a great asset in the kitchen. Try to get plain white towels without any texture or patterns.

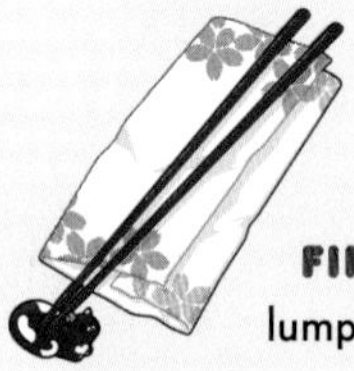

COOKING CHOPSTICKS OR TONGS: Handy for plating food and moving things easily between pans.

FINE-MESH STRAINER: Good for straining lumps and bumps out of sauces and batters.

INFRARED THERMOMETER: When making desserts, a good thermometer is an invaluable tool. Infrared thermometers are the easiest to use in the kitchen to get a quick read on your candies and cakes.

OFFSET SPATULA: A spatula that's perfect for frosting cakes due to the fact that it's offset, so your knuckles won't drag in the frosting.

PALETTE KNIFE: Similar to an offset spatula but not offset, which might seem pointless, but I find that small palette knives are awesome for helping to release cakes from tins or to do small frosting work without leaving weird lines like butter knives sometimes do.

PARCHMENT PAPER: Paper useful for lining pans and molds to allow for easy release of delicate baked items. This has saved the life of my cakes more times than I can count.

PARING KNIFE: A shorter knife useful for cutting fruit and trimming away excess skin.

POTS AND PANS: A heavy-bottomed saucepan is a great addition to your kitchen, especially for desserts. A big pot for boiling water wouldn't go amiss here, either. An 8-inch round cake pan will be a big help for many of the cake recipes, and a 9 x 13-inch baking dish with high sides is always useful. A loaf pan (mine is 8 x 4 x 4 inches) will be useful for many of these recipes, as will an 8-inch square baking pan. Cupcake pans are useful even for projects that don't involve making cupcakes. Finally, a baking sheet or two can be used not only for cookies but also for making decorations or baking free-form desserts, or as a portable work surface.

RULER: A good old-fashioned measuring tool, useful for leveling cakes perfectly and for measuring dimensions of baking dishes.

SERRATED KNIFE: A nice, long one is perfect for slicing layers of cake, bread, or anything with a crumbed texture.

SKIMMER SPOON: A long-handled metal tool, the base of which ends in a wide, fine-mesh spoon, perfect for removing delicate things like balls of mochi from a pot of boiling water.

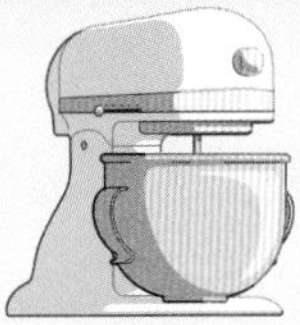

STAND MIXER OR HANDHELD MIXER: A stand mixer is always going to help you out in the kitchen, but if you don't have space or money for one, I find a handheld mixer to be just fine. I used a handheld mixer in all of these recipes.

Recipe-Specific Tools

BATTENBERG CAKE PAN: A baking pan characterized by its three horizontal dividers, which allow the baker to bake all the layers of a Battenberg cake at once, in the same pan. If you can't find one, you can use foil dividers to make two, three, or four separate wells in your cake pan.

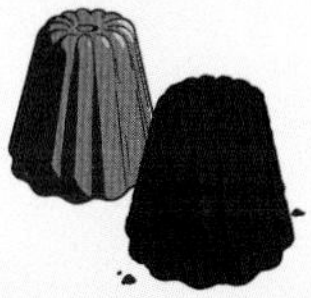

CANELÉ MOLD: Traditionally made of copper, this mold is used to produce the distinctive French pastry of the same name.

COOKIE CUTTERS: A set of round cutters gets a lot of use in my kitchen, but novelty shapes sometimes also come in handy for baking projects.

IMAGAWAYAKI PAN: Similar to a waffle iron and sometimes called an obanyaki pan, this is a stovetop mold that creates the oval imagawayaki shape.

JELLY-ROLL PAN: A long, shallow pan with sides used for making long, flat cakes to be filled and rolled up into logs. Slightly smaller than a baking sheet.

KITCHEN SCALE: Every once in a while, having a scale to measure out perfectly equal portions of dough is very handy.

MADELEINE PAN: A pan used to give madeleine cakes their distinctive, shell-like shape.

PIPING TIPS AND PASTRY BAGS: These are used together to produce frosting designs, pastry shapes, and perfect peaks of whipped cream.

PUDDING BASIN: A bowl with tall sides and a lipped top used for British puddings.

PUDDING CUPS: Usually made of metal, these are useful for making Japanese-style pudding.

SILICONE CAKE MOLD: A pliable mold good for baking cakes, or for using to make mirror cakes.

SILICONE SPHERE MOLD: A pliable mold good for making chocolate spheres.

SHAVED ICE MACHINE: Small, household-size machines are available. Getting one to make the Japanese treat kakigori is never a bad idea.

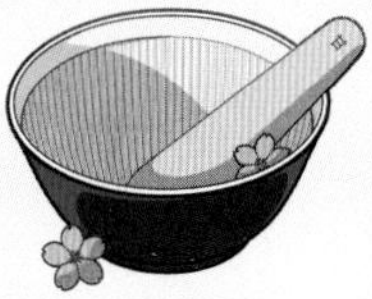

SURIBACHI AND SURIKOGI: A Japanese mortar and pestle that is great for grinding sesame seeds. A regular mortar and pestle or food processor will also do the trick.

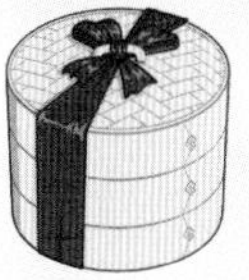

STEAMER BASKET: Made of bamboo and placed over a pot of boiling water, the steamer basket is perfect for cooking buns and other treats.

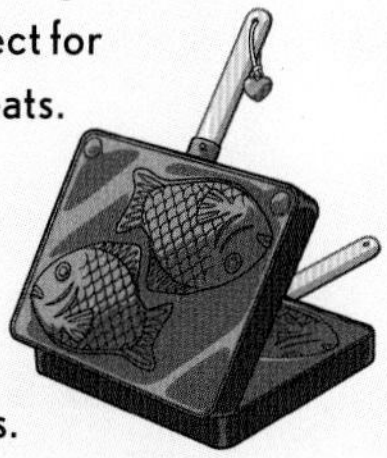

TAIYAKI PAN: Much like a waffle iron, a taiyaki pan is used to cook batter into those iconic fish shapes.

TART PAN: These come in various sizes. Whatever you buy, make sure they have a removable bottom for best results. These molds allow you to get that perfect fluted crust iconic to tarts with minimal fuss.

Japanese Desserts

Should you find yourself in Japan, you might be surprised by the number of Western sweets available. Convenience stores, train stations, and cafés are all rife with cakes and cookies that originated in Europe or America. Yet underneath all the dazzle of Western desserts is a no less astonishing abundance of traditional Japanese sweets. Japanese desserts tend to be fairly simple (often featuring bean paste) and generally less sweet than Western desserts. In fact, you might bite into a fresh, fluffy slice of castella or a piping-hot imagawayaki and be a little underwhelmed, especially if you're used to eating American levels of sugar.

But don't assume that less sweet means less tasty. Japanese desserts employ restraint in order to enhance the natural flavors of their ingredients, rather than overpower them. This approach has remained popular in Japan, so while many Japanese people appreciate Western treats, Japanese desserts stay in demand. For many, Japanese sweets are familiar reminders of childhood. As a result, Japanese hearts have continued to burn fiercely for traditional Japanese sweets.

Animators use this love to their advantage. Putting beloved food at the center of important moments—a conversation with a friend, as a quiet moment of indulgence, or as a snack during a shopping trip—is one of the easiest ways to build a connection between the audience and the characters. So, in the following pages, I've included a variety of recipes that (1) pop up in anime and (2) are either traditionally significant, culturally significant, or just plain tasty. Some of these are wagashi—traditional Japanese sweets usually enjoyed with a cup of tea—and some are dagashi—cheaper Japanese sweets and snack foods. These Japanese sweets and their nuanced take on flavor in desserts are integral to Japanese culture. With that in mind, I've tried to keep these recipes as faithful as possible. *Itadakimasu!*

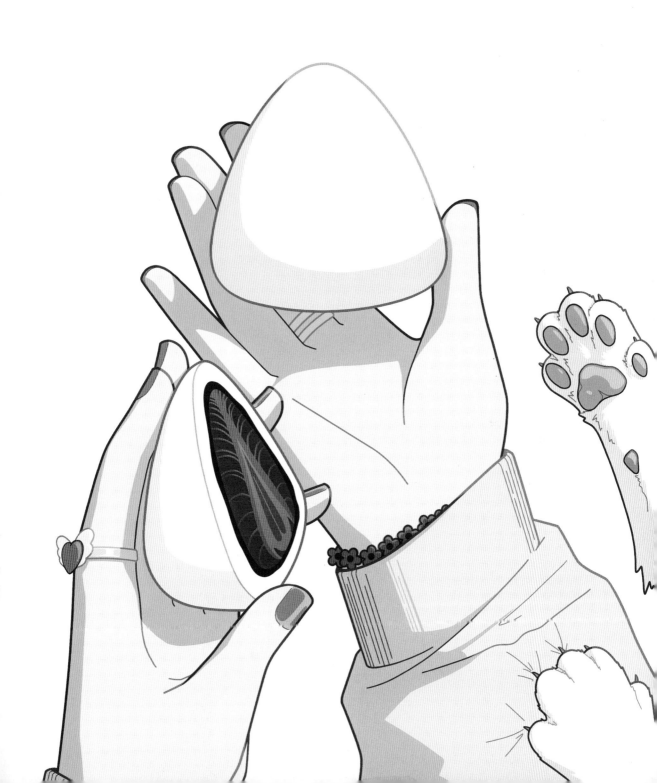

MARCH COMES IN LIKE A LION

ICHIGO DAIFUKU

March Comes in Like a Lion follows high schooler Rei Kiriyama and his friendship with the lively Kawamoto sisters and their grandfather. Rei is a loner who avoids his complicated family; instead, he uses his earnings as a professional shogi player to rent his own apartment. After a chance encounter with the Kawamoto sisters, however, Rei is soon welcomed into their family and becomes a frequent dinner guest.

In one episode, the Kawamoto sisters brainstorm a new variation of daifuku for the wagashi shop their grandfather owns. *Daifuku* refers broadly to a round mochi ball with a filling (usually red bean paste, although modern takes include fillings such as whipped cream, custard, or ice cream). While their grandfather is partial to ichigo daifuku (strawberry and bean paste mochi), the sisters convince him to make little mochi figures each filled with different-flavored bean pastes. As Rei watches them develop new products for the shop, he realizes a treat is never far off and that every hardship usually has a sweet silver lining.

30 MINUTES

MAKES 6 PIECES

DAIRY-FREE, GLUTEN-FREE, NUT-FREE, VEGAN

1 cup koshian (smooth red bean paste)

6 strawberries, hulled

½ cup potato starch

¾ cup shiratamako (sweet rice flour)

2 tablespoons sugar

⅔ cup water

1. Divide the koshian into 6 equal pieces. Cover each strawberry with koshian, coating them completely. Set the coated berries aside on plastic wrap or aluminum foil.

2. Spread half the potato starch over a plate so it evenly dusts the surface. Set aside.

3. In a microwavable bowl, whisk together the shiratamako and sugar until combined. Add the water and stir until the shiratamako mixture has completely dissolved. Cover the bowl tightly with plastic wrap and microwave on high for 1 minute, then stir thoroughly for 20 seconds. Cover the bowl with the plastic wrap and repeat; if the spatula starts to stick as you stir, run it under water to dampen the surface and prevent the mochi from clinging. Cover the bowl once more, microwave for a final 30 seconds, then stir the mixture one last time.

4. Pour the mochi mixture onto the plate with the potato starch and dust the remaining potato starch over the surface of the mochi. Using a bench scraper or knife, divide the mochi into 6 equal pieces. Allow to cool for about 5 minutes.

5. Take a piece of cooled mochi and spread it out into a flat disc in your hands. Put a koshian-coated strawberry in the center, pointed end down, then bring the sides of the mochi up to enclose the berry and pinch the edges to seal. Use your hands to round the mochi and shape it over the berry. Repeat to fill the remaining mochi.

6. Serve and enjoy. Eat within the day for best results!

RECIPE TIP: Depending on the brand you use, koshian can be a little goopy, which causes it to stick to your hands when you're trying to wrap it around the berries. If you find yourself struggling with this, pop the koshian in the freezer for about 30 minutes before using it.

SUBSTITUTION TIP: Strawberries not to your taste? Try a different fruit, or just go for a 100 percent bean paste filling.

FOOD FACT: While most types of wagashi were invented much further in the past, ichigo daifuku was invented in the '80s and is therefore a relatively new form of wagashi!

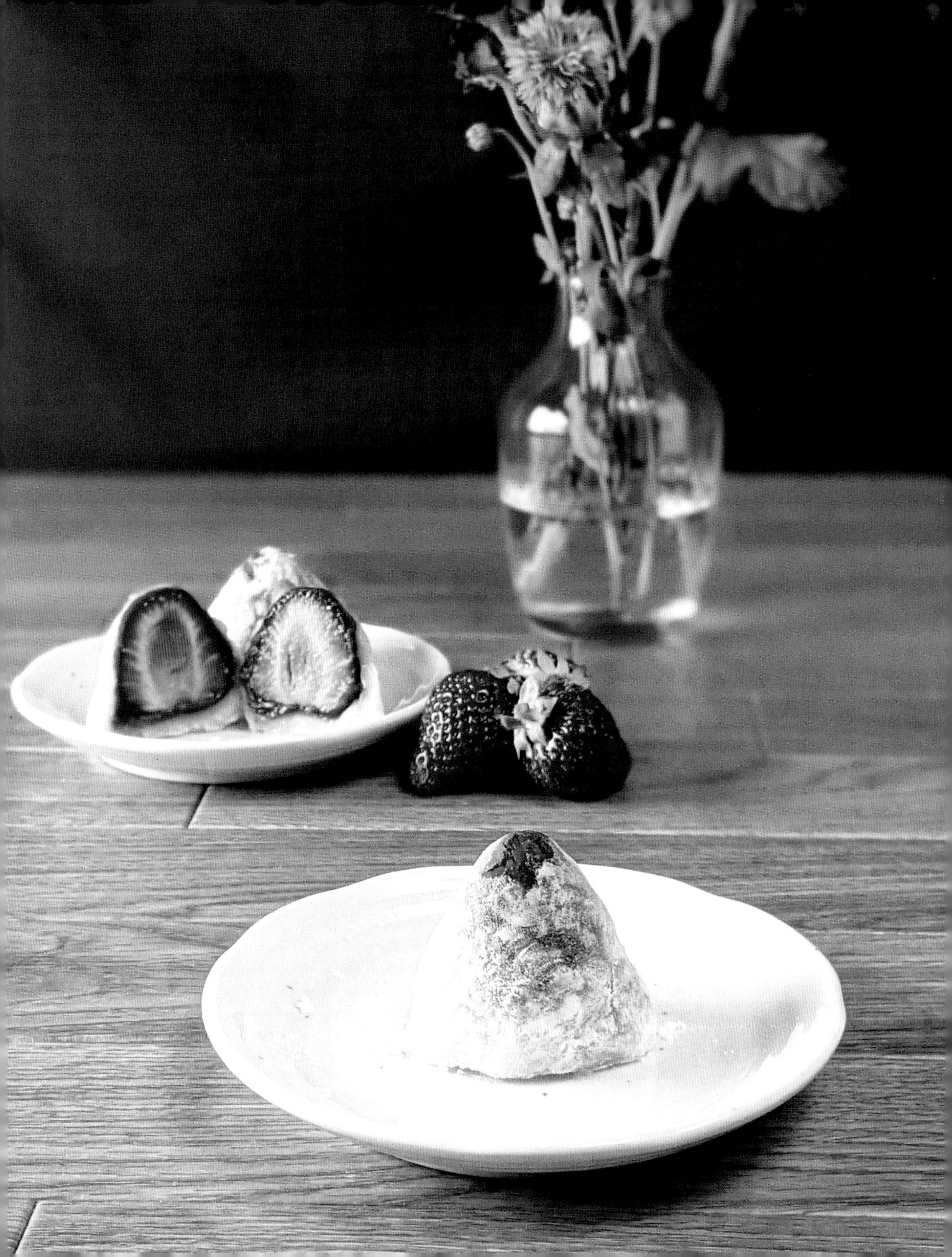

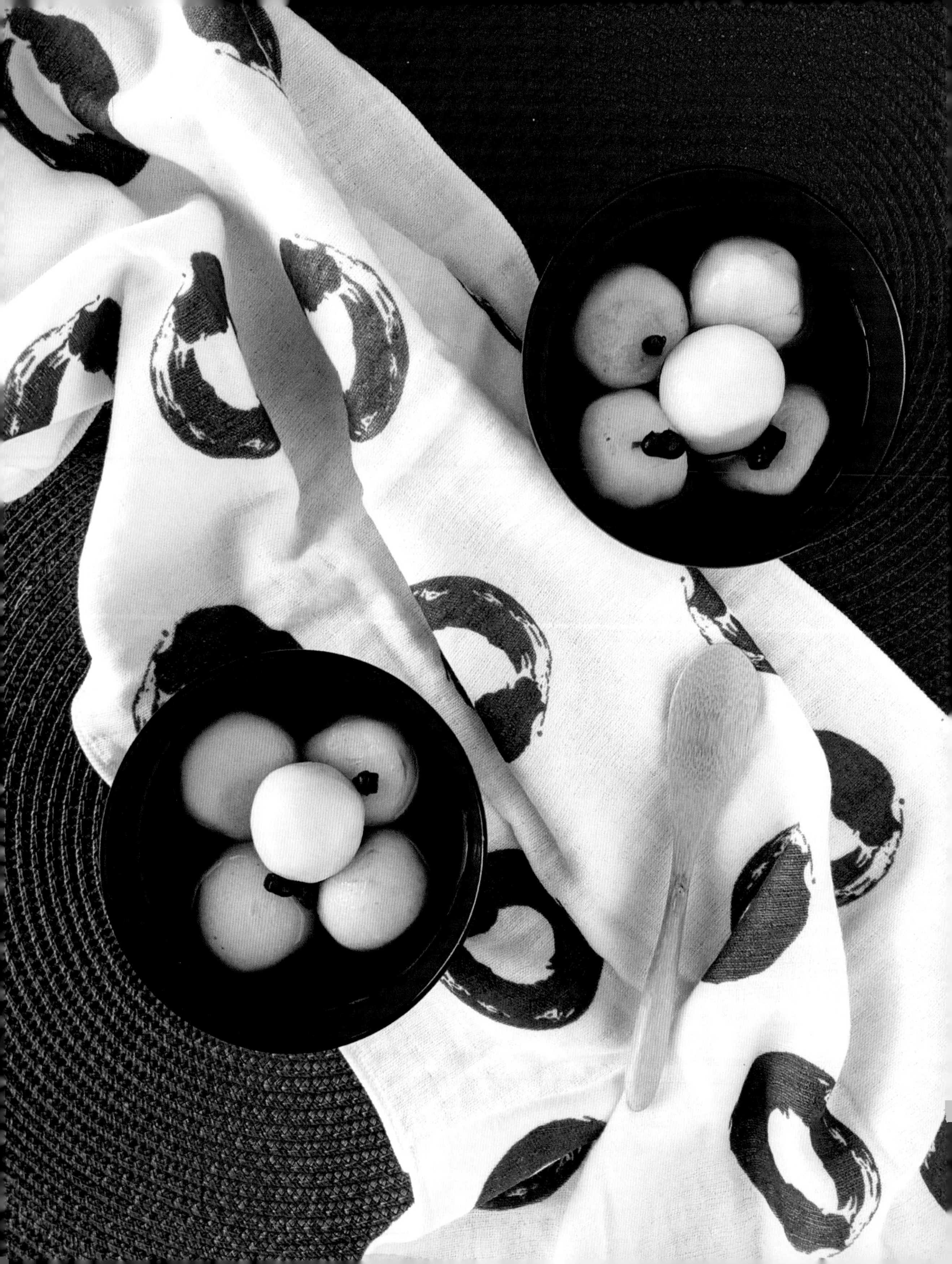

MARCH COMES IN LIKE A LION

OSHIRUKO

Hina Kawamoto considers her future as she makes a riff on oshiruko. Should she pursue wagashi-making as a career, or does she only want to avoid difficult schoolwork? As she contemplates, she and her sisters design a new food item to serve at a summer festival.

The sisters make shiratama dango served in soup. They sample different dipping sauces to use, such as the more traditional bean paste soup (oshiruko), green tea syrup, and plum syrup. This recipe is for shiratama dumplings and a red bean soup base. If you have other syrups you'd like to try, experiment and find one you like. Served cold, this recipe will become a summer go-to for a light, easy treat. Served warm, it'll be a winter staple to chase away any weather-induced chills.

1 HOUR

SERVES 2

DAIRY-FREE, GLUTEN-FREE, NUT-FREE, VEGAN

SUBSTITUTION TIP: You can use koshian instead of tsubuan. I personally like the texture of the beans in this soup, as it pairs nicely with the smooth mochi, but go with what you want!

⅓ cup shiratamako (sweet rice flour)

½ teaspoon sugar

1 cup plus 3 tablespoons water

¾ cup tsubuan (whole red bean paste)

1. Place the shiratamako and sugar in a small bowl. Add 2 tablespoons of the water, then stir to combine. The dough should become soft and pliable; it should be delicate and soft, like an earlobe. If the dough still feels a little crumbly and dry, stir in another tablespoon of water.

2. When the dough is the proper consistency, divide it into 10 equal pieces. Roll each piece into a ball.

3. Bring a pot of water to boil. Fill a bowl with ice and water and set it nearby.

4. When the water comes to a boil, stir it so it swirls around the pot, then drop in the dumplings one at a time. Cook, nudging the dumplings every 30 seconds to keep them from sticking to the bottom of the pot, until they float to the surface, 3 to 4 minutes, then cook for 1 minute more. Use a skimmer or slotted spoon to transfer them to the ice bath to cool. When cooled, transfer the dumplings to a plate and set aside.

5. Stir together the remaining 1 cup water and the tsubuan in a small saucepan. Heat over medium heat until the soup froths and becomes foamy at the edges of the pan, then remove the pot from the heat.

6. Divide the oshiruko soup between two bowls and add 5 dumplings to each bowl. Enjoy warm or let cool slightly before chilling in the fridge to eat later as a cold dessert.

SAMURAI CHAMPLOO

MITARASHI DANGO

Records of dango, a dumpling made out of different rice flours, go back as far as the tenth century! Mitarashi dango is said to be named after mitarashi, a well placed in front of a shrine that bubbles with fresh water. In Japan, dango are still used as offerings to gods to show respect, especially during festivals. So when Fuu, one of the protagonists of *Samurai Champloo*, offers up one hundred dango to a man named Mugen in exchange for his aid in dispatching rude customers from her dumpling shop, you can see the irony. She makes an offering to Mugen, who is not a god at all but rather just a renegade with a no-nonsese attitude who's Fuu's best hope for help.

Traditionally, the dango are made with five round dumplings on a skewer, toasted and brushed with soy sauce syrup. Their taste is complex, just like Fuu, Mugen, and Jin's relationship—a little salty, a little sweet, and just a tiny bit of bitter char. As they set forth to find Fuu's mystery samurai "who smells of sunflowers," dango are the perfect fortifying snack to get them started. Unlike the face of the man Fuu seeks, the taste of these treats is unforgettable.

1 HOUR

MAKES **5 SKEWERS (15 DANGO)**

SPECIAL EQUIPMENT: **5 WOODEN SKEWERS**

DAIRY-FREE, GLUTEN-FREE, NUT-FREE, VEGAN

FOOD FACT: A popular variant of dango is hanami dango, which are three different-colored (green, pink, and white) dango pieces on a skewer. These are traditionally seen in the springtime in Japan, and the colors of the dango reflect the beautiful cherry blossom flowers.

FOR THE DANGO

$1\frac{1}{4}$ cups dangoko (a mix of glutinous and non-glutinous rice flours), or $\frac{2}{3}$ cup joshinko (non-glutinous rice flour) plus $\frac{3}{4}$ cup shiratamako (glutinous rice flour)

$\frac{2}{3}$ cup water

Wooden skewers

FOR THE SOY SAUCE SYRUP

3 tablespoons sugar

2 tablespoons gluten-free soy sauce

2 tablespoons mirin (rice wine)

$\frac{2}{3}$ cup water

2 tablespoons potato starch

1. Make the dango: In a medium bowl, combine the dangoko and all but about 2 tablespoons of the water and mix with your hands until the dough becomes soft, like an earlobe. Add the reserved 2 tablespoons water only if the dough feels a little dry and crumbly. The dough shouldn't be sticky at all.

2. Divide the dough into 15 equal pieces. Roll each piece into a ball and set aside.

3. Bring a pot of water to a boil. Fill a bowl with ice and water and set it nearby.

4. When the water comes to a boil, stir it so it swirls around the pot, then drop in half the dango. Cook, nudging them every 30 seconds so they don't stick to the bottom of the pot, until they float to the surface, 3 to 5 minutes, then cook for 1 minute more. Use a skimmer or slotted spoon to transfer them to the ice bath to cool. Repeat to cook and cool the second batch of dango.

5. Thread 3 cooled dango onto each wooden skewer. If desired, turn on the broiler, place the dango on a baking sheet, and crisp the dango under the broiler until lightly charred, 30 seconds to 1 minute (or skip the broiler and char over a lit burner on your gas stovetop). This adds both color and flavor, but please use an abundance of caution! Set the skewers on a serving plate and set aside.

6. Make the soy sauce syrup: Whisk together the sugar, soy sauce, mirin, water, and potato starch in a medium saucepan to combine. Cook over medium-high heat, stirring continuously as the mixture heats. Patches of it will start to go clear—this is a sign that it's time to take it off the heat. It'll boil and go clear very quickly, so remove the pot from the heat as soon as you see the signs. Allow the sauce to cool before serving.

7. When you're ready to eat, spoon the sauce over the dango and serve. Best eaten the same day they're made.

VARIATION TIP:
If you'd like to make hanami dango instead, split the dango dough into thirds. Use matcha powder to color one-third green and powdered dehydrated strawberries or red food coloring to color another third pink; the remaining dough should be kept white. Roll into balls and cook as directed in the recipe, then thread one dango of each color onto each skewer and serve (omit the sauce from the original recipe).

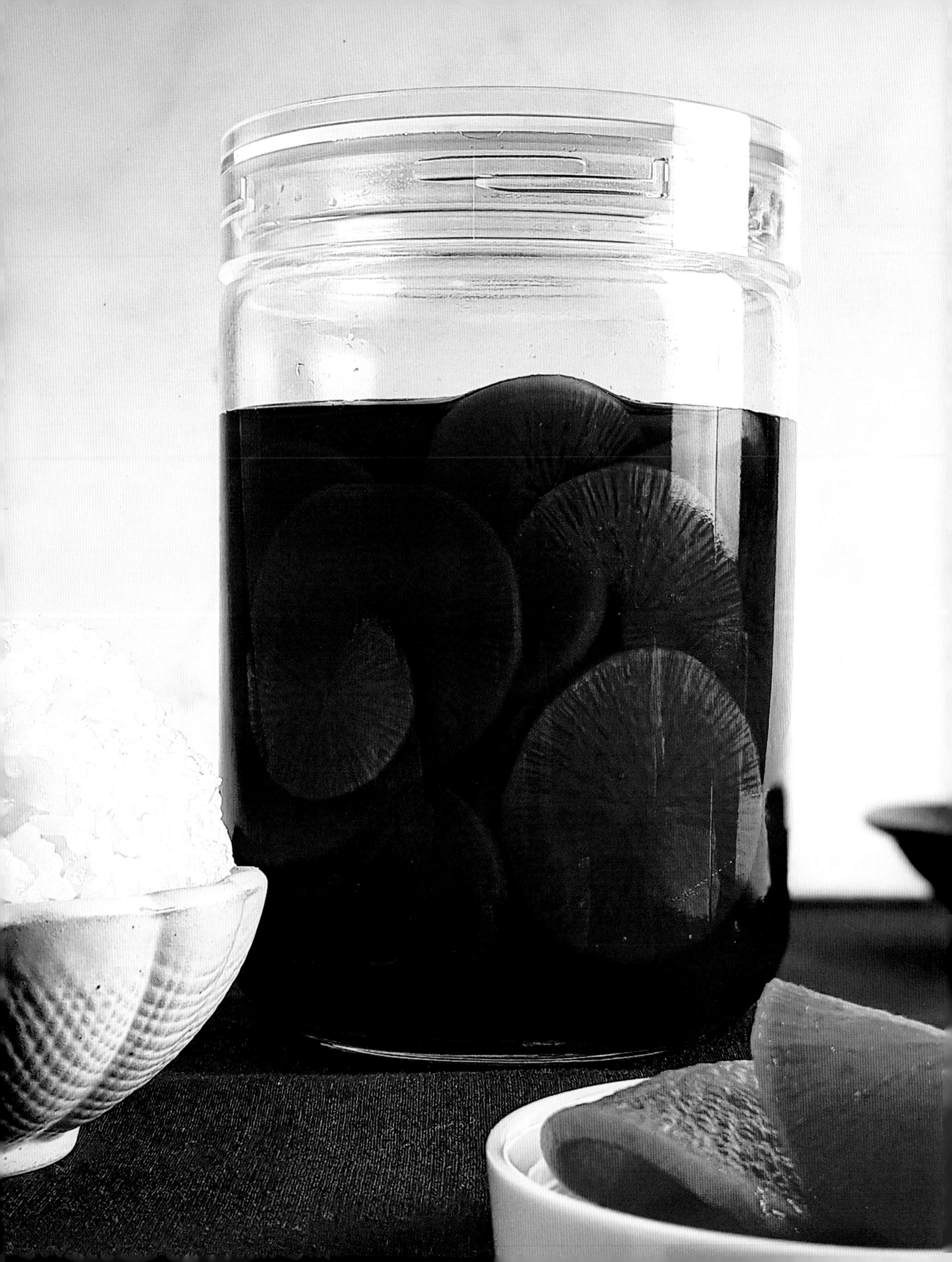

DAGASHI KASHI

SAKURA DAIKON

Hotaru's quest to get Kokonotsu to take over the family dagashi shop also serves as an important narrative technique for the audience. In trying to convince Kokonotsu, Hotaru shares her intense love for dagashi. In one episode, she gleefully opens a package of sakura daikon and wastes no time explaining that these treats are multifaceted—they can be eaten alone as a sweet, or paired with rice.

Sakura daikon are an interesting dagashi for this reason. If you look at the ingredients, they don't really scream *sweet*. Daikon is a type of vegetable, after all. However, when removed from the brine, they have a tasty and refreshing salty-sweet quality. If you like sweet pickles, you're going to love these! The color of this snack is out of this world, too. The umeboshi vinegar is colored with beefsteak (red perilla) leaves and lends the daikon a gorgeous magenta tone. Shove those sweet dill pickles aside and have a few of these—you'll never look back.

20 MINUTES PLUS 12 HOURS REFRIGERATION TIME

MAKES 1 JAR

DAIRY-FREE, GLUTEN-FREE, NUT-FREE, VEGAN

SERVING TIP: For extra fun, try adding these to sandwiches, serving them alongside Japanese curry, or using them in salads to bring some punchy flavors to your favorite dishes.

STORAGE TIP: These pickles will keep in the fridge for up to a month.

1 (8-inch) daikon radish

1 tablespoon kosher salt

2 cups rice vinegar

1 cup umeboshi vinegar

1 cup sugar

1. Peel the daikon and sprinkle with the salt, then set aside on a plate for 10 minutes to draw out moisture.

2. Pat the daikon dry with a paper towel and wipe off as much salt as you can. Using a mandoline or knife, thinly slice the daikon into discs.

3. Combine the daikon slices, rice vinegar, umeboshi vinegar, and sugar in a jar. Stir until the sugar has dissolved, then cover the jar and refrigerate for 12 hours.

4. Serve as a snack (with rice, if you wish) and enjoy.

MONAKA

The defining features of monaka are the crisp patterned rice crackers that sandwich the luxurious filling. This is probably why Soma from *Food Wars!* opted to use a traditional monaka shell not as a container for a sweet but as a vehicle for a savory appetizer in the BLUE (Bishoku Leading Under-25 Entrance) cooking competition. The appetizer subverts the judges' expectations—two wafer-thin shells containing seasoned monkfish liver? The contrast of the light shell against the flavor-packed fish is enough to send the judges to heaven!

Traditionally, monaka is filled with bean paste or something similar, and while the shells are a little more difficult to make at home, they can be ordered online. I've included a spin on the usual bean paste filling, inspired by monaka I found right here in Japan. Bean paste is combined with umeboshi and perilla to create a sweet filling that's lightened by the tartness of plum and made complex by the minty licorice perilla. If that doesn't appeal to you, stick to the more usual bean paste, or use the monaka shell in a savory way as Soma did. The choices are endless—have fun experimenting!

20 MINUTES

MAKES **4 PIECES**

DAIRY-FREE, GLUTEN-FREE (IF MONAKA SHELLS ARE 100 PERCENT RICE-BASED), **NUT-FREE, VEGAN**

½ cup koshian (smooth red bean paste)

1 umeboshi (Japanese pickled plum), pitted and finely chopped

1 fresh perilla leaf

8 monaka shells

1. Place the koshian in a bowl. Add the umeboshi and mix thoroughly.
2. Roll the perilla leaf tightly into a cigar shape and cut it crosswise into thin strips.
3. Take one monaka shell and fill it with some of the koshian-plum mixture. Do the same with another shell. Sprinkle one half with perilla, then sandwich the two shells together. Repeat to fill and sandwich all the shells.
4. Serve immediately! Monaka shells are delicate and thin and will absorb moisture quickly.

RECIPE TIP:
Premade monaka shells can be purchased online, but if that doesn't appeal to you, you can make them like Soma did: Whip up a batter using 3 tablespoons shiratamako, 2 tablespoons cornstarch, and 3 tablespoons water. Sandwich a dollop of the batter between two silicone or aluminum cupcake liners and bake in a preheated 475°F oven for about 12 minutes, until crisp.

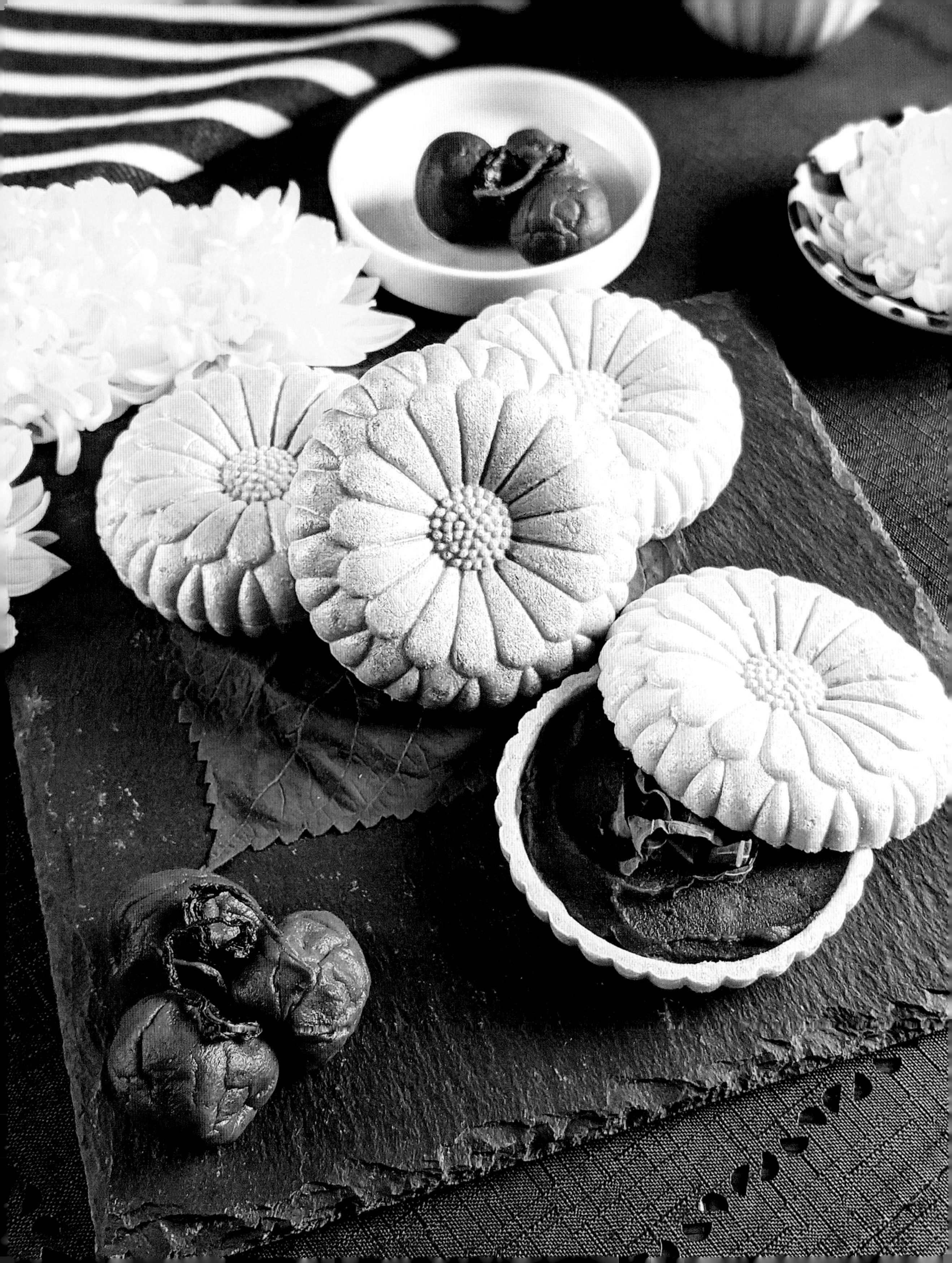

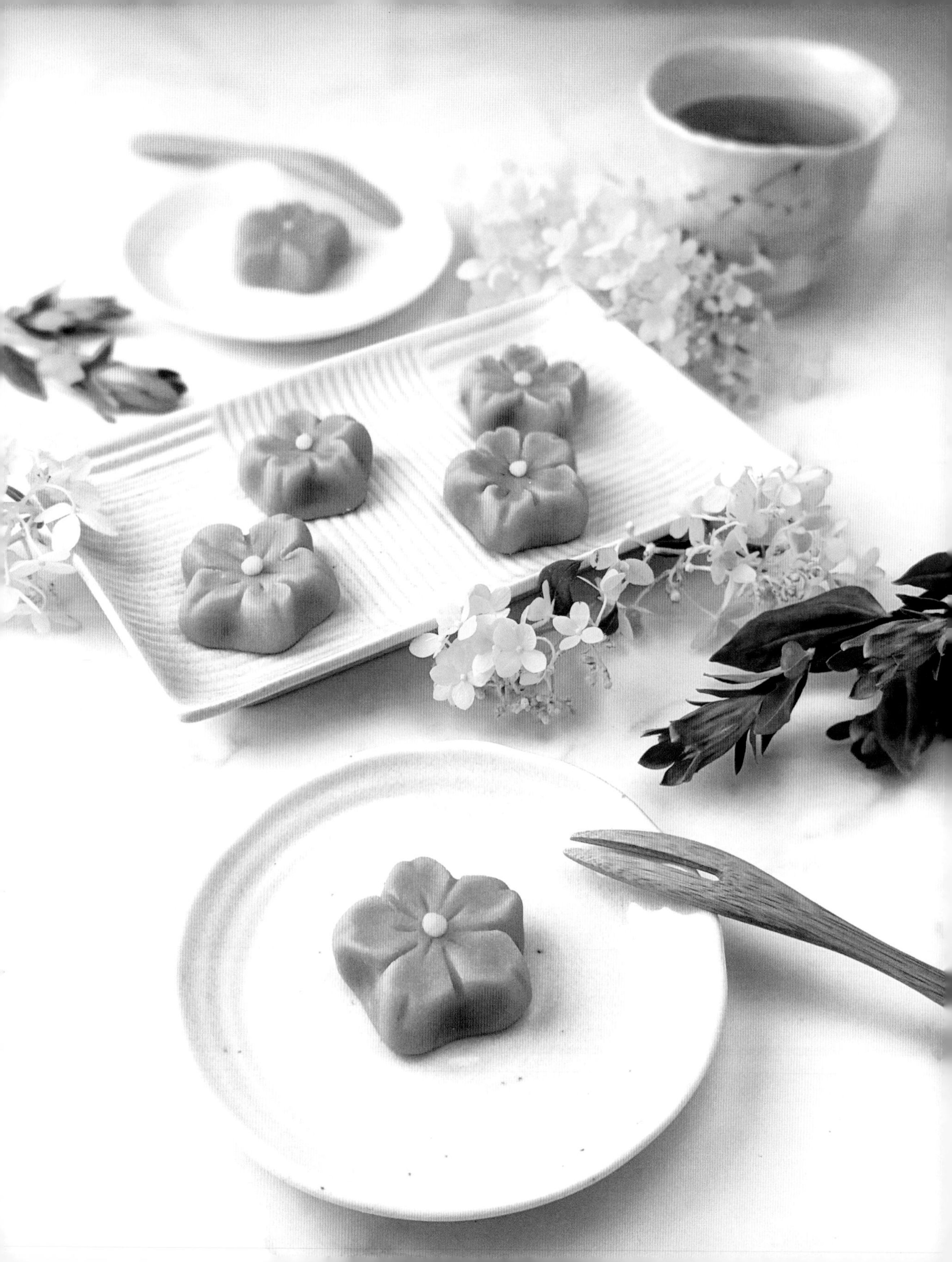

CARDCAPTOR SAKURA: CLEAR CARD

NERIKIRI

1 HOUR 30 MINUTES

MAKES 10 PIECES

DAIRY-FREE, GLUTEN-FREE, NUT-FREE, VEGAN

Cardcaptor Sakura is a story about one girl's mission to put the world to rights. Her journey highlights a unique kind of girl power: looking cute while being tough and overcoming obstacles. Sakura's love for cooking, eating sweets, and being adorable doesn't mean she's weak or childish—it just means she likes to eat good things and save the day with style.

One of the more traditional Japanese sweets that pops up in the anime is nerikiri. In the age of social media, these are the ultimate post-worthy desserts. The art and tradition of nerikiri making comes from the Edo period. Basically, this dessert is *old*, but it's remained extremely popular as a teatime treat. The shape, color, and fillings change depending on the season, and the designs can get complicated. Sakura shares her name with the Japanese cherry blossom, which produces star-shaped, pastel-pink flowers every spring. Because of this, we'll be shaping these nerikiri into sakura blossoms. As you become comfortable handling the dough, feel free to experiment with other shapes and colors. While the shaping process can take time and practice, once you get the hang of it, you'll never fail to impress!

Because of the beautiful nature of the dish and the simplicity of the recipe, it's important that your measurements are precise so each final piece looks the same. With this in mind, I recommend using a kitchen scale to portion the dough equally. Keep in mind that the soft nerikiri will take on the impression of the cloth it's shaped on, so use a dish towel with a smooth weave.

RECIPE TIPS: Keeping your hands dry and dusted with a light layer of cornstarch will help you during the molding process, especially if you have warm hands.

SUBSTITUTION TIP: Not interested in koshian as a filling? Substitute shiroan and flavor it with powdered freeze-dried strawberries or raspberries. Shiroan has a much milder flavor and takes on flavorings well.

1 tablespoon shiratamako (sweet rice flour)

1½ tablespoons water

⅔ cups shiroan (white bean paste)

Pink and yellow food coloring gels

⅓ cups koshian (smooth red bean paste)

Cornstarch, for dusting

1. Stir together the shiratamako and water in a small saucepan until the shiratamako has completely dissolved. Add the shiroan and mix until the shiratamako mixture has been absorbed. Cook the shiroan mixture over medium heat while stirring, allowing the water to cook off, until the dough is no longer sticky to the touch and feels soft, like an earlobe, about 3 to 5 minutes.

2. Turn the dough out onto a clean cotton dish towel. The towel should be smooth so the dough doesn't develop divots. Allow the dough to cool slightly, then knead the dough with the towel until it becomes cool to the touch. The dough shouldn't stick to the towel too much; if it does, place it back in the pot to cook more of the water off. When the dough is ready, it will be soft and moldable, like Play-Doh.

3. Set the towel aside and split the dough into thirds. Roll two-thirds of the dough into a ball and set aside. Pinch off a piece the size of a penny from the remaining third of the dough and roll both pieces into balls. Knead 1 to 2 drops of the pink food coloring into the biggest ball, and add a tiny bit of yellow food coloring to the smallest ball. The medium-size ball will remain

Continued

naturally white. Wear food-safe gloves if you're worried about the food coloring staining your hands and make sure your workspace is covered. If you want each tinted piece to be more saturated, knead in a few more drops of the food coloring. Set the yellow dough aside and split the pink and white doughs into 10 equal pieces each.

4. Divide the koshian into 10 equal pieces.

5. Place a piece of pink dough in your hand and roll it into a ball. Using a knuckle, press a dent into the middle of the ball. Roll a white piece into a small cone and press it into the dent, pointed side down. Spread out the edges of the white dough so it melds and blends into the pink dough, pressing the dough out to widen the disc. At this point, the disc has a thick center that's pink on the bottom and white on top; the edges of the white dough should fade into the pink dough. Place a piece of koshian in the center of the disc and bring the edges of the disc up and over the koshian. Pinch the edges of the dough together to enclose the koshian. Turn the ball over so that the closed end is on the bottom. You should see the white center that bleeds out to the pink edges on top. Use the palms of your hands to round the edges and gently flatten the dough into a half-dollar-size disc.

6. At this point, your piece of nerikiri should be flat on top with rounded edges. Use the side of your pinkie finger to create five equally spaced indentations along the rounded edges of the nerikiri. Hold your pinkie vertically to the side of the dough and gently press your pinkie tip in, rolling up as you do. These will be the petals.

7. Place your pointer finger on one edge of a petal and your thumb on the other and gently pinch. While holding this pinch shape, use your other thumb to gently press on the dough to spread the petal outward into the pinched corner of your fingertips. It should fan into a soft pear shape, with the smaller part by your fingertips and the larger base near the center of the blossom. Repeat for each petal.

8. Define the petals. Place a toothpick vertically between where two petals join and roll the toothpick up and slightly onto the flat surface of the nerikiri itself to create distinctions between the petals, about one-third of the way toward the center. Repeat until you have five indentations, one per petal.

9. Use the toothpick to press a short, shallow indentation into the center of the petal tips to emulate how sakura petals are slightly bisected at their outer edge. Hold the toothpick vertically against the point of the petal and roll it up and slightly over the top edge.

10. Make five little lines, one per petal, near the center of the flower to suggest the middle vein of the petal. Pinch off a small piece of yellow dough, roll it into a little ball, and place it in the center of the flower to create the blossom's anther.

11. Repeat to fill and form the remaining nerikiri. Store in an airtight container at room temperature for up to 1 week.

OHAGI

After demons tore his family apart, Sanemi Shinazugawa has become a hotheaded demon slayer motivated by rage. Skeptical of demons living harmoniously among humans, Sanemi doesn't trust Tanjiro, the protagonist of *Demon Slayer*, or Tanjiro's demon sister, Nezuko. When audiences see Sanemi gleefully eating ohagi, it's a surprising moment of levity that exposes a sweet crack in his hardened armor.

For a long time, ohagi was an important Japanese dessert. Whether it was served to visiting guests as a special treat or used in offerings for the dead, ohagi was the kind of sweet that most people rarely indulged in. To see Sanemi go to town on ohagi underscores his wayward nature—he grew up without parents, which means he made his own rules.

When you could die at any point fighting demons, the little things become that much sweeter. See what the hype is about and try out ohagi for yourself. The kinako-coated ones are my favorite, but all three varieties are tasty!

1½ cups mochigome (sweet rice)	1 tablespoon sugar
⅓ cups Japanese short-grain rice	½ cup ground black sesame seeds
2⅔ cups water	1 teaspoon kosher salt
3 tablespoons kinako (roasted soybean flour)	1 cup tsubuan (whole red bean paste)

1. Combine the mochigome and short-grain rice in your rice cooker. Wash the rice thoroughly, then empty out the water and wash the rice again until the water is no longer cloudy.

2. Add 1⅔ cups of the water to the rice and soak for 30 minutes, then start the rice cooker.

3. Combine the kinako powder and the sugar in a shallow bowl and whisk to combine. Grind the sesame seeds using a suribachi and surikogi or food processor, then set aside in a separate small bowl.

4. When the rice is cooked, transfer it to a large cutting board. Stir the salt into the remaining 1 cup water until dissolved. Dip or coat a rolling pin into the salt water, then use the rolling pin to pound the rice so the grains break down and become stickier. The longer you pound, the smoother the grains will become. I personally enjoy textured ohagi, so I only pound until the rice clings together but the individual grains are still visible.

5. Flatten the rice into an even layer and cut lines with a spatula or knife to split the rice into 18 equal portions. You can measure or weigh the portions to ensure each is exactly the same weight, it you d like.

6. Wet your hands with the salt water and mold the rice into ovals, pressing each portion gently between your cupped hands to achieve the desired shape.

Continued

1 HOUR 30 MINUTES

MAKES 18 PIECES

SPECIAL EQUIPMENT: RICE COOKER, SURIBACHI AND SURIKOGI (OR OTHER TOOL FOR GRINDING THE SESAME SEEDS)

DAIRY-FREE, GLUTEN-FREE, NUT-FREE, VEGAN

RECIPE TIPS:
Shaping ohagi can be tricky if you aren't careful—keep your hands dampened with a bit of water to stop the rice from sticking. Alternatively, a piece of plastic wrap can go a long way toward helping you shape the rice without getting messy.

The toppings for this are optional. If you don't like kinako or black sesame seeds, skip them and just get extra koshian for all the ohagi.

7. Roll one-third of the ohagi in the kinako mixture; this will result in a slightly sweet, slightly nutty ohagi bite. Roll half the remaining ohagi in the ground sesame seeds. The remaining ohagi can be coated with tsubuan: Spread 3 tablespoons of the tsubuan on a piece of plastic wrap in a thin layer. Put an ohagi on top, then wrap the tsubuan around the rice to shape and smooth it down. Repeat to coat the remaining ohagi.

8. Serve fresh, and if you want to be traditional, enjoy it with a cup of tea. Eat these, ideally, within a day, or store in an airtight container in a cool spot.

ROKUHOUDOU YOTSUIRO BIYORI

MATCHA WARABI MOCHI

Rokuhoudou Yotsuiro Biyori follows four friends who run a traditional Japanese tea shop. In one episode, they serve a matcha warabi mochi set to a customer and the audience is invited into her experience of eating it. Her facial expressions let us know she's tasting some form of nirvana.

Warabi mochi, despite the name, is not actually made with rice flour: it's composed of bracken starch, which comes from a type of fern. The texture of warabi mochi is similar to its rice-based counterpart, but it notably melts more quickly in the mouth. Popular since before the Heian period, it's typically eaten with kinako and kuromitsu (black sugar syrup), but other variations are also popular. This recipe for matcha warabi mochi is soft, bouncy, and pleasantly chewy. When you cover it with kuromitsu, the caramelized sweetness contrasts perfectly with the slight bitterness of the matcha. These little bites of happiness are sure to delight!

1 HOUR

SERVES 6 TO 8

DAIRY-FREE, GLUTEN-FREE, NUT-FREE, VEGAN

RECIPE TIP: The warabi mochi can be sticky—a bench scraper or butter knife will go a long way toward helping you handle the mochi in step 3 without getting your hands sticky.

SUBSTITUTION TIP: Potato or tapioca starch can be used if you can't find bracken starch.

Matcha (green tea powder), for dusting

1¼ cups water

⅓ cup plus 1 tablespoon bracken starch

⅓ cup plus 1 tablespoon sugar

Kuromitsu (black sugar syrup), for serving (optional)

1. Dust a baking sheet liberally with matcha.

2. Combine the water, bracken starch, and sugar in a heavy-bottomed pan. Stir to dissolve any lumps, then set the pan over medium-low heat and cook, stirring continuously with a wooden spoon. After about 3 minutes of stirring, you'll see wisps of a clear, gel-like substance floating around. After another minute of cooking, the mixture will thicken quickly; it'll go from being a cloudy white color to a sticky, clear gel. Beat the gel with the wooden spoon until the entire mixture has turned clear, then immediately tip the mixture onto the matcha-dusted baking sheet. Dust the top of the mixture with more matcha and allow to cool for about 30 minutes, then transfer to the refrigerator to finish cooling, 10 to 20 minutes more.

3. When ready to serve, put some matcha in a bowl. Cut the warabi mochi into 1-inch pieces and toss each piece in the matcha to coat. This dessert is best eaten fresh. Serve with kuromitsu syrup, if desired.

SAKURA QUEST

MANJU

In *Sakura Quest*, Yoshino gets roped into becoming the spokeswoman for an aging Japanese town that desperately needs more visitors to revitalize the local economy. A common issue for many country-bound townships, Manoyama Village is finding that the change they need to attract tourists is at odds with maintaining their rich culture and traditions. Yoshino's job is to figure out a way to create that change while still respecting the local charm. Her solution? Branding a traditional edible souvenir with a made-up mascot—a sea monster.

The souvenir she chooses is manju, a tea snack that's both affordable and delicious. Originating in China, manju are steamed buns filled with bean paste. Nowadays, you can find manju filled with all sorts of things, and they can be baked or steamed. Yoshino's manju don't gain much traction, mostly because they're a little scary. This recipe is for a more traditional version of manju. Decorating it with the face of the chupacabra using a food coloring marker is optional, but I do find it adds a certain . . . *something*.

1 HOUR 30 MINUTES

MAKES 12 PIECES

SPECIAL EQUIPMENT: **STEAMER BASKET, FOOD COLORING MARKER (OPTIONAL)**

DAIRY-FREE, NUT-FREE, VEGAN

½ cup packed light brown sugar

¼ cup plus 1 teaspoon water

½ teaspoon baking soda

1¼ cups cake flour, plus more for dusting

1 cup koshian (smooth red bean paste)

1. Combine the brown sugar and ¼ cup of the water in a small pot over medium heat. Stir until the sugar has dissolved, then turn off the heat and allow to cool.

2. Combine the baking soda and remaining 1 teaspoon water in a small bowl. Stir to dissolve the baking soda, then set aside.

3. When the sugar syrup is cool, add the baking soda mixture and whisk together. Add the cake flour and stir with a spatula until just combined and no dry pockets of flour are visible. Don't overmix. Refrigerate the dough for 30 minutes.

4. Divide the koshian into 12 equal portions (use a scale to get precisely the same amount per portion), then roll each portion between your palms into a ball. Set aside.

5. Cut twelve 2-inch squares of parchment paper for the manju to sit on in the steamer. Sprinkle a clean work surface with flour. Turn the cooled dough out onto the surface and knead gently until the dough is no longer sticky. Do not overwork the dough. Divide the dough into 12 equal portions (use a scale to get precisely the same amount per portion) and roll each portion into a ball.

6. Flatten one ball of dough between well-floured palms. Use your fingers to thin out the dough around the edge until the ball is roughly 2 inches in diameter, with a center that's slightly thicker. Place a piece of koshian in the center of the dough and fold the sides up to enclose the koshian, pinching the dough together at the top. Smooth out any wrinkles, then flip the manju over so the smooth side is facing up. Place the manju on a square of parchment and use the sides of your palms to round the sides and flatten the top. Repeat to fill and form the remaining manju.

RECIPE TIP: Don't overestimate how much these will puff up, and don't overcrowd the steamer or you'll find that the buns start to merge together.

REHEATING AND STORAGE TIP: If you have leftovers, gently microwave the manju in a damp paper towel for about 30 seconds to warm them back up. These buns can be stored in an airtight container on the counter overnight, but should be eaten the next day or they will go stale. You can also freeze them and then revive them in a steamer when you're ready to eat them.

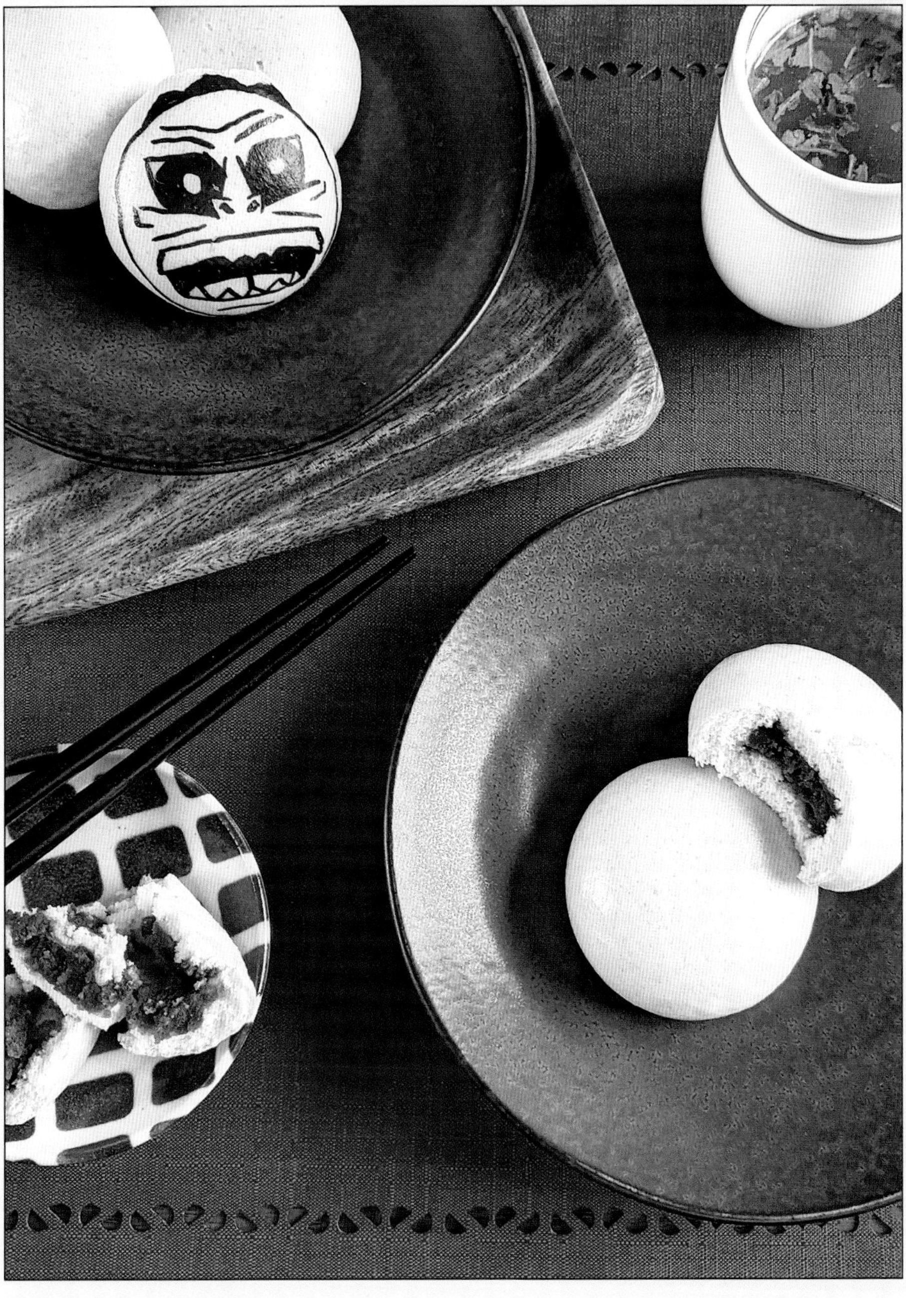

7. Bring an inch or two of water to a boil in a medium saucepan. Working in batches, place the manju in a steamer basket with an inch of space around each and set the basket in the pot. Reduce the heat until the water is simmering, cover the pot, and steam for 10 minutes. Repeat until all the manju have been steamed.

8. If you'd like, decorate the manju to be as fearsome as possible with a black food coloring marker before serving.

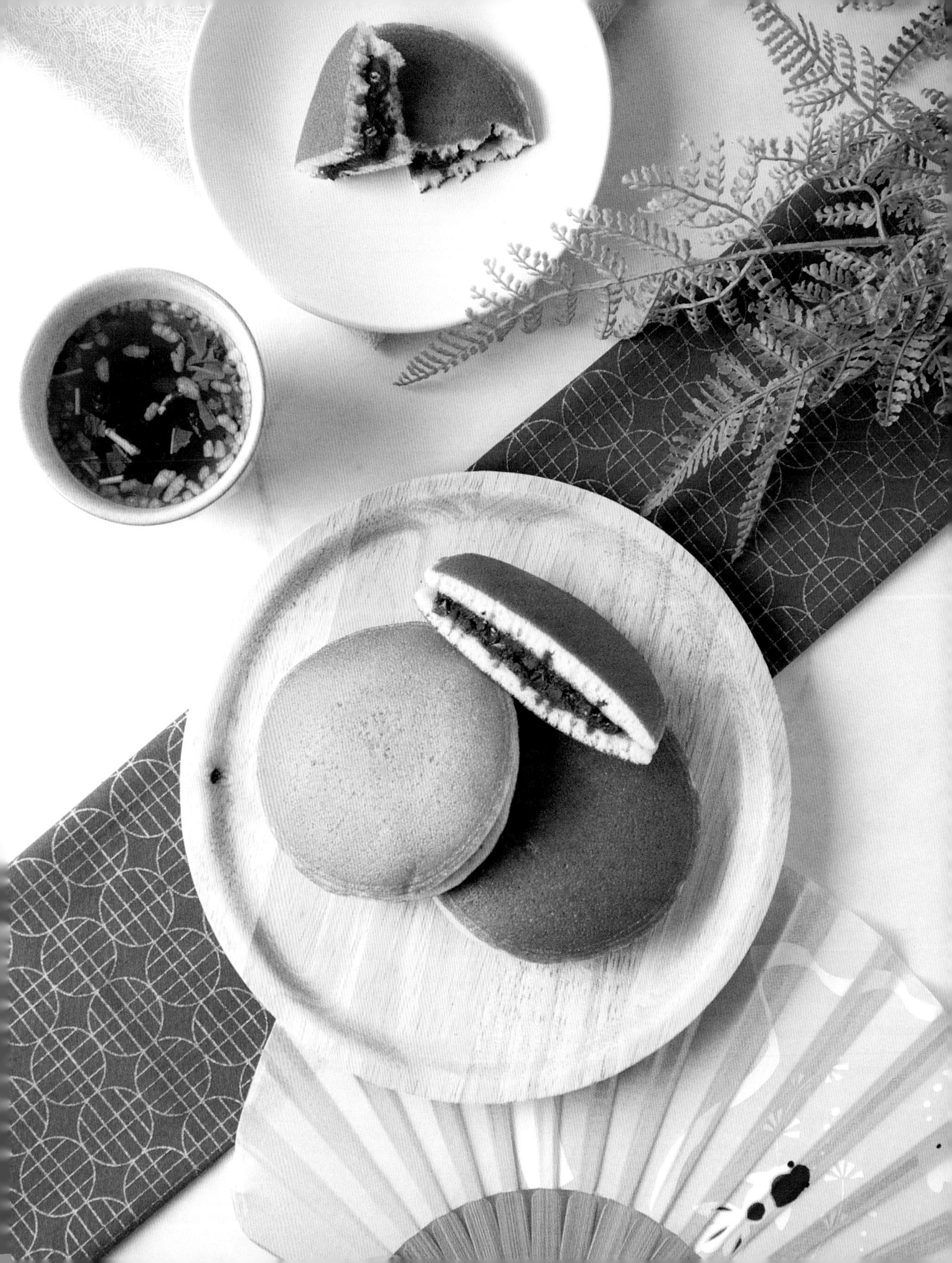

DORAYAKI

Everyone loves a good enemies-to-lovers story, and *Nisekoi* provides this trope in a reverse *Romeo and Juliet* scenario. The children of two separate gang leaders are forced to date to keep the peace between their rival families, and of course, the two immediately clash. In one early interaction, Raku purchases dorayaki for Chitoge as an apology for getting off on the wrong foot.

Dorayaki are two small honey pancakes traditionally sandwiching bean paste. It's not uncommon to find them filled with extras like fruit, too. It's also popular to see them filled with flavored creams. After Raku runs off, Chitoge remarks that she hates dorayaki. Maybe it's because she's from America and isn't used to the traditional Japanese sweet, or maybe it's because she doesn't like bean paste. Whatever the case may be, in Japan, dorayaki are loved by everyone—they're the perfect handheld treat. This is a standard recipe for the honey cakes with bean paste filling, but don't be afraid to experiment!

3 large eggs	1 teaspoon baking powder
¾ cup sugar	1½ cups cake flour, sifted
1 tablespoon honey	2 tablespoons vegetable oil
1 tablespoon mirin (rice wine)	2 cups anko (red bean paste)
3 tablespoons water	

1. Whisk together the eggs, sugar, honey, and mirin in a medium bowl. Allow to rest for 10 minutes.

2. Mix the water with the baking powder in a small bowl. Stir to dissolve, then pour the baking powder mixture into the egg mixture and whisk together.

3. Add the sifted cake flour and mix until just combined, then refrigerate for 30 minutes.

4. When the batter is ready, it should be slightly thick and smooth; if you dip a whisk into the batter then hold it over the bowl, the batter should fall back into the bowl in ribbons. If you find it's too thick, whisk in water as needed to thin it out, one tablespoon at a time.

5. Dampen some paper towels and set them near the stove—you'll rest each cooked dorayaki between two damp paper towels to help them retain moisture. Heat a nonstick skillet over low heat. Dip a pastry brush in the oil, then lightly brush the bottom and sides of the pan. Using a ¼-cup measuring cup, pour the batter into the pan from 3 to 4 inches above the surface to allow it to pool out. Each pancake should be 3 inches across. Cook on the first side for 2 to 3 minutes, or until bubbles start to form and pop on the surface of the pancake. Run the spatula around the edge to loosen the pancake from the pan, and then flip and cook for just 1 minute more, or until the other side has browned and the cake is cooked through. Transfer the dorayaki to a damp paper towel and drape a second dampened paper towel over the top.

Continued

1 HOUR 30 MINUTES

MAKES 8 TO 10 PIECES

DAIRY-FREE, NUT-FREE

COOKING TIP:
To get perfectly browned pancakes, cook them low and slow. If you want to make the process go faster, you can raise the heat under the pan, but don't expect them to have the same uniform color.

SUBSTITUTION TIP:
Tired of bean paste? Add a different filling and don't be afraid to get creative. Think: flavored whipped cream, a nut butter and jelly, some custard or pudding, or anything you think would taste nice sandwiched between two honey-flavored pancakes.

FOOD FACT:
In Japanese, *yaki* basically means grilled or cooked over direct heat.

Repeat to cook the remaining batter, leaving the cooked dorayaki between the dampened paper towels to ensure they stay tender and pliable.

6. Remove one dorayaki from the paper towels and set it darker side down. Spoon 2 tablespoons of the anko into the center of the dorayaki, then spread the anko to the edges, leaving more in the center to create a slight lump between the two dorayaki. Sandwich the anko with a dorayaki, darker side up. Repeat to fill the remaining dorayaki.

7. Eat immediately, or wrap in plastic wrap and store at room temperature for up to 3 days to keep the dorayaki moist.

THE ECCENTRIC FAMILY

MIZU-YOKAN

Yokan, a dessert conceived in China and popularized in Japan during the Edo period, is essentially a block of solidified bean paste with an impressive shelf life. It was originally made with sheep by-products, ingredients Japanese people of the time were strictly forbidden to consume. (True story: Meat derived from cows and other land animals was outlawed in Japan from 675 AD until after the Meiji Restoration in the nineteenth century; Emperor Meiji ate beef to celebrate the new year in 1872, which effectively lifted the ban on eating animals.) To make yokan permissible to eat, Japanese cooks swapped out the animal-based gelatin for agar, a firming agent derived from seaweed, giving us the vegan jellied dessert we know today.

In *The Eccentric Family*, an anime that follows a family of tanuki who live in a shrine in Kyoto, mizu-yokan makes an appearance as a refreshing afternoon treat. It serves as a nod to the family's appreciation for the traditional, comforting aspects of Japanese life, especially in the face of the modern world. If you're hot and looking to cool off, try a chilled slice of this yokan. It'll become a summer dessert favorite!

3 HOURS, PLUS 30 MINUTES SETTING TIME

MAKES 4 PIECES

DAIRY-FREE, GLUTEN-FREE, NUT-FREE, VEGAN

⅓ cup koshian (smooth red bean paste)

¼ cup water

3 tablespoons sugar

1 teaspoon agar powder

1. Combine the koshian, water, and sugar in a small saucepan over medium-high heat. Whisk until smooth, then add the agar and whisk until fully combined.

2. Remove the pot from the heat and pour the mixture into a standard 8 x 4-inch loaf pan. The mixture should be about an inch deep. Allow it to set on the counter for 30 minutes, then chill in the refrigerator for 2 hours.

3. To unmold the yokan, run a knife around the edges of the loaf pan, then tip the yokan out onto a plate or cutting board. Cut the yokan into 4 slices and serve chilled.

RECIPE TIP: This yokan is going to *seem* like it won't pop out of the pan, but trust the process—if prepared properly, it will! If, however, you find yourself struggling, draw some hot water into your sink and let the bottom of the pan rest in it for about 30 seconds. That should help the yokan melt a tiny bit around the edges, enough to slide right out.

STORAGE TIP:

This treat will keep in an airtight container in the refrigerator for up to 1 week.

MY HERO ACADEMIA

CUSTARD TAIYAKI

As Deku attends U.A. High School to learn how to be a hero, he finds mastering his new superpower comes with challenges. In one episode, he microwaves frozen taiyaki for his mentor, Gran Torino, who complains that they haven't been cooked through. Because Deku put a large plate in the microwave, there wasn't enough room for it to spin, so the taiyaki were only partially heated. Deku suddenly realizes how he can better control his quirk—like the taiyaki on the overly large plate, he's been focusing on using the power in one or two key areas. Instead, he needs to be sending power throughout his whole body!

Between the cute shape and the endless possibilities for fillings, there's a taiyaki out there for everyone. Traditionally, these Meiji-era treats are stuffed with bean paste, but I chose a custard filling here, since that's how I prefer them.

3 HOURS 30 MINUTES

MAKES 8 PIECES

SPECIAL EQUIPMENT: TAIYAKI PAN

NUT-FREE

FOR THE CUSTARD FILLING

¼ cup sugar

2 tablespoons cake flour

⅛ teaspoon kosher salt

¾ cup whole milk

1 large egg

¼ teaspoon vanilla extract

FOR THE TAIYAKI BATTER

¾ cup cake flour

2 teaspoons baking powder

1 tablespoon sugar

¼ teaspoon kosher salt

⅔ cup water

⅓ cup whole milk

Vegetable oil or butter, for the pan

1. Make the custard filling: Whisk together the sugar, cake flour, and salt in a microwave-safe bowl. In a separate bowl, whisk together the milk, egg, and vanilla to thoroughly combine. Slowly pour the wet ingredients through the whisk into the dry ingredients (this helps break up any egg white that hasn't been fully mixed). Mix together until smooth.

2. Cover the bowl with plastic wrap and microwave at 50 percent power for 2 minutes 30 seconds, then whisk the mixture thoroughly to evenly distribute the heat, cover, and microwave for 2 minutes 30 seconds more. Whisk again to make the mixture smooth, then refrigerate for a minimum of 2 hours to chill.

3. An hour before you plan to cook the taiyaki, make the taiyaki batter: Whisk together the cake flour, baking powder, sugar, and salt in a bowl. Mix the water and milk together in a separate small bowl, then add them to the dry ingredients in a slow, steady stream, whisking thoroughly to combine. Chill in the refrigerator for at least 1 hour.

4. Lightly grease the taiyaki pan with oil or butter and heat over medium-low heat. Spoon 2 tablespoons of batter into each cavity, making sure to fill out the tail and the fins. To the center of the fish, add 1 to 2 teaspoons of the custard filling, then add another tablespoon of batter to the top so it covers the custard. Anoint the fins and tail with more batter, then close the pan. Cook for 3 minutes per side, or until golden brown. Remove the taiyaki from the pan and repeat to cook the remaining batter. Serve hot and fresh!

REHEATING TIP:
These can be frozen and reheated in the microwave, just like in the anime! For best results, throw the taiyaki under the broiler for a minute after you microwave it to crisp up the exterior.

SUBSTITUTION TIP:
Looking for a different flavor? Make your custard chocolaty with some cocoa powder, add a spoonful of jam along with the regular custard, or take it easy on yourself and go for a nice dollop of Nutella or cookie butter instead of making a filling from scratch.

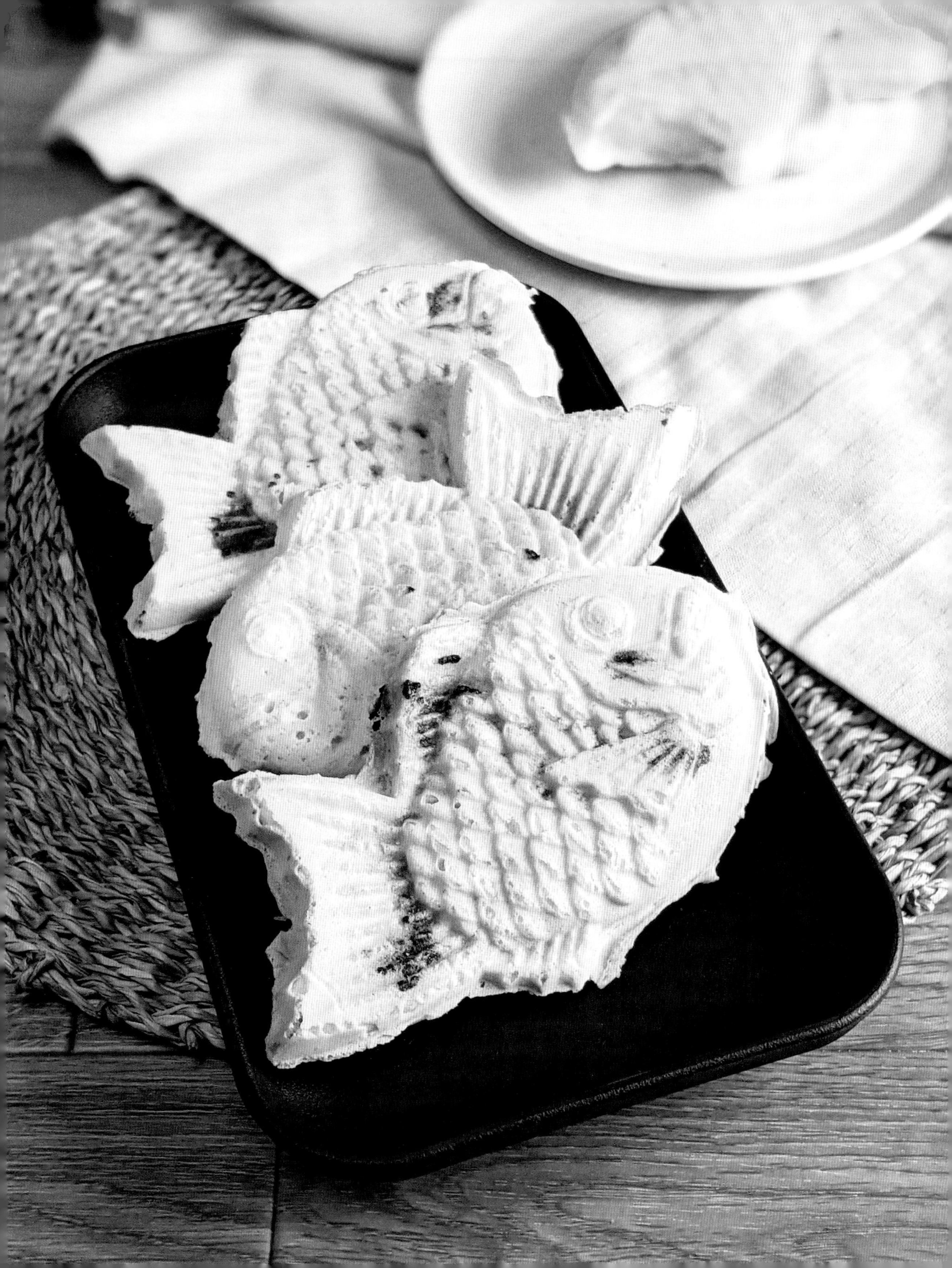

KINAKO BOU

Imagine you're an only child and your dad wants you to inherit the family business. Now imagine you have *no* desire to do so. Well, that's exactly what happens to Kokonotsu, whose father wants him to take over his dagashi shop. When Hotaru comes to town and insists Kokonotsu's father come work for *her* family's confectionery business, Kokonotsu is forced to decide his future much more quickly.

Hotaru employs all manner of charms to persuade Kokonotsu's father. In one memorable moment, she sticks kinako bou between her fingers like Wolverine's claws and eats them with such intensity and ferocity that she accidentally chokes herself. Absolutely iconic and also, incidentally, highly relatable for me personally (except when I choked, it wasn't on kinako bou, and I had to be given the Heimlich. Very fun. Don't worry, I'm fine.)

These treats are delicious. Made out of simple and inexpensive ingredients, the kinako bou has a taste similar to peanut butter, with a consistency similar to an energy bar. Try these out—you might be surprised by how often you find yourself snacking on them.

¾ cup kinako (roasted soybean flour), plus more for dusting

3 tablespoons honey

1 tablespoon sesame seeds

1. Place the kinako, honey, and sesame seeds in a bowl and mix together. Use a spatula to knead the honey through the dry ingredients. When the mixture clumps together in a ball that sticks together easily, it's ready.

2. Split the mixture into 16 equal pieces (eyeball it or use a scale). Take a toothpick and squeeze one piece of the mixture around the end. Use your hands to shape it into a little log, then set aside. Repeat with the other 15 pieces.

3. Shake some kinako onto a plate or into a shallow bowl and roll each log in the kinako to coat. Enjoy!

1 HOUR 30 MINUTES

MAKES 16 PIECES

DAIRY-FREE, GLUTEN-FREE, NUT-FREE

RECIPE TIP: Because this recipe is so simple, don't be afraid to add more or less honey, depending on your environment. If you live in an especially dry climate or you like your desserts sweeter and stickier, you might find you need more honey in the mixture. Alternatively, if you live in a humid climate, you might find the 3 tablespoons the recipe calls for are adequate.

FOOD FACT: Dagashi is a catchall name for cheap, popular Japanese snacks and candies. Unlike wagashi, they aren't always eaten with tea; they're meant to be a more on-the-go snack.

MILK CARAMELS

While Hotaru tries to get Kokonotsu to take over the family shop, Kokonotsu falls for her. As a result, he tries to impress her with his knowledge of Japanese sweets. This is so effective that romance actually begins to bloom! (I'll put this out there now, for anyone interested in getting my attention: Forget about pickup lines. Instead, regale me with facts about sweets.)

Anyway, in an attempt to impress Hotaru, Kokonotsu recites the history of Morinaga milk caramels. These caramels were slow to gain popularity in Japan. One reason was their cost. Another was their ingredient list. For much of Japan's history, the consumption of animal products was illegal; when this taboo was lifted, dairy products weren't immediately embraced, and people complained of the caramels' milky odor (you might not notice it if you're used to dairy products and consume them regularly). Eventually, though, the caramels gained popularity, enough so that the company issued specialty flavors to meet demand.

Hotaru is suitably impressed, but if you try making *my* copycat recipe, you'll be blown away. Milk caramels are easy to make, and the kuromitsu adds a unique depth of flavor to the recipe. If you're looking to woo hearts, this treat will do the trick.

2 cups packed dark brown sugar

1 cup (2 sticks) unsalted butter, plus more for the pan

1 cup kuromitsu (black sugar syrup)

2 tablespoons corn syrup

1 (14-ounce) can sweetened condensed milk

1 teaspoon kosher salt

1 teaspoon vanilla extract

1. Generously butter a 9 x 13-inch baking pan.

2. Combine the brown sugar, butter, kuromitsu, and corn syrup in a heavy-bottomed pot. Bring to a boil over medium heat, stirring continuously, then cook until the butter has melted and the ingredients are incorporated. Reduce the heat to low and stir in the condensed milk. Sprinkle in the salt, then stir until completely combined. Allow the caramel to bubble away until it reaches 255°F to 260°F. Remove from the heat and stir in the vanilla. Pour the caramel into the prepared pan and allow it to set, about 1 hour.

3. When fully set, slice the caramel into 1-inch pieces with a sharp knife. Wrap in parchment or waxed paper and store in a cool, dry spot until ready to be eaten.

30 MINUTES, PLUS
1 HOUR SETTING TIME

MAKES 32 CARAMELS

SPECIAL EQUIPMENT:
INFRARED
THERMOMETER

GLUTEN-FREE,
NUT-FREE

RECIPE TIP: An infrared thermometer really helps here, but if you don't feel like buying one, fill a glass with cold water and drop in little spoonfuls of the caramel as you cook to check its progress. It's done when the caramel in the glass hardens into a stiff but pliable droplet.

STORAGE TIP:

When properly stored, these will keep for 6 to 9 months, but will probably disappear faster than that once you get a taste of the finished product.

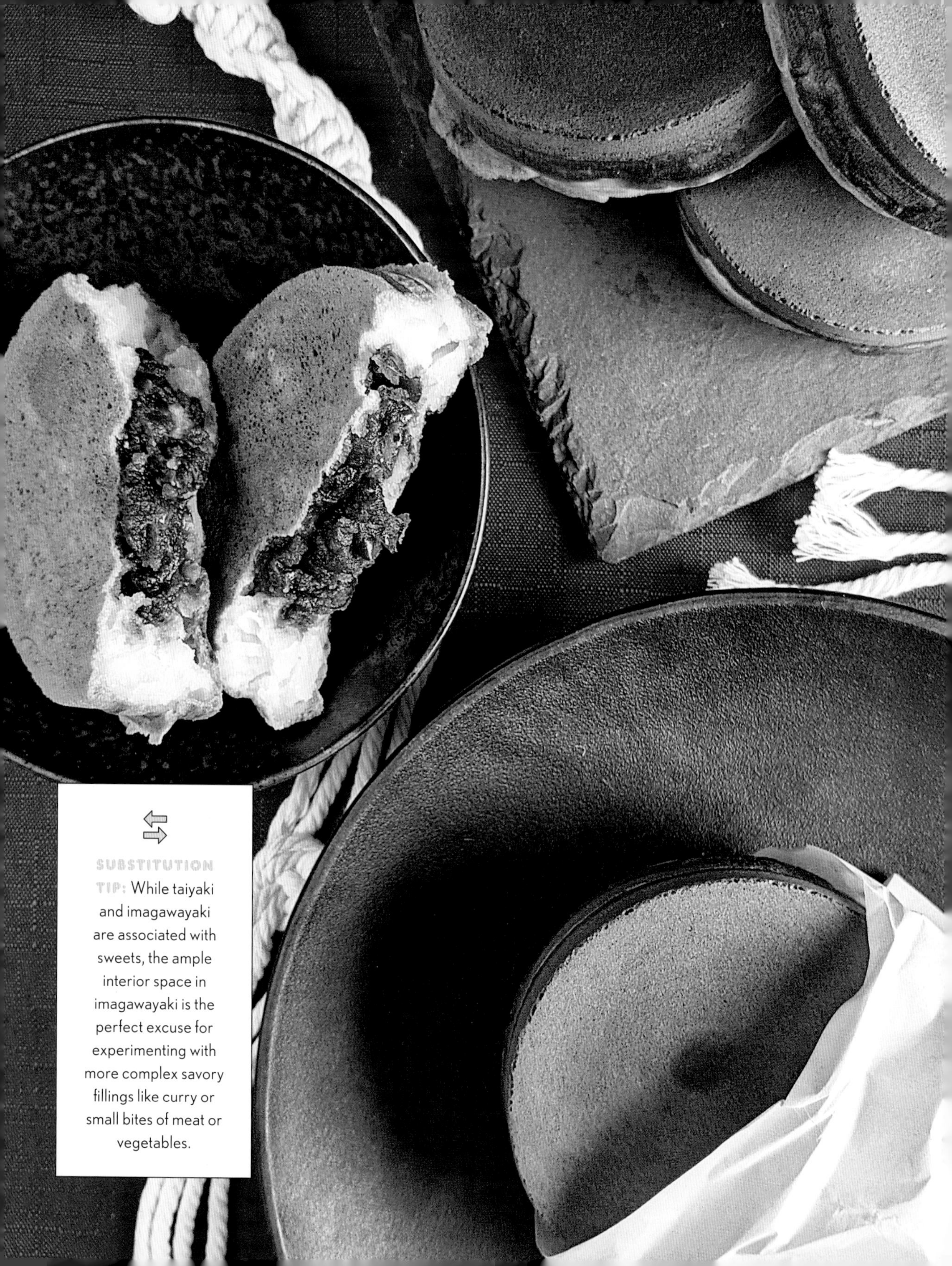

SUBSTITUTION TIP: While taiyaki and imagawayaki are associated with sweets, the ample interior space in imagawayaki is the perfect excuse for experimenting with more complex savory fillings like curry or small bites of meat or vegetables.

TODAY'S MENU FOR THE EMIYA FAMILY

IMAGAWAYAKI

Today's Menu for the Emiya Family is anime fan fiction at its best. The *Fate* franchise is huge, and the characters are usually in a fight for their lives. *Today's Menu*, however, depicts the series' characters cooking and eating together. It's random, but it works surprisingly well. While the show has many recipes, I wrote one for a dessert they don't provide a recipe for—the first episode's imagawayaki.

Imagawayaki (also called obanyaki or kaitenyaki) are soft, round cakes filled with everything from bean paste to chocolate to custard, and can be eaten cold or warm. They're similar to taiyaki in their composition, but more straightforward in shape and construction. They also precede taiyaki by at least one hundred years. I would choose imagawayaki if you're a big fan of fillings, because the shape of these little cakes allows for more room inside. Hearkening all the way back to the Edo period, they were traditionally stuffed with bean paste, but as with most Japanese desserts, you can get creative with the fillings!

1 HOUR 30 MINUTES

MAKES 12 PIECES

SPECIAL EQUIPMENT: IMAGAWAYAKI PAN, SKEWER

NUT-FREE

2 large eggs

2 cups whole milk

⅓ cup sugar

2 tablespoons honey

2 tablespoons vegetable oil, plus more for the pan

2⅔ cups cake flour, sifted

2 teaspoons baking powder

1 cup tsubuan (whole red bean paste)

1. Whisk together the eggs, milk, sugar, honey, and oil in a large bowl. Mix in the cake flour and baking powder until combined, then refrigerate the batter for 30 minutes.

2. Heat an imagawayaki pan over low heat. Using a pastry brush, coat the wells of the pan lightly with oil. Fill one set of the wells halfway with batter. Cook until bubbles form and pop on the surface of the batter, about 1 to 2 minutes. Then add 1 tablespoon of tsubuan to the batter in the pan, which should be just set on the outside but still wet in the middle. While you allow that to cook through, fill the other set of wells halfway with batter and cook for 2 minutes, or until bubbly on top and mostly set through.

3. Use a knife to loosen the edges of the imagawayaki in the second set of wells (the ones without filling). Pierce the interior of the cakes with a skewer, then use the skewer as a hook to flip them onto the filled imagawayaki halves to form a complete shell. Press down gently to marry the two halves together and continue cooking for 2 to 3 minutes until the outside is nice and bronzed and the inside is set. Use a knife to remove the imagawayaki from the pan and transfer to a wire rack to cool. Then enjoy!

RECIPE TIP: Some imagawayaki pans are hinged, much like taiyaki pans. If you have one of these, follow the instructions but fill all the wells with batter and filling. Allow to become mostly set through, then close the pan and flip it so the raw batter is closest to the heat source. Cook until evenly browned, an additional 2 to 3 mintues.

EQUIPMENT TIP: If you don't want to buy a special pan for this, you can use a metal cupcake pan to get the round shape you're looking for, as long as it's stable on your stovetop and won't accidentally slip off the burner. However, be careful if you do this—make sure the cupcake tin can withstand the heat and won't melt or deform.

CASTELLA

The Tatami Galaxy is a coming-of-age story that focuses on Watashi as he embarks on his first college experience. Determined to experiment and try it all, he signs up for a variety of clubs and meets a whole host of characters, but despite his efforts, he becomes increasingly frustrated with his perceived failures. According to his college friend Ozu, "You can't get any lonelier than eating a giant castella by yourself." Later, alone in his room, Watashi shoves fistfuls of the cake into his mouth.

Originating in Portugal, castella became a popular dessert when the Portuguese began trading with Japan in the sixteenth century. It's boldly yellow, with vivid brown layers of caramelization at the top and bottom of the cake. When prepared properly, it's a moist, rich honey cake with a springy texture. It's typically saved for special occasions, to be shared with friends alongside a cup of tea.

I'm not saying that if you make this cake, you'll also be shoving fistfuls into your face, but it's pretty good with a cup of tea or coffee. Try it and you might find a new favorite afternoon snack. The good news? You won't have to endure an existential crisis to enjoy it.

Butter, for greasing	6 large eggs, at room temperature
⅓ cup honey	1 cup sugar
2½ tablespoons warm water	1⅔ cups bread flour, sifted

1. Preheat the oven to 320°F. Grease the sides and bottom of an 8-inch square cake pan with butter and line the bottom with parchment paper cut to fit. Press the parchment against the butter so it sticks.

2. Combine the honey and water in a bowl and whisk until the honey has dissolved. Set aside.

3. Using an electric mixer, beat the eggs in a large bowl to break them apart. Pour in the sugar and beat on high speed for 5 to 10 minutes, until the batter has quadrupled in size and is pale and fluffy; the batter should fall in a ribbon from a spoon into the bowl.

4. With the mixer running on its lowest setting, slowly drizzle in the honey mixture through the whisk attachment and mix until you don't see any unincorporated honey water.

5. Sprinkle one-third of the flour lightly over the surface of the batter. With the mixer running on its lowest speed, beat until there's no loose flour, then add another ½ cup and mix. Once that's been beaten in, add the remaining flour and mix until you no longer see any loose flour.

6. Pour the batter into the prepared pan and tap the pan lightly on the counter to pop any air bubbles. Bake for 50 minutes, or until the top is relatively flat and browned, the cake is springy to the touch, and a toothpick inserted into the center comes out clean. Remove the cake from the pan immediately (don't forget your oven mitts!). Peel off the parchment paper and wrap the cake in plastic wrap. Allow the cake to cool.

7. Slice the cooled cake into two 4 x 8-inch rectangles and trim off the edges to get clean sides before cutting into slices. To make the cake even softer and more tender, allow it to sit in the refrigerator overnight, then slice the next day. Enjoy!

---

2 HOURS, PLUS 12 HOURS RESTING

MAKES 16 1-INCH-THICK SLICES

DAIRY-FREE, NUT-FREE

RECIPE TIP: You can brush a honey syrup over the top of the cake for additional moisture, if you really like your cakes to be less fluffy and sturdier.

FOOD FACT: For a long time, castella was quite an expensive product—it couldn't be made without sugar imported from Portugal—and its status as a specialty dessert has held strong for centuries.

STORAGE TIP: Keep leftover cake moist by wrapping it in plastic wrap. It will keep in the fridge for about 5 days.

SIBERIA CAKE

In this fictionalized biography of aircraft designer Jiro Horikoshi, the audience watches as one man pursues the creation of beauty. *The Wind Rises* is a bittersweet story; Horikoshi achieves his dreams with the help of the government, but ultimately wonders about the cost. After all, his designs were used to bring death to hundreds of thousands during World War II.

In one scene, Horikoshi purchases Siberia cake on his way home, then stops to share it with some children on the street. His purchase is a little ironic, considering Russian and Japanese relations weren't very friendly at the time, but Siberia cake actually has very little to do with Siberia. There are many suggestions of how the name came to be, each more suspect than the last. One theory claims the lines of the cake look like the tracks of the Trans-Siberian Railway, but others think the name refers to the fact that this cake is the perfect summer treat to help cool you down (and Siberia is cold, so, you know. Look, I never said these theories were *good*). Whatever the origins of the name, Siberia cake is actually a combination of two Japanese sweets—yokan and castella. In this case, the two treats work together to make for an impressive, sweet cake sandwich that holds up well to travel.

3 HOURS 30 MINUTES

MAKES 8 LARGE TRIANGULAR SLICES

DAIRY-FREE, NUT-FREE

SERVING TIP: I find smaller slices to be better here for serving purposes, as the cake, while delicious, can be a bit overwhelming in its richness.

FOOD FACT: After *The Wind Rises* came out, demand for this product increased wildly in Japan, and you can now find Siberia cake on shelves in grocery and convenience stores.

FOR THE SPONGE CAKE

Nonstick cooking spray

⅓ cup honey

2½ tablespoons warm water

6 large eggs, at room temperature

1 cup sugar

1⅔ cups bread flour, sifted

FOR THE MIZU YOKAN FILLING

1⅔ cups koshian (smooth red bean paste)

1¼ cups water

3 tablespoons sugar

2 teaspoons agar powder

1. Make the sponge cake: Preheat the oven to 320°F. Grease the sides and bottom of an 8-inch square cake pan with nonstick spray and line the bottom with parchment paper cut to fit. Press the parchment into the spray so it sticks.

2. Whisk together the honey and water in a small bowl until the honey has dissolved. Set aside.

3. Using an electric mixer, beat the eggs in a large bowl to break them apart. Add the sugar and beat on the highest speed for 5 to 10 minutes, until the mixture has quadrupled in size and become pale and fluffy; it should fall from a spoon in a ribbon that sits on top of the mixture in the bowl.

4. With the mixer running on its lowest setting, slowly drizzle in the honey mixture through the whisk attachment and mix until you no longer see any unincorporated honey water.

5. Sprinkle one-third of the flour lightly over the surface of the batter. With the mixer running on its lowest speed, beat until you can't see any loose flour, then add another ½ cup. When that's beaten in, add the remaining flour and mix until you don't see any loose flour.

Continued

6. Pour the batter into the prepared pan. Tap the pan lightly on the counter to pop any air bubbles. Bake for 50 minutes, or until the top is flat and browned, the cake is springy to the touch, and a toothpick inserted into the center comes out clean. Let cool completely, then remove the cake from the pan. Peel off the parchment and wrap the cake in plastic wrap to lock in the moisture; set aside. Wash and dry the pan.

7. Make the mizu yokan filling: Whisk together the koshian, water, and sugar in a small pot. Set over medium heat, then whisk in the agar. When the edges of the mixture are bubbling and foamy, cook for 1 minute, stirring to keep the mixture from burning. Pour the contents of the pot into the cleaned cake pan and refrigerate for an hour to set.

8. Assemble the cake: Use a serrated knife to trim off the sides of the cake, leaving the top and bottom caramelization but removing the caramelization from the sides. Slice the cake horizontally into two even layers (use a ruler to measure the height of the cake and find the midpoint).

9. Remove the yokan from the fridge. Run a knife around the outer edge of the pan to loosen the yokan, then flip the pan over onto a cutting board and tap the bottom to pop the yokan out.

10. Place one cake layer on your work surface, cut side up. Set the yokan on top, trim it as necessary, then put the second cake layer on top, cut side down. Cut the cake into quarters, then cut each quarter in half diagonally to make 8 triangular slices in total. Serve and enjoy!

MIKAN AME

After the Rain (Koi wa Ameagari no You ni in Japanese) is a coming-of-age story about a girl named Akira. Akira is an incredible runner, but she sustains an injury that ruins her chances of becoming a professional athlete. During her moment of grief at the news, a manager at a family restaurant serves her a drink with a warm, friendly smile. Akira then quits the track club and becomes a part-time employee at the restaurant. She also finds herself falling in love with that same manager.

In one episode, Akira goes to a festival with a friend. One of the treats Akira grabs is mikan ame—tart wedges of orange encased in a thin shell of sugar. In Japan, great emphasis is put on seasonal foods, and candied fruit is a popular festival and summer snack. Like Akira, who has to break through the shell of her own misgivings and disappointments, the fruit inside the candy coating is juicy, refreshing, and brimming with life.

If oranges, clementines, or tangerines aren't in season, try this with strawberries or grapes, which are other popular options in Japan. This dessert embellishes something that's already exceptional, so choose whatever fruit looks best at the market. These are perfect on a hot summer's night, especially if you happen to find yourself on the porch, admiring the stars and dreaming of your future.

30 MINUTES

MAKES 5 PIECES

SPECIAL EQUIPMENT: INFRARED THERMOMETER, WOODEN SKEWERS

DAIRY-FREE, GLUTEN-FREE, NUT-FREE, VEGAN

RECIPE TIP: A thinner coating of sugar syrup is preferable, as it makes for an easier bite.

2 mikan oranges, clementines, or tangerines

¾ cup sugar

⅓ cup water

1. Peel the oranges and split them into individual segments. Remove the white pith, then place 5 orange segments on each skewer.

2. Pull out a piece of parchment paper and set it near the stove. Combine the sugar and water in a small heavy-bottomed pot and heat over medium-high heat, without stirring, until the sugar syrup reaches 295°F, 5 to 8 minutes. Don't stir, even if you're tempted to.

3. Turn off the heat and immediately dip the orange skewers in the sugar syrup, then place them on the parchment to set. Be very careful—this syrup will burn you if you touch it. Depending on the pot's size, you may need to tilt the pot to pool the sugar syrup on one side to get a better angle for dipping. If the syrup in the pot starts to harden before you can dip all the skewers, reheat over low heat until it softens again.

4. Serve the mikan ame the day they are made.

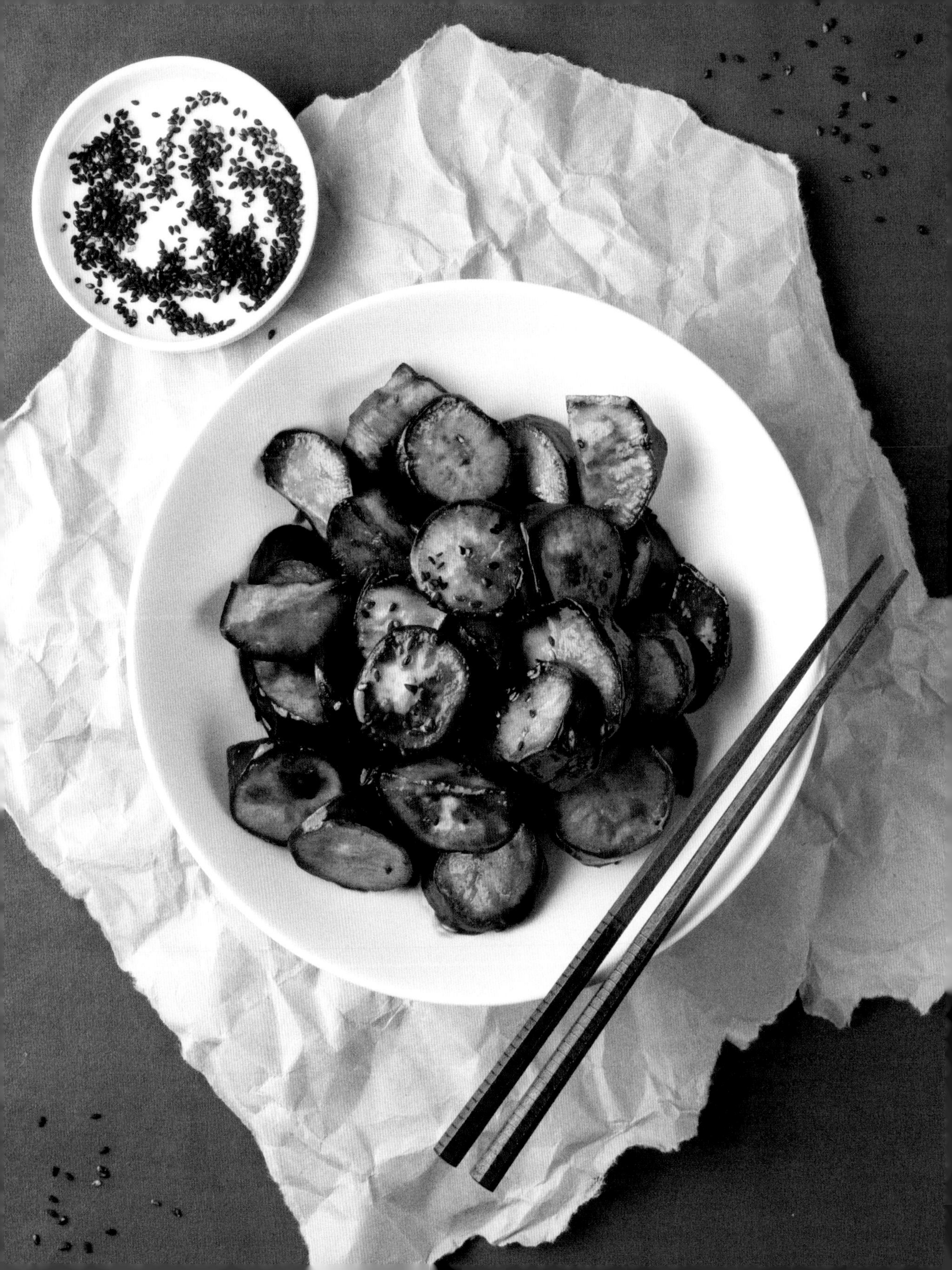

DORAEMON

DAIGAKU IMO

No cookbook focusing on Japanese sweets would be complete without at least one recipe using satsumaimo. The Japanese sweet potato is a favorite here, and while it can be prepared in savory ways, it's also beloved as a sweet winter treat. Here I've opted to share the recipe for my favorite sweet potato dessert, daigaku imo. To American tastes, the idea of eating a potato for dessert might seem a little odd. I had my own misgivings, but when I tried this dish for the first time, I was floored at how warm and tasty (and surprisingly healthy) it really was!

Shizuka, one of the children in *Doraemon*, isn't afraid to claim her love for daigaku imo, going so far as to chase the potato seller's car down the street to buy one for herself. Though we don't see this *exact* dessert in *Doraemon*, I think you'll find it engaging. The key here is to treat the potato with love and reverence. Give it the time it needs to crisp up in the pan, and you'll fall in love with the melty interior, crisp exterior, and salty-sweet sauce.

30 MINUTES

SERVES 4 TO 6

DAIRY-FREE, GLUTEN-FREE, NUT-FREE, VEGAN

3 medium satsumaimo (Japanese sweet potato)

3 tablespoons sugar

2 tablespoons mirin (rice wine)

1 tablespoon gluten-free soy sauce

¼ cup vegetable oil

1 teaspoon kosher salt

Black sesame seeds, for garnish

1. Scrub the satsumaimo and cut them into bite-size pieces. Soak the pieces in a bowl of water for 5 minutes to draw out the extra starch.

2. Place the satsumaimo in a microwave-safe dish. Cover loosely with a lid and microwave for 8 to 10 minutes, until fork-tender. Meanwhile, combine the sugar, mirin, and soy sauce in a small bowl and set aside.

3. Heat the oil in a large skillet over medium heat for 3 to 5 minutes, until the oil is shimmering. Place the satsumaimo in the pan so the largest surface of each piece is facing the pan and season with the salt. Fry for 4 to 5 minutes, until the first side is browned and crispy, then turn the pieces and fry until crisp on all sides, 5 to 10 minutes more. Transfer to paper towels to drain off excess oil.

4. Clean the pan and set it over low heat. Pour in the soy sauce mixture and cook, stirring, until the sugar has dissolved. Add the satsumaimo to the pan and toss to coat in the sauce.

5. Serve immediately, garnished with a sprinkling of sesame seeds.

RECIPE TIP: Okay, fine, so let's say you just wanted a roasted sweet potato recipe to keep things really traditional. Preheat the oven to 375°F. Scrub the satsumaimo and prick them with a fork to allow steam to vent. Set them on a baking sheet and bake for anywhere from 50 to 90 minutes (depending on the size of the potatoes), until easily pierced with a wooden skewer or fork. Allow to cool slightly, then serve topped with cold butter. If you want to get fancy, halve each potato lengthwise and scoop the flesh into a bowl (set the skins aside). Mash the flesh with butter, cream, and brown sugar, then return it to the skins. Arrange them on a baking sheet and crisp the tops under the broiler.

Non-Japanese Desserts

As beloved as Japanese sweets are, Western desserts run rampant in Japan. Pop into any Japanese convenience store and behold the endless "Western" choices available. Would you like a cream puff with a crackled cookie topping filled with strawberry puree, cream cheese frosting, and whipped cream? How about caramel pudding in a container designed with a tab that breaks the air seal inside, releasing the pudding from the mold without damaging the treat?

Once Japan's sakoku policy ended in 1853—drawing to a close a 214-year isolationist period during which foreigners were largely prohibited from entering Japan—all bets were off. A myriad of Western sweets entered the country for the first time, and many of them took off. Possibly the humblest of sweet treats was bread. Once a curiosity for the wealthy, bread exploded in popularity in 1875 in the form of the sweet anpan—a bread bun stuffed with bean paste. From there, Western desserts boomed and became staple treats for many. Today, while some commonly seen Western sweets are direct imports, others often contain an element of Japanese innovation. Take melon pan, for example: made of sweetened bread with a crackly cookie crust, it's not found anywhere besides Japan, but it's made up of foreign parts.

Non-Japanese sweets can represent many things, but mostly they're seen and used in anime for their "special" and "other" qualities. A dessert's specialness might be compounded by a character unlocking incredible new Japanese techniques to create a Western dessert (see Bûche de Noël on page 77). The dessert's admirable qualities could instead be simply put on display in a most mouth-watering way—with scrumptious art and animation so tempting, it'll make your stomach rumble (like mine is right now, just *thinking* about the fluffy pancakes from *Your Name* on page 70). Whatever the case may be, the recipes you'll find here either follow the anime as closely as possible, or (if the anime's recipe is totally out-there) are modified for your home kitchen *and* for the ingredients you're likely to find in your local grocery store.

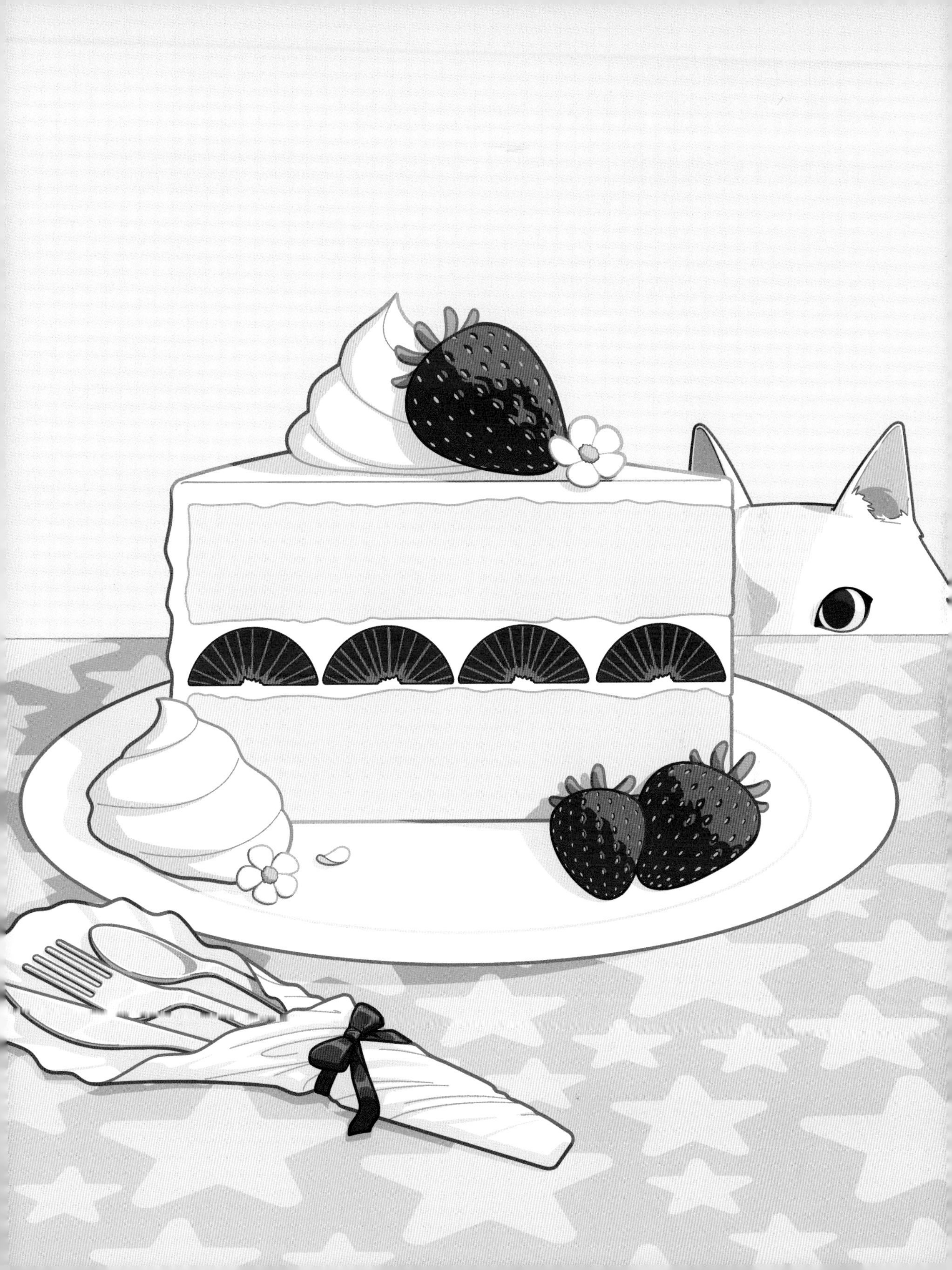

OURAN HIGH SCHOOL HOST CLUB

JAPANESE STRAWBERRY SHORTCAKE

Haruhi, a new scholarship student at the prestigious private Ouran High School, doesn't quite know what she's going to find when she enters the music room. One thing's for sure—she certainly wasn't expecting to see a host club!

After a tragic mishap with an expensive vase, Haruhi finds herself indebted to the club and becomes their newest host. She learns that behind their polished exteriors, these new friends are desperate to just be kids and live life to the fullest. Honey-senpai is a prime example. Pushed by his family to become a martial arts guru, Honey instead longs to enjoy the things he loves in life—sweets and everything cute. His favorite treat? This Japanese strawberry shortcake.

Japanese strawberry shortcake can be found pretty much year-round but is especially popular in December, as its red and white coloring is evocative of Christmas. As a result, you may have also seen this cake in anime by its secondary name—Christmas cake. *But wait!* you're probably thinking. *Strawberries aren't in season in December!*

You are correct. However, Japan has a dedicated hothouse strawberry season from late November to the end of April. To me, though, this is a summer cake, and one I make at least once a year.

4 HOURS

MAKES ONE 8-INCH CAKE

SPECIAL EQUIPMENT: **INFRARED THERMOMETER, PASTRY BAG AND PIPING TIPS**

NUT-FREE

FOOD FACT: When my mom lived in Japan back in the late '80s, there was a term for unmarried women over the age of twenty-five: Christmas cakes! Because, like this special cake, no one wants them after the 25th. *Yikes.*

ANIME FACT: In Japan, host clubs are businesses where adults pay a fee to sit with a companion, play games, and make small talk (and drink lots and lots of alcohol). It's unheard-of for a host club to be staffed with actual high school students, but I suppose if you go to a private school for the very rich, anything is possible.

FOR THE CAKE

6 tablespoons (¾ stick) unsalted butter, plus more for greasing

¼ cup whole milk, at room temperature

7 large eggs, at room temperature

1¼ cups granulated sugar

2 cups cake flour, sifted twice

FOR THE SIMPLE SYRUP

2 tablespoons water

3 tablespoons granulated sugar

1 tablespoon liquor of choice (citrus liqueurs are nice; optional)

FOR THE FILLING AND GARNISH

32 ounces strawberries (about 4 cups)

2½ cups heavy cream

1 teaspoon vanilla extract

5 tablespoons confectioners' sugar

1. Make the cake: Preheat the oven to 350°F. Set an oven rack in the lowest position. Grease the bottom and sides of two 8-inch round cake pans with butter and line the bottoms with parchment paper cut to fit.

2. Place the butter and milk in a small microwave-safe bowl and microwave on high in 20-second intervals, stirring after each heating, until the butter is completely melted. Set aside and keep warm.

3. Fill a pot with 3 inches of water and bring to a boil over high heat. Whisk together the eggs and granulated sugar in a tempered glass or metal bowl. Place the bowl over the pot to make a bain-marie (make sure the bottom of the bowl does not touch the water), lower the heat so the water remains at a simmer, and cook, whisking continuously, until the mixture reaches 110°F to 120°F. Remove the bowl from the pot.

4. Strain the egg mixture through a fine-mesh sieve into a bowl to remove any cooked egg if you notice lumps. Using an electric mixer, beat the mixture on high speed until it has tripled in size and falls from the beaters in ribbons. (If using a handheld mixer on level 5, this will take 8 to 10 minutes. If using a stand mixer on the highest speed, it'll take about half the time.)

5. Cover the surface of the batter with half the flour. Gently fold the flour in with a spatula, lightly scooping down, up, and over the batter. Make sure you're really digging down into the bowl to ensure you're mixing everything. Repeat with the remaining flour.

6. Take a few spoonfuls of cake batter and stir them into the bowl of butter and milk. Gently drizzle this mixture onto the surface of the batter, then use the spatula to fold it in, scooping down one side of the bowl, around the bottom, then up the other side.

7. Divide the batter between the prepared pans. (If you'd like, use a scale to ensure you're pouring exactly the same amount into each pan.) Tap the pans on the counter to release any air bubbles from the batter. Bake the cakes on the bottom rack for 25 to 30 minutes, until a toothpick inserted into the center comes out clean. If you can't fit both pans on the lowest rack, swap their positions halfway through baking. If they start to darken quickly during baking, place a sheet of foil loosely over the top.

8. Remove the cakes from the oven and tap the pans on the counter to stop them from overly shrinking. Allow to cool for 10 minutes, then run a knife around the edges of one cake and flip it over onto a wire rack. Remove the parchment paper, then flip it onto another rack so it's right side up. Repeat with the second cake. Allow to cool completely.

9. Prepare the simple syrup: Place the granulated sugar, water, and alcohol (if using) in a small microwave-safe bowl and microwave on high for 1 minute. Stir until the sugar has completely dissolved, then set aside.

10. Make the filling: You'll need 7 to 10 berries for the top of the cake; they should be as uniform in size and shape as possible. Wipe them down with a damp paper towel and cut off the leafy green tops; set aside. For the filling, cut 7 to 8 berries in half lengthwise, then set them cut side down on a paper towel (to remove excess moisture).

11. Using an electric mixer, beat the cream in a large bowl until it begins to thicken. Add the confectioners' sugar and vanilla and whip until you get medium peaks (when you lift the beaters from the bowl, the cream should form peaks that mostly hold their shape but tip over at the top).

12. Assemble the cake: Trim off the caramelization on the top (and bottom and sides, if you'd like) of both cake layers, making sure the layers are even. Brush the cakes generously with the simple syrup and let stand for 5 minutes to allow the syrup to soak through. The cakes should look wet with moisture before you let the syrup soak in; this will make the final product nice and luxurious.

Continued

13. Place one cake layer on a cake plate or cake board. Spread a layer of the whipped cream over the top, then place the sliced berries cut side down on the cream. Start with a ring of berries around the outer edge of the cake, then make a second ring just inside the first. If there's room, make a third inner ring with the smallest berries. Place a few scoops of whipped cream on top and use a spatula to gently nudge the cream into the gaps between the berries.

14. Place the second cake layer on top. Set aside 1 cup of whipped cream for finishing the cake, then spoon the rest onto the top of the cake and use the spatula to smooth it over the top and sides of the cake, covering it evenly.

15. Transfer the reserved whipped cream to a pastry bag fitted with a closed star piping tip. Pipe 8 cream swirls around the edge of the cake, leaving an equal space between each swirl. Place one cream swirl in the middle as well, then place a whole berry on top of each swirl. Serve and enjoy!

TIRAMISU

Piacevole is Italian for "enjoyable." It's usually used in sheet music to direct the feeling of the sound, but *Piacevole!* the anime truly fulfills the meaning of the word. Each brief episode offers a small, pleasant peek into the lives of the staff of at a Japanese-owned Italian restaurant. Morina Nanase, the main character, is new to Trattoria Festa. While she learns about her eccentric coworkers, she also learns about Italian food.

One of the earlier dishes she's introduced to is tiramisu. After learning all about it, she recommends the dessert to a flirty frequent customer of the restaurant. He tells her that *tiramisu* means "pick me up," and then proceeds to do just that by flirting with Nanase! Tiramisu is a sophisticated, coffee-flavored cake made up of ladyfingers, fluffy enriched cream, and chocolate. It's decadent and rich without being heavy. Best of all, it's a refrigerator cake, meaning you don't need to bake anything—just assemble it and let the moisture in the cream soften the ladyfingers overnight.

40 MINUTES, PLUS RESTING OVERNIGHT

SERVES 9

SPECIAL EQUIPMENT: INFRARED THERMOMETER

NUT-FREE

RECIPE TIP: For an extra kick, add some coffee liqueur to your cup of coffee!

6 large egg yolks, at room temperature

1 cup confectioners' sugar

1¾ cups heavy cream

1¼ cups mascarpone cheese, at room temperature

28 ladyfingers (get the cookie kind, not the cakey kind; I like Italian savoiardi)

1 cup cold coffee

Unsweetened cocoa powder, for dusting

Fresh mint, for garnish

1. Fill a pot with 3 inches of water and bring to a boil over high heat. Whisk together the egg yolks and confectioners' sugar in a tempered glass or metal bowl. Place the bowl over the pot to make a bain-marie (make sure the bottom of the pot does not touch the water) and cook, beating with a handheld mixer on its highest setting, until the egg mixture is light and fluffy and has reached between 110°F and 120°F, 5 to 10 minutes. Remove the bowl from the pot and allow the mixture to cool slightly.

2. Clean the beaters, then use the mixer to beat the cream in a large bowl on high speed until you achieve soft peaks. Add the mascarpone and whip until you achieve medium peaks.

3. When the egg mixture has cooled, carefully fold in the mascarpone mixture carefully until evenly incorporated. Set aside.

4. Dip each ladyfinger into coffee briefly (the longer you let the ladyfinger sit, the more moisture it sucks up, and the more delicate it becomes), placing them in a single layer over the bottom of an 8-inch square cake pan as you go. Add half the mascarpone mixture, using a spatula to smooth the cream into an even layer. Repeat with another layer of coffee-dunked ladyfingers, then top with the rest of the mascarpone mixture. Cover with aluminum foil or plastic wrap and refrigerate overnight.

5. When ready to serve, sprinkle cocoa powder over the top in an even layer (a small sieve can help you get an even coating), slice, and serve garnished with a sprig of fresh mint.

LEMON-ALMOND CHIFFON CAKE

Chihiro and her parents are on their way to their new home when a supposed shortcut leaves them trapped in the spirit world. When her parents are turned into pigs, Chihiro strikes a bargain with the owner of a bathhouse for spirits. She's given a new name and subsequently loses her identity. Her nights become riotous affairs overcome with bossy spirits, and her days are filled with endless chores and making fruitless plans to rescue her family. By the time she finds a train ticket to visit the witch at Swamp Bottom, Chihiro is lost and looking for comfort.

At Swamp Bottom, she's given a warm reception and a warm meal. Unlike the feasts served every night at the bathhouse, the meal laid before her is simple and comforting. The table is filled with rustic, lovingly handcrafted sweets. Of all the desserts on the table, one stands out—a plain cake with white frosting.

In the film, there's no clear-cut answer to what kind of cake this is meant to be, but I picked a sponge for the jiggly nature of the cake. I decided to infuse it with lemon and almond, two refreshing and bright flavors. Try this out and eat a few slices for yourself—your problems may not be completely solved, but like Chihiro, you'll definitely walk away with a better mindset and a more positive outlook after eating some.

5 HOURS

SERVES 8

SPECIAL EQUIPMENT: 8-INCH ROUND NONSTICK ALUMINUM CAKE PAN, CAKE STAND (OPTIONAL)

RECIPE TIP: Why do we flip the cake to cool it? Since the cake is anchored to the bottom of the pan, flipping it helps the cake cool while maintaining the delicate air bubble structure inside. Furthermore, the steam that's trapped inside the pan loosens the edges and bottom of the cake, so turning it out of the pan is much easier.

FOOD FACT: This cake is a spin on Japanese jiggly cheesecake, a spongy cheesecake that wiggles and wobbles.

FOR THE CAKE
5 large egg yolks

1/3 cup whole milk

3 tablespoons vegetable oil

1 teaspoon pure almond extract

2/3 cup plus 2 tablespoons cake flour

Grated zest of 1 lemon

5 large egg whites

1/2 cup granulated sugar

FOR THE GLAZE
1 cup confectioners' sugar

Juice of 1 lemon

1 to 2 tablespoons milk, as needed

FOR THE FROSTING
1 cup whole milk

5 tablespoons all-purpose flour

1 cup (2 sticks) unsalted butter, at room temperature

1 cup granulated sugar

1 teaspoon pure almond extract

Pinch of kosher salt

1. Make the cake: Preheat the oven to 325°F. Set an oven rack in the lowest position.

2. Whisk together the egg yolks, milk, oil, and almond extract in a medium bowl until uniform.

3. Sift the flour into a separate large bowl, then whisk in the lemon zest.

Continued

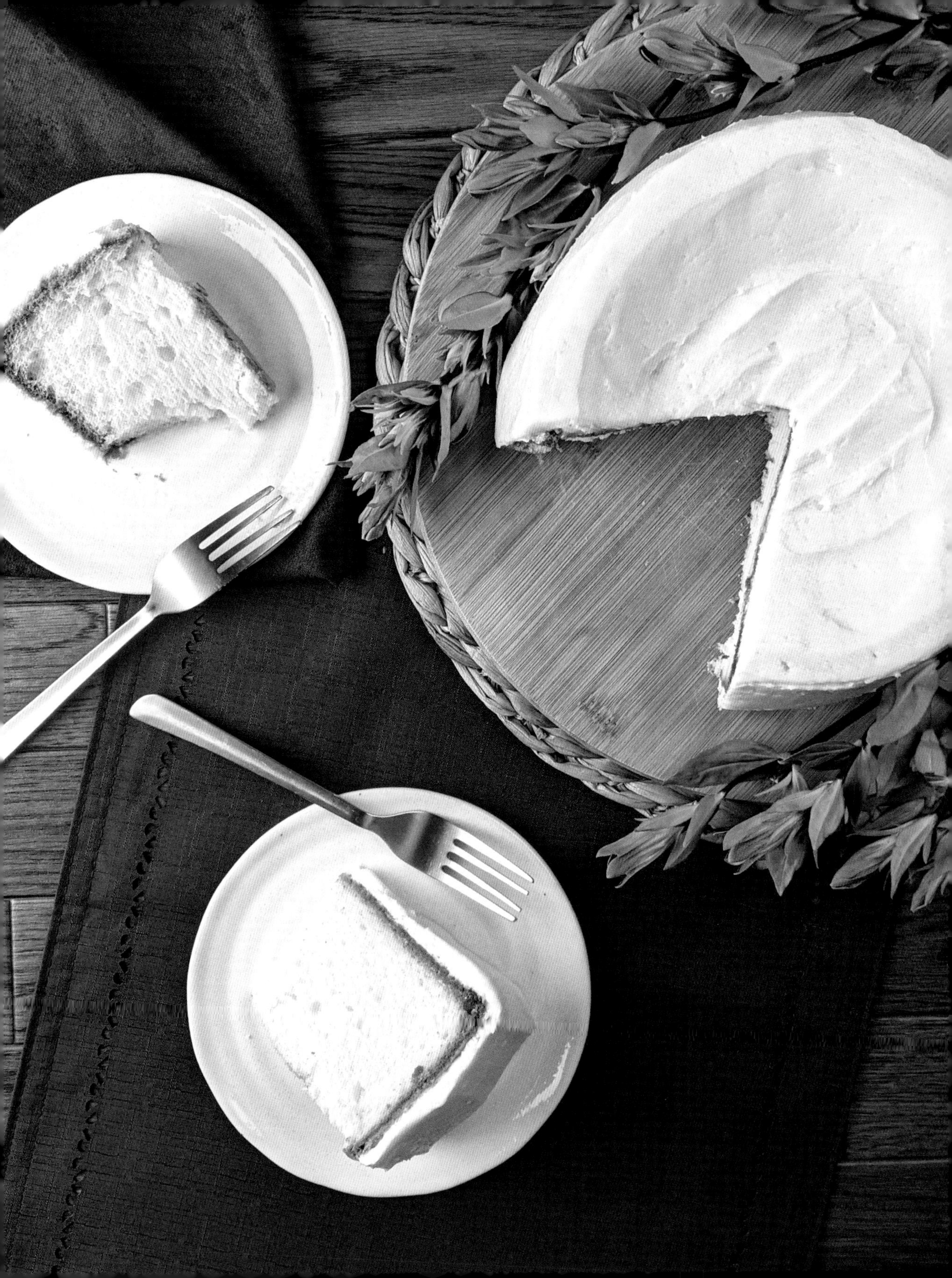

4. Add the egg mixture to the flour mixture, then whisk to combine. Set aside.

5. Place the egg whites in a clean bowl. The bowl and the beaters must be free of water and oil; make sure no egg yolk ends up in the egg whites, or they won't whisk properly. Using an electric mixer, beat the egg whites on medium speed until large bubbles form on the surface. With the mixer running, shake in the granulated sugar a little at a time and beat until the sugar is fully incorporated. Beat on high speed for 5 to 10 minutes, until stiff peaks form and the egg whites are glossy and fluffy.

6. Add a quarter of the egg white mixture to the yolk mixture, then whisk to combine. Pour half the yolk mixture into the bowl with the remaining egg whites and use a spatula to fold the two together until you see only wisps of white, then fold in the remaining yolk mixture until there are no white lumps remaining and the batter is pale yellow.

7. Pour the batter into an 8-inch round nonstick aluminum cake pan and tap the pan gently on the counter to release any air bubbles. Bake for 45 to 50 minutes, until the top is a pale brown and a toothpick inserted into the center comes out clean.

8. Get out a cake stand (or make one out of three overturned cups). Remove the cake from the oven and immediately flip it over onto the cake stand. Allow it to cool in the pan, upside down, for 3 to 4 hours.

9. Make the glaze: Stir together the confectioners' sugar and lemon juice in a small bowl. Thin with a tablespoon or two of milk until you have a runny glaze. Set aside.

10. Make the frosting: Combine the milk and flour in a saucepan and cook over medium heat, stirring continuously with a whisk or spatula to avoid burning, until the mixture is thick and pudding-like, 3 to 5 minutes. Use a spatula to pass the mixture through a fine-mesh sieve into a bowl. Cover with plastic wrap, pressing it directly against the surface of the mixture to prevent a skin from forming, then refrigerate until completely cooled.

11. Using an electric mixer, beat the butter and granulated sugar in a large bowl on high speed until combined, light in color, and fluffy. Add the almond extract and salt and beat to incorporate. Beat in the cooled flour mixture a little at a time until it's all incorporated and the frosting is light and white.

12. Assemble the cake: Run a knife around the edge of the cake to loosen it from the side of the pan. Place a plate or a cake stand on the top of the cake and then flip both the cake and the plate or stand over together. Tap firmly on the bottom of the pan with the heel of your hand so the cake pops out, then remove the pan.

13. Using a spatula, coat the top and sides of the cake in a thin layer of the glaze and allow to set in the fridge, about thirty minutes. Then, pile all the frosting onto the top of the cake and use a spatula to spread it out and down, covering the top and sides evenly. Serve and enjoy.

ORANGE-CINNAMON GÂTEAU MILLE-CRÊPES

Kino's Journey: The Beautiful World—The Animated Series is an introspective anime that explores humanity through the unbiased eyes of a perpetual newcomer. Kino spends their days traveling by motorcycle, visiting new towns and villages and venturing into different countries to learn about the world and the people inhabiting it. Their sole rule is to only stay two nights and three days in any one place.

In one episode, Kino rolls into a town where murder isn't outlawed and most people carry firearms. But while everyone carries a gun for self-defense, the town comes down hard on anyone *unjustly* seeking to harm others (which really makes you wonder what the township considers *justified* harm toward others). In direct contrast to this plotline is the second thing this town is famous for: gâteau mille-crêpes, a stack of crepes layered with crème pâtissière (pastry cream). The townspeople recommend that Kino try it, and Kino is impressed by the intricacy of the cake's many layers and its refreshing taste.

Whether you want to debate the pros and cons of one's right to bear arms for self-defense, this cake is the perfect snack to enjoy with a cup of tea or coffee. Though the flavor isn't specified in the anime, I wanted to do something more exciting than vanilla, so I took inspiration from the sepia filter used in this episode and selected cinnamon and orange flavors.

FOR THE CREPES

3 cups whole milk, warmed

8 large eggs

½ cup (1 stick) unsalted butter, melted, plus more for the pan

Grated zest of 1 orange

2 cups all-purpose flour

¼ cup granulated sugar

1 teaspoon ground cinnamon

Pinch of kosher salt

FOR THE PASTRY CREAM

3 cups whole milk

Grated zest of 1 orange

1 cinnamon stick

6 large egg yolks

¾ cup granulated sugar

⅓ cup plus 2 tablespoons cornstarch, sifted

3 tablespoons unsalted butter

2 tablespoons orange liqueur (optional)

Pinch of kosher salt

FOR THE TOPPING

1 cup heavy cream

2 tablespoons confectioners' sugar

Pinch of ground cinnamon

Continued

3 HOURS, PLUS RESTING OVERNIGHT

SERVES 8

SPECIAL EQUIPMENT: PASTRY BAG AND ROUND PIPING TIP

NUT-FREE

RECIPE TIP: Patience is key to get the precise layers on this cake. Don't rush things by going in with lukewarm or even room-temperature pastry cream or crepes, as they'll start to slide all over the place and make a horrible mess before you know it.

FOOD FACT: *Mille-crêpes* means "one thousand crepes," in reference to the cake's many layers.

1. Make the crepe batter: Whisk together the milk, eggs, melted butter, and orange zest in a large bowl. Sift the flour, granulated sugar, cinnamon, and salt over the wet ingredients, then whisk until there are no lumps and the batter is smooth. Refrigerate for at least 30 minutes.

2. Prepare the pastry cream: Combine the milk, orange zest, and cinnamon stick in a small heavy-bottomed pot. Bring to a low simmer over medium heat, then turn off the heat and allow the mixture to steep for 30 minutes.

3. Place the egg yolks and granulated sugar in a bowl and whisk until thoroughly combined. Sift the cornstarch over the mixture and whisk until no lumps remain. Set aside.

4. Discard the zest and cinnamon stick from the pot of milk. Bring the milk to a low simmer over medium heat, stirring every so often to avoid burning. While whisking continuously, slowly pour a ladleful of the hot milk (¼ to ⅓ cup) into the egg mixture and whisk to combine, then repeat. (This is called tempering the eggs—we do it to slowly heat the eggs so they don't curdle when they come in contact with the hot liquid.) The egg mixture should now be warm to the touch.

5. While whisking, pour the egg mixture into the pot with the rest of the milk and whisk to combine. Switch the whisk for a rubber spatula, raise the heat to medium-high, and cook, stirring continuously and scraping the bottom and sides of the pot to ensure nothing sticks. Within a minute or two, the mixture will thicken. Stop stirring at that point to see whether the mixture is coming to a boil—when it does, you'll notice bubbles fighting their way to the top and popping thickly and the mixture will have a pudding-like consistency; if you dip a spoon into it and run your finger along the back, it should make a distinct stripe in the cream. When this stage is reached, remove the pot from the heat.

6. Add the butter, orange liqueur (if using), and salt and whisk until the butter has melted and the pastry cream is smooth and well combined. If you're worried about bits of cooked egg in the cream, strain it through a fine-mesh sieve in a bowl; otherwise, just transfer it to the bowl. Cover with plastic wrap, pressing it directly against the surface of the pastry cream to prevent a skin from forming, and refrigerate until completely cooled.

7. Cook the crepes: My first crepe always cooks terribly—too browned on one side, or horribly misshapen—so use your first crepe to figure out how to optimize the rest. Fiddle with the heat, or adjust how much batter you put in the pan at the start. Melt a little butter in a nonstick skillet over low heat. Pour in ¼ cup of the crepe batter and swirl the pan until the bottom is completely coated. Cook until the edges become crispy and the surface becomes dry, 1 to 2 minutes, then carefully wiggle a spatula under the crepe and flip it quickly. Cook for another minute to brown the second side, then slide the crepe onto a plate. Stick the plate in the freezer between crepes. Repeat until the batter is gone, then place the full plate in the refrigerator to chill before assembling the cake.

8. When everything is sufficiently cooled, assemble the cake: Place one crepe on a cake stand or serving plate, then top with 2 to 3 tablespoons of the pastry cream and use a knife or an offset spatula to spread the pastry cream into a thin, even layer. Repeat, stacking the crepes and layering with the pastry cream, then chill the cake in the refrigerator overnight. (This helps you get perfect slices when you cut the cake.)

9. Make the topping: Just before you're ready to present the cake, whip the heavy cream in a large bowl until soft peaks form, then add the confectioners' sugar and whip until medium peaks form. Place the cream in a piping bag with a round piping tip and pipe little blobs of cream across the top of the crepe cake, making sure not to leave any space between blobs. Sprinkle a little cinnamon on top to add some color, and serve.

CHOCOLATE CHECKERBOARD CAKE

Momo is a standout chef at school. While most students specialize in some form of savory cookery, she's a master of all things sweet. Famous for her whimsical apple tart and her formidable roll cake castles, her chocolate checkerboard cake is nothing but pure class— it's glossy and sleek and the interior is breathtaking in its complexity.

Momo uses military precision to assemble her desserts, which is reflected in this recipe. This checkerboard cake is no joke—in order to get the right look, it's important to get the measurements and the cutting correct. The damask rose made of modeling chocolate for the top of the cake is optional—after the checkerboard assembly, you might be worn out. However, if you're going for a professional look, this is a final touch you can't skip.

2 HOURS 40 MINUTES

SERVES 8

SPECIAL EQUIPMENT: CIRCLE CUTTERS OR TEMPLATES

NUT-FREE

RECIPE TIP: There's no denying it—this recipe is long, but you don't have to do it all in a day! Take it in stages: I made the modeling chocolate one week and the cakes the next week, then assembled everything a week later.

Store the modeling chocolate in a plastic bag in a cool, dry space. The cakes can be wrapped in plastic wrap and stored in a plastic bag in the freezer. When ready to use, simply allow them to thaw slightly until very chilled, and assemble from there.

FOR THE MODELING CHOCOLATE (OPTIONAL)
12 ounces milk chocolate candy coating wafers, such as Candy Melts

¼ cup corn syrup

FOR THE CAKE
1 cup (2 sticks) unsalted butter, at room temperature, plus more for greasing

½ cup unsweetened Dutch-process cocoa powder

½ cup unsweetened natural (not Dutch-process) cocoa powder

2 cups boiling water

2²/₃ cups all-purpose flour

2 teaspoons baking powder

1½ teaspoons baking soda

1 teaspoon kosher salt

2½ cups sugar

4 large eggs

FOR THE CHOCOLATE GANACHE
2 cups heavy cream

16 ounces good-quality dark chocolate (72 percent cacao), chopped into small chunks

1. Make the modeling chocolate (if using): Place the candy coating wafers in a microwave-safe bowl and microwave in 30-second intervals, stirring after each, until most of the chocolate has melted, then microwave for 10-second stints, stirring after each, until the chocolate is completely melted and smooth. The melted chocolate should be warm but not hot. If the bowl feels hot to the touch, transfer the chocolate to a new bowl to stop it from scorching from the residual heat.

2. Pour in the corn syrup and stir with a rubber spatula to combine. Scrape carefully all around the bowl, making sure all the chocolate comes in contact with the corn syrup. Don't overmix— stop as soon as the corn syrup looks mostly incorporated and the mixture has started to cling together rather than to the sides of the bowl. It should look wet and the consistency should be similar to soft-serve ice cream. Pour the mixture into a zip-top plastic bag. Squeeze the air out,

Continued

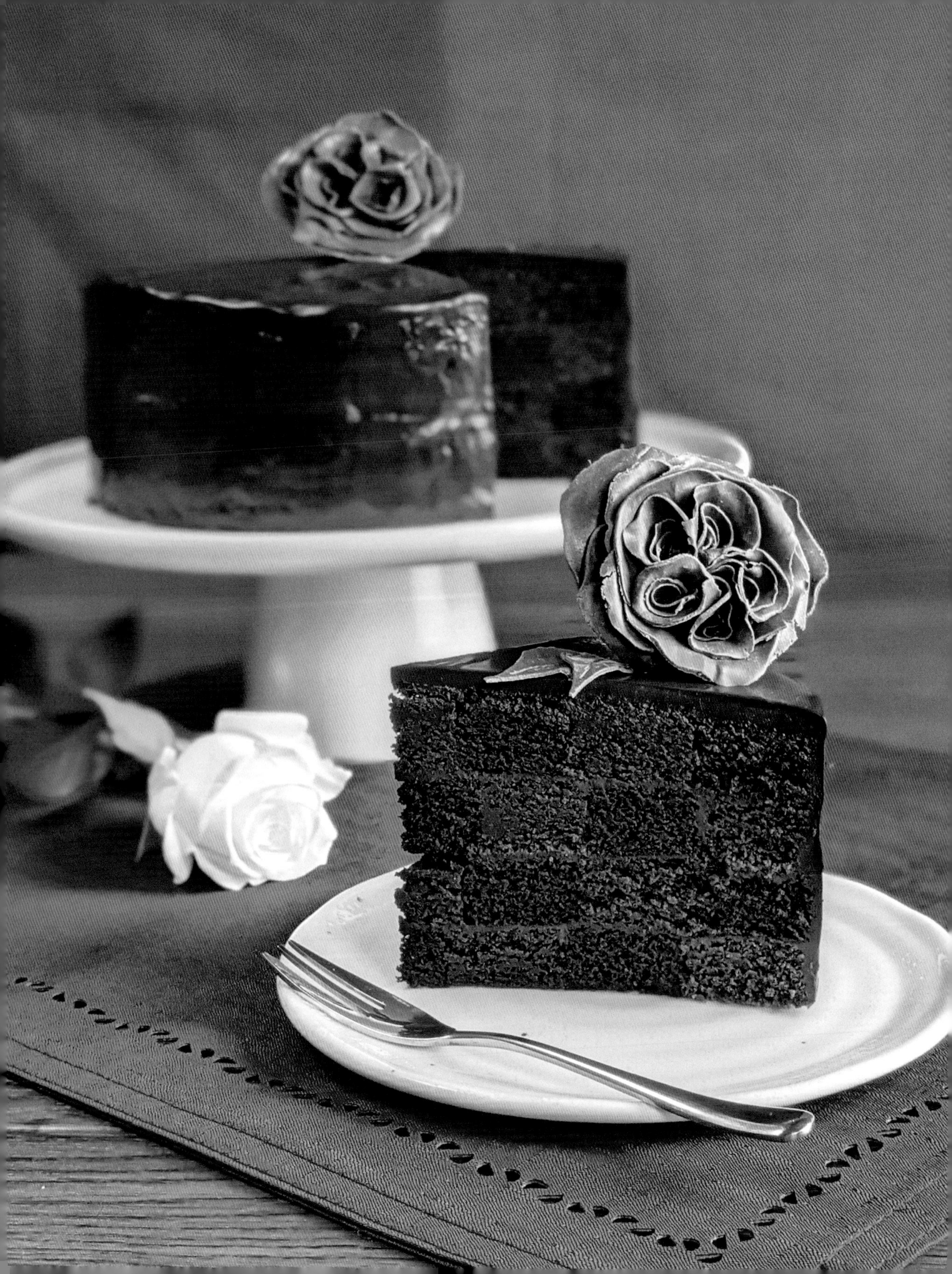

seal, and set aside to harden in a cool, dry place. (The modeling chocolate can be made 1 to 2 weeks ahead.)

3. Make the cake: Preheat the oven to 350°F. Grease the bottom and sides of two 8-inch round cake pans with butter and line the bottoms with parchment paper cut to fit.

4. Put the Dutch-process and natural cocoa powders in separate small bowls. Add 1 cup of the boiling water to each bowl and whisk to combine. Set aside.

5. Sift 1⅓ cups of the flour, 1 teaspoon of the baking powder, ¾ teaspoon of the baking soda, and ½ teaspoon of the salt together into a medium bowl. Set aside.

6. Using an electric mixer, cream ½ cup (1 stick) of the butter and 1¼ cups of the sugar together until lightened in color and fluffy, about 2 minutes. Add 2 eggs, beating them in one at a time. Add about ⅓ of the flour mixture, then about ½ of the Dutch-process cocoa mixture, then another ⅓ of the flour mixture, then the remaining Dutch-process cocoa mixture, then the remaining flour mixture and mix until entirely combined. Pour the batter into one of the prepared pans and set aside.

7. Repeat steps 5 and 6 with the remaining ingredients, adding the natural cocoa mixture in step 6 (this will tint the batter a lighter brown than the first batch). Bake the cakes for 1 hour, or until a toothpick inserted into the center comes out clean. Rotate the pans after 30 minutes to make sure they bake evenly. Allow to cool in the pans on the counter, then turn them out of the pans, wrap the cakes in plastic wrap, and refrigerate.

8. To achieve the checkerboard effect, you'll need to cut the cakes into rings of decreasing sizes: a 7-inch ring, a 5-inch ring, a 3-inch ring, and a 1-inch round. To guide your cuts, make sure you have templates or round cutters of the correct sizes. Trim a thin layer off the top of the cake using a long serrated knife, making sure the top is level (you can discard the scraps or eat them). With a ruler, measure up the side of one cake to find the midpoint. Use the serrated knife to split the cake perfectly in half horizontally, but leave the cut halves stacked together.

9. Set a 7-inch circular template on top of the cake and cut around the outside of the template, making sure the edge is even. Remove the template and set the 5-inch template on top of the cake. Carefully cut into the cake around the outside of the 5-inch template to form a ring. Repeat with the 3-inch template. Carefully lift and separate the outer rings, then repeat with the 1-inch template and the 3-inch round of cake that remains. Separate the cake layers so you have two rings of each size. Repeat with the second cake. If you're worried about the layers ripping during assembly, chill them in the freezer for an hour to add strength.

10. Assemble the cake layers: To achieve the checkerboard look, you'll alternate the darker- and lighter-brown rings: Place a 7-inch light brown ring on your serving plate or cake stand, then nestle a 5-inch dark brown ring in the center. Nestle a 3-inch light brown ring in the center of that, and finish with a 1-inch dark brown round. It will look like a bull's-eye when you're done. Assemble a second layer in the same fashion, then repeat, starting with a 7-inch dark brown ring, to make two more layers. Refrigerate the layers for about 30 minutes before assembling the cake.

11. Make the chocolate ganache: Place the heavy cream in a microwave-safe bowl and microwave for 1 minute or until hot. Add the chocolate and let it sit for 10 minutes, then stir to melt the chocolate and combine it with the cream. At this stage, the ganache will be thick and runny.

12. Assemble the cake: Pull the cake layers out of the refrigerator. Place one layer with a light brown outer ring on a cake board. Spoon on some ganache and spread it into a thin layer over

Continued

RECIPE TIP: Not interested in buying two types of cocoa powder? You can use natural (not Dutch-process) cocoa powder for both layers if you'd like to cut a corner here, and simply add a small drop of black food coloring to half the batter to tint it slightly darker.

STORAGE TIP: If you can't eat all the cake within a few days (doubtful), wrap with plastic wrap and store at room temperature for up to a week.

the top of the whole cake. Place a cake layer with a dark brown outer ring on top, spread a thin layer of ganache over it, and repeat with the remaining cake layers. The assembled cake should look striped.

13. Using a rubber spatula, crumb-coat the whole cake with a thin layer of ganache, working it into any uneven cracks or surfaces on the top and sides of the cake and locking down any crumbs. This layer doesn't need to look nice; it just serves to trap any crumbs in place so they don't get into the top layer of frosting. Chill the cake in the refrigerator for 30 minutes.

14. Set up a ganache pouring station: Line a baking sheet with parchment paper and set a wire rack on top. Remove the cake from the refrigerator and set it on the wire rack. If the ganache has firmed too much, warm it in the microwave in 10-second bursts, stirring after each, until it's smooth and pourable. Working quickly, pour a generous helping of ganache onto the middle of the cake. Use a cake spatula to gently smooth out the ganache to cover the top, and then urge it over the sides. Use your spatula to smooth the ganache around the edges, coaxing it anywhere that needs more coverage.

15. If the cake needs a second or third coating of ganache, return it to the fridge, collect the ganache that fell under the cake, microwave if necessary to soften it, and repeat until you're happy with the coverage. When it's coated to your liking, chill the cake in the refrigerator to allow the ganache to harden.

16. Make the roses: You'll need round cutters in four sizes for the roses—3 inches, 2 inches, 1½ inches, and 1 inch. Take out that modeling chocolate and take some time to massage it into a workable state, kneading it with your hands until it's pliable. Separate about one-eighth of the modeling chocolate. Use a third of that to make a base for your rose, rolling it into a ball and then squashing it flat. Taper the edges inward so the top is thicker than the bottom, creating a slight cone. Set aside.

17. Roll out the rest of the chocolate as thinly as possible. A damask rose has an interior unlike that of other roses—instead of having the petals bunched around one center, a damask rose has petals bunched together in clusters. To replicate this, start from the middle of the flower and work your way outward. We'll start by making five interior clusters of petals.

18. For the interior petals, you'll need to cut five 2-inch circles, five 1½-inch circles, and five 1-inch circles of the modeling chocolate. Line the petals up in three rows, grouping the same size petals together. Use a finger to thin the top edge of each petal—pick one half of each circle to be the top and squash it down to make the edge look more natural.

19. Place a 1-inch circle of modeling chocolate directly in the center of the 1½-inch circle, with the tops of the petals aligned. Then place this stack on a 2-inch circle so the 1½-inch circle is just shy of the top. At this point, you should have three circles stacked on top of each other. Fold the whole thing in half like a taco so the smaller circle is on the inside and all the petal tops are on one end of the taco. Repeat with the four other circle sets to make five petal tacos total. Using your fingers, flip the petal edges outward to make them look more realistic.

20. Take the five petal tacos and fit them together in a circle, insides together, with the tops of the petals all flipped outward. Cut off the bottom end to even the rose off and squish it onto the flower base you made in step 19. Use the largest circle cutter to cut more circles. Cut each circle in half with a knife, then use your fingers to thin the rounded part of each petal. Wrap these petals around the inner petals, flipping out the top edge of each petal when you're done affixing it to the base.

21. Repeat with the remaining modeling chocolate to make as many roses as you'd like. If you use all the chocolate, you should be able to make 7 or 8 roses that are roughly 3 inches in diameter.

22. When ready to serve, cut clean slices of the cake, wiping off the knife after each cut. Garnish each slice with a damask rose and serve.

CARDCAPTOR SAKURA: CLEAR CARD

RARE HONEY CHEESECAKE WITH A RASPBERRY SAUCE

Sakura is a young girl who gains a special ability—using a key, she can invoke the power of the mystical Clow Cards to give herself magical powers. When the Clow Cards suddenly go clear, Sakura goes on a quest to find out what's wrong. Along the way, however, she has plenty of time to cook tasty recipes.

In one episode, Sakura's friend Chiharu gives her a recipe for rare cheesecake (the Japanese name for no-bake cheesecake). Out of all the anime food I've ever made, this is a personal favorite. The contrast of the honey cheesecake with the raspberry sauce is truly enlightening. Sakura's eagerness to try her friend's recipe in the middle of a personal disaster is a charming reminder that no matter our circumstances, there's always time for cheesecake.

1 HOUR, PLUS RESTING OVERNIGHT

SERVES 8

NUT-FREE

RECIPE TIP: If the cream cheese isn't completely soft, you'll likely end up with obnoxious little lumps in the batter that are impossible to get rid of. Save yourself from this problem by letting the cream cheese reach the correct temperature before you try to work with it, and be sure to whip it by itself to further soften it before adding anything else to the bowl.

FOR THE CHEESECAKE

4 tablespoons (½ stick) unsalted butter, melted

1½ cups graham cracker crumbs or Biscoff cookie crumbs

1¾ teaspoons unflavored powdered gelatin

¼ cup warm water

2 cups heavy cream

2 (8-ounce) packages cream cheese, at room temperature (very soft)

⅔ cup sugar

¼ cup honey

Juice of 1 lemon

FOR THE RASPBERRY SAUCE

6 ounces fresh or frozen raspberries

¼ cup sugar

¼ cup water

Fresh mint, for garnish (optional)

1. Make the cheesecake: Line the bottom of an 8-inch springform pan with parchment paper cut to fit. Stir together the melted butter and graham cracker crumbs in a bowl until the crumbs are evenly moistened, then transfer the crumb mixture to the prepared pan and press it firmly and evenly over the bottom. Refrigerate the crust until you're ready to assemble the cheesecake.

2. Pour the warm water into a small bowl, sprinkle the gelatin over the top, and mix together. Set aside for 3 to 5 minutes to bloom.

3. Using an electric mixer, whip the heavy cream in a large bowl until medium peaks are achieved, 3 to 5 minutes. Set aside.

4. In a separate large bowl, use the mixer to beat the cream cheese briefly until there are no lumps. Add the sugar, honey, and lemon juice and beat until completely incorporated.

Continued

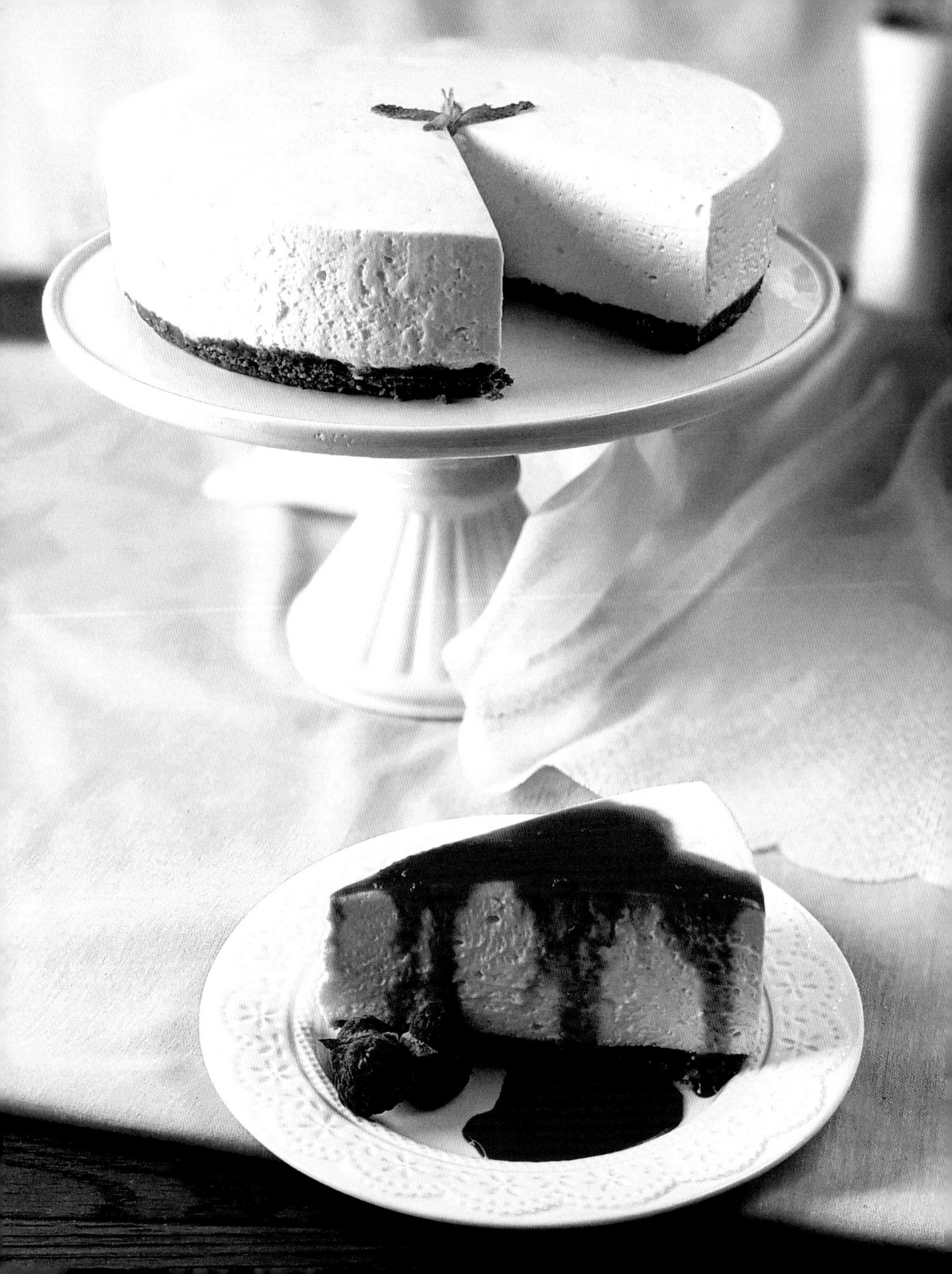

5. Microwave the gelatin mixture for 10 seconds. Allow it to cool slightly, then whip it into the cream cheese mixture.

6. Add half the whipped cream and beat on low speed until fully combined, then repeat to incorporate the remaining whipped cream.

7. Pour the cream cheese mixture over the graham cracker crust. Smooth it into an even layer with a spatula, then cover with plastic wrap and gently press the plastic wrap against the surface of the filling so a skin doesn't form. Refrigerate for at least 4 hours, but ideally overnight.

8. Make the raspberry sauce: Combine the berries, sugar, and water in a small saucepan and bring to a simmer over medium heat. Cook until the berries are soft and falling apart, then remove from the heat and use a spatula to smash them into pulp. Strain the raspberry sauce through a fine-mesh sieve into a bowl. Refrigerate to cool.

9. To serve, unfasten the springform ring and remove it from the cake. Slide the cake off the bottom of the springform tin and onto a serving platter. If the parchment paper starts to peel off during the transfer, you can carefully tug it out from under the cheesecake. If it doesn't budge, simply remove it after slicing the cake. Garnish with a sprig of mint in the center, if desired. Serve each slice with a generous spoonful of the raspberry sauce and enjoy!

YOUR NAME

BOUNCY SOUFFLÉ PANCAKES

In *Your Name*, Mitsuha and Taki are two teenagers tied by the red thread of fate: they wake up one morning having switched bodies! Taki wakes up in Mitsuha's body and experiences her country life, steeped in family and tradition. Mitsuha, on the other hand, wakes up in Taki's body and is let loose in Tokyo, caught up in the sparkle and flash of the city. She also gets to enjoy the most gorgeous plate of fluffy pancakes ever animated.

Food fads come and go in Japan, but there's a particular love for pancakes that's endured for years. The current trend is fluffy soufflé pancakes, and the ones Mitsuha eats fall into this category: they're large, jiggly, and drenched in fresh fruit, butter, and syrup. Making these pancakes takes some practice—the batter is delicate and can collapse easily—but once you nail it, you'll be rewarded with the softest pancakes ever.

40 MINUTES

MAKES 6 PANCAKES

NUT-FREE

RECIPE TIP: This recipe is simple in practice, but it can quickly frustrate you. Make sure you don't overfold the batter—you want to trap as many air bubbles in the batter as possible. Also make sure you understand your stove. Try cooking a test pancake before you commit to doing all of them in one go. Keep in mind that my stove's lowest setting—which heated my pan to 300°F—might not be the same as yours, so adjust your timing as needed. Finally, confirm that you have a well-fitting lid for the pan. This traps steam inside, which helps cook the pancake perfectly. Without this element, your pancakes will fall flat and be gummy inside.

FOR THE PANCAKES

4 large eggs

3 tablespoons whole milk

½ teaspoon vanilla extract

½ cup cake flour

1 teaspoon baking powder

¼ cup granulated sugar

Neutral oil, such as vegetable or canola, for greasing the pan

FOR THE TOPPINGS

1 mango, peeled and cut into chunks

1 banana, sliced

Handful of raspberries

Handful of blueberries

Confectioners' sugar

Salted butter

Maple syrup

1. Make the pancake batter: Separate the eggs into two medium bowls, taking care not to get any yolk in the whites. Refrigerate the whites.

2. Add the milk and vanilla to the bowl with the egg yolks. Beat with an electric mixer to combine, then sift in the cake flour and baking powder and mix again until just combined. Set aside.

3. Clean the beaters thoroughly, then whip the egg whites on high speed. When they start to froth, add the granulated sugar little by little until it's all incorporated. Keep beating until you achieve stiff, glossy peaks.

4. Take a hefty scoop of the egg white mixture and add it to the yolk mixture. Beat with the mixer until incorporated. Add another scoop of whites and mix again.

5. Add half the remaining egg white mixture to the egg yolk mixture. Fold the two together with a rubber spatula until only wisps of egg white remain. Pour in the rest of the egg white mixture and fold together again until everything's incorporated. Make sure to scrape the bottom of the bowl so that no egg white is left behind during mixing.

6. Lightly grease a nonstick pan with oil, then set it over a burner on its lowest heat setting. Use some kind of scooper—I prefer a 4-ounce, ½-cup ice cream scoop, but a ladle will do—to scoop 3 pools of batter onto the pan. Don't spread the batter out. Pour 1 to 2 tablespoons water into the empty spaces around the pancakes (this will create steam to help cook them), then cover the pan with a lid. Set a timer for 2 minutes and let them cook. Don't open the lid until the timer goes off.

7. When the timer goes off, uncover the pan and top each pancake with an additional half scoop of batter. Add a little more water to the pan if you notice it is dry, then cover and set a timer for 6 minutes.

8. When the timer goes off, remove the lid and test the pancakes: Gently wiggle a spatula under one of them. The top will look uncooked, but the bottom should be golden brown. If it's still clinging to the pan or seems to be raw underneath, put the lid back on and cook for a few more minutes before attempting to flip the pancakes. When you get the spatula under a pancake, pull back to move the pancake a little to clear some space in the pan, then flip it over. Repeat to flip the remaining pancakes.

9. Add another tablespoon of water to the pan, then cover it with the lid and cook for 6 minutes. Plate the pancakes, cover with toppings, and serve immediately. Repeat with the remaining batter, serving each batch of pancakes as soon as they are done.

SERVING TIP: As these pancakes cool, they'll deflate. Like a regular soufflé, the hot air trapped inside is what helps puff the pancakes. As they cool, they lose air, so eat them immediately for the most pillowy pancakes you've ever had.

FOOD FACT: These fluffy pancakes are so popular, you can find restaurants in Japan totally devoted to them, serving both sweet and savory versions.

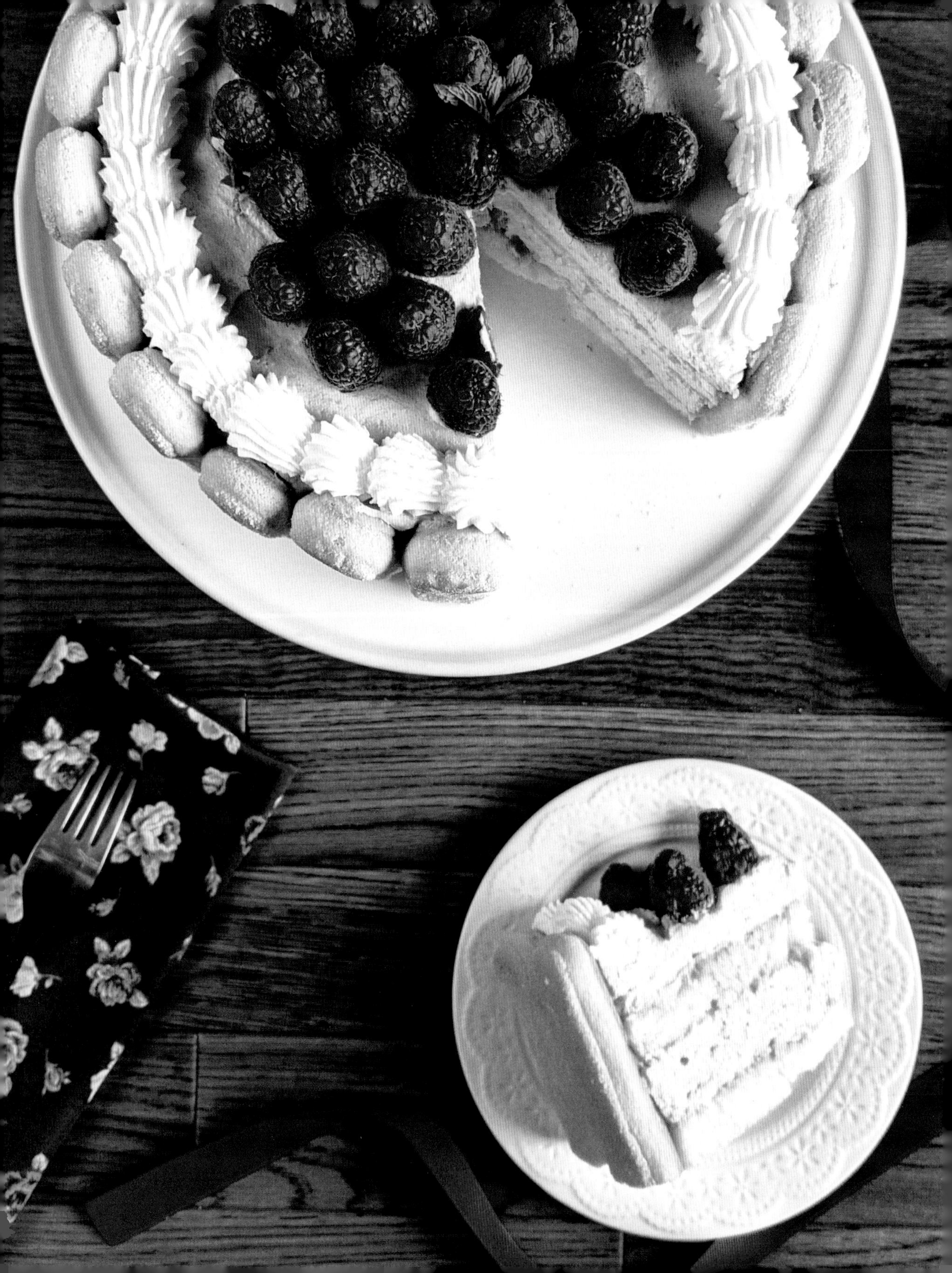

CHARLOTTE RUSSE CAKE

Middle-schoolers Madoka and Sayaka are on a walk one day when they encounter the catlike creature Kyubey. Kyubey offers the girls a contract: any wish granted in exchange for their service as magical girls. Curious about what it means to be a "magical girl"—and tempted by the idea of having any wish of theirs come true—they agree.

On one mission, they run into the witch Charlotte, an extremely tenacious sorceress of sweets. Charlotte's labyrinth is populated by all kinds of desserts. If you look closely at the background during this episode, you can see that the walls are made of charlotte russe, a type of layered mousse cake. Charlotte russe layers can be made with just about anything bready—sponge cake, cookies, even actual bread—and are glued together with a rich, creamy mousse. While it looks difficult, this cake is actually a no-bake masterpiece. Simply assemble it the day before, rest it overnight, and eat it, in excess, the next day.

1 HOUR, PLUS RESTING OVERNIGHT

SERVES 8

NUT-FREE

RECIPE TIPS:
Using stale bread might be a little weird for you, but this isn't as unusual as you'd think. Plenty of older recipes use bread as an ingredient for sweets (bread pudding, anyone?). If you can't get around it, bake up a sponge cake and slice it into layers, or just use ladyfingers instead.

If you don't have day-old bread, leave your slices on the counter overnight to let them dry out.

FOR THE CAKE

¼ cup plus 3 tablespoons water

1 tablespoon unflavored powdered gelatin

12 ounces fresh raspberries

½ cup granulated sugar

Juice of 1 lemon

¼ cup strawberry jam

6 slices stale white bread

2 (7-ounce) packages Savoiardi ladyfingers

3 cups heavy cream

⅓ cup confectioners' sugar

FOR TOPPING

1 cup heavy cream

2 tablespoons confectioners' sugar

6 ounces fresh raspberries

Fresh mint leaves, for garnish

1. Make the cake: Pour 3 tablespoons of the water into a small bowl, sprinkle the gelatin over the top, and mix together. Set aside to bloom for 3 to 5 minutes, or until the water has been absorbed.

2. Cook the raspberries and granulated sugar in a small saucepan over medium heat, stirring occasionally. When the berries have broken down, remove the pan from the heat. Strain through a fine-mesh sieve to remove the seeds, then pour the raspberry sauce back into the pan. Set the pan over low heat, then add the lemon juice and bloomed gelatin. Stir until the gelatin has melted and everything is thoroughly combined. Set aside to cool.

3. Mix the strawberry jam and remaining ¼ cup water together in a small bowl. Cut the crusts off the bread, then arrange 2½ slices of the bread to fit snugly over the bottom of an 8-inch springform pan and brush with the jam mixture to add moisture. Arrange the ladyfingers around the edge of the pan, standing them up vertically and using the bread to keep them pushed up along the pan's inner edge.

Continued

4. Using an electric mixer, whip the cream in a large bowl until you achieve soft peaks, then add the confectioners' sugar and whip to medium peaks. Pour in the cooled raspberry sauce and mix on low speed until everything is uniform. If the cream gets too stiff, switch to a spatula to finish folding everything together.

5. Spoon half the raspberry mousse into the pan and smooth it over the bread. Add another layer of bread, using what you have left. Brush the bread with more strawberry jam, then pile on the remaining mousse and spread it evenly. Cover with plastic wrap, pressing it directly against the surface of the mousse to prevent a skin from forming, then refrigerate overnight.

6. Make the topping: The next day, using an electric mixer, whip the cream in a large bowl until you achieve soft peaks, then add the confectioners' sugar and whip until you get medium peaks.

7. Pop the cake out of the pan by unfastening the springform ring and removing it. Set the cake on a serving platter and decorate the top with the whipped cream. (If desired, use a pastry bag fitted with a star tip to pipe the cream in little dollops.) Arrange the raspberries on top as desired and garnish with mint leaves. Enjoy generous slices—trust me, you'll want to go back for more.

ROKUHOUDOU YOTSUIRO BIYORI

MONT BLANC

Tsubaki, the pâtissier of the Japanese tea shop Rokuhoudou, goes out one afternoon to sample another shop's Mont Blanc, a favorite dessert in Japan year-round. Made with cake or biscuit, chantilly cream, chestnut paste, and chestnuts in syrup, the dish has a mature, refined taste. Tsubaki is inspired by the Mont Blanc he samples, and especially by the complexity of the chestnut cream. He decides to feature the dessert in Rokuhoudou, and when he does, he's surprised to find that his first customer is the maker of the very same Mont Blanc that inspired him in the first place.

To reflect his recipe, each step in mine draws on the flavor of chestnuts to heighten the overall autumnal effect. If you've got someone to impress with your sophisticated maturity like Tsubaki, this is the perfect dessert to make for them.

1 HOUR 45 MINUTES

MAKES 8 MINI MONT BLANCS

SPECIAL EQUIPMENT: 2-INCH ROUND CUTTER, INFRARED THERMOMETER, PASTRY BAG AND MONT BLANC PIPING TIP

RECIPE TIP: The only thing that can be tricky about this recipe is mastering the piping work with the chestnut cream. Do a few practice runs making little piles of chestnut frosting on a piece of plastic wrap. You can easily reuse it by scraping the cream back into the pastry bag afterward.

FOOD FACT: *Mont blanc* is French for "white mountain," and is also the name of a specific snowcapped mountain in Europe. Traditionally, the dessert has a thick sprinkling of confectioners' sugar on top to mimic the snowy mountain.

FOR THE SPONGE CAKE BASE

2 large egg yolks

1 cup granulated sugar

1 cup all-purpose flour

FOR THE CHANTILLY CREAM

2 cups heavy cream

2 tablespoons confectioners' sugar

FOR THE CHESTNUT CREAM TOPPING

2 cups chestnut paste

2 tablespoons light rum (optional)

2 tablespoons whole milk

TO ASSEMBLE

8 kuri kanroni (chestnuts in heavy syrup)

Confectioners' sugar, for dusting

1. Preheat the oven to 350°F. Line the bottom of an 8-inch square baking pan with parchment paper.

2. Make the sponge cake base: Fill a pot with 3 inches of water and bring to a boil over high heat. Whisk together the egg yolks and granulated sugar in a tempered glass or metal bowl. Place the bowl over the pot to make a bain-marie (make sure the bottom of the bowl does not touch the water), reduce the heat to medium, and cook, beating with a handheld mixer to keep the eggs moving in the bowl, for about 5 minutes, until the mixture reaches 110°F to 120°F.

3. Remove the bowl from the pot and beat the mixture on high speed until the bowl has cooled to the touch and the mixture is fluffy and has at least doubled in size, 8 to 10 minutes.

4. Sift the flour over the surface of the mixture and fold it in with a rubber spatula until you no longer see streaks of flour. Do so carefully, scraping the bottom and sides of the bowl to ensure all the flour is incorporated. Pour the mixture into the prepared baking pan and tap the pan briskly on the counter to release any bubbles, then bake for 12 to 15 minutes, until the top is golden brown and a toothpick inserted into the center comes out clean. Set aside to cool in the pan.

Continued

5. Make the chantilly cream: Using an electric mixer, beat the heavy cream in a large bowl on medium-low speed for 4 to 5 minutes, until you achieve soft peaks. Add the confectioners' sugar and mix on low for another 30 seconds or so, until you get medium peaks. Refrigerate until chilled.

6. Make the chestnut cream topping: Combine the chestnut paste, rum (if using), and milk in a large bowl. Using an electric mixer, blitz everything just long enough to combine. With a rubber spatula, fold in ⅔ cup of the chilled chantilly cream to lighten the mixture.

7. Transfer the chestnut cream to a pastry bag fitted with a Mont Blanc piping tip, then refrigerate until ready to use.

8. Assemble the Mont Blancs: Use a 2-inch cutter to cut rounds of sponge cake. Pop open the kuri kanroni jar and dab or brush the heavy syrup from the jar onto the cake rounds to add moisture and flavor. Top each cake round with one of the kuri kanroni, then use a small butter knife or cake spatula to spread chantilly cream on top of the chestnut into a cone shape. Smooth out the cream so it comes to the edges of the cake.

9. Place the cakes in individual cupcake liners or small cake boards and arrange on a serving platter. Working with one cake at a time and starting from the base of the cake, pipe the chestnut cream around the cake, spiraling up the Mont Blanc until you reach the top. The key is to move steadily and without rushing so you can achieve clean, unbroken lines. Using a sieve, dust the Mont Blancs with confectioners' sugar and serve!

FOOD WARS! SHOKUGEKI NO SOMA

BÛCHE DE NOËL

In *Food Wars!*, Soma fights to be selected as the top chef in the BLUE (Bishoku Leading Under-25 Entrance) competition. It's a warm midsummer day when Soma is tasked with making a showstopping Christmas dessert, but that doesn't stop him. In order to impress the judges, he makes a cake that's simultaneously impressive (with "exploding" white chocolate ornaments) and weather appropriate (made from light, refreshing, in-season ingredients).

While I can appreciate the ingenuity of this recipe, it's not particularly user-friendly, nor does it overwhelm in taste or appearance. What we see in the anime is a stretch: Soma uses silken tofu, soy milk, banana, and avocado to create two different creams, but in reality these ingredients lack the proper fats necessary to trap air, so the "creams" end up more like pudding. Also, avocado and banana both oxidize quickly, tingeing the cream an odd off-white color. Soma uses yamaimo in the cake, but I find it weighs down the batter and compresses the sponge. Long story short, there are a variety of tweaks we can make here that will result in a better-tasting and better-looking dessert. Soma's goal was to make a showstopping cake that wasn't too heavy on the palate, and we can keep that goal in mind while making this cake user-friendly (and tasty) for the average cook.

2 HOURS 20 MINUTES

SERVES 8

SPECIAL EQUIPMENT: **INFRARED THERMOMETER, 12 X 8-INCH JELLY-ROLL PAN, 2-INCH SPHERE MOLD, SYRINGE, METAL SKEWER**

RECIPE TIP:
The components of this recipe can (and, in my opinion, should) be made on separate days. Put the roll cake in the freezer, leave it there overnight, and move on to the other steps the next day. The ornament sauce, shells, and granola can also be prepared in advance, but assemble everything the day you plan to serve it. To make sure the ganache is the right consistency, make it the day you plan to decorate the bûche de Noël.

FOR THE SWISS ROLL CAKE

Nonstick cooking spray

3 large eggs, at room temperature

⅓ cup granulated sugar

1 teaspoon vanilla extract

½ teaspoon baking powder

½ cup cake flour

FOR THE WHIPPED CREAM FILLINGS

1 cup heavy cream

4 tablespoons confectioners' sugar

1 tablespoon grated orange zest

2 tablespoons unsweetened Dutch-process cocoa powder

FOR THE WHITE CHOCOLATE ORNAMENTS

5 ounces white chocolate

2 tablespoons grated orange zest

¼ cup of your favorite granola (should contain sweetened oats, dried fruit, and nuts)

1 teaspoon ground coffee beans or granulated instant coffee

⅓ cup heavy cream

⅓ cup soft caramel candies, plus more if needed

1 tablespoon unsweetened Dutch-process cocoa powder, if needed

1 vanilla bean

FOR THE GANACHE FROSTING

1 cup heavy cream

8 ounces dark chocolate

Rosemary sprigs, for garnish

Continued

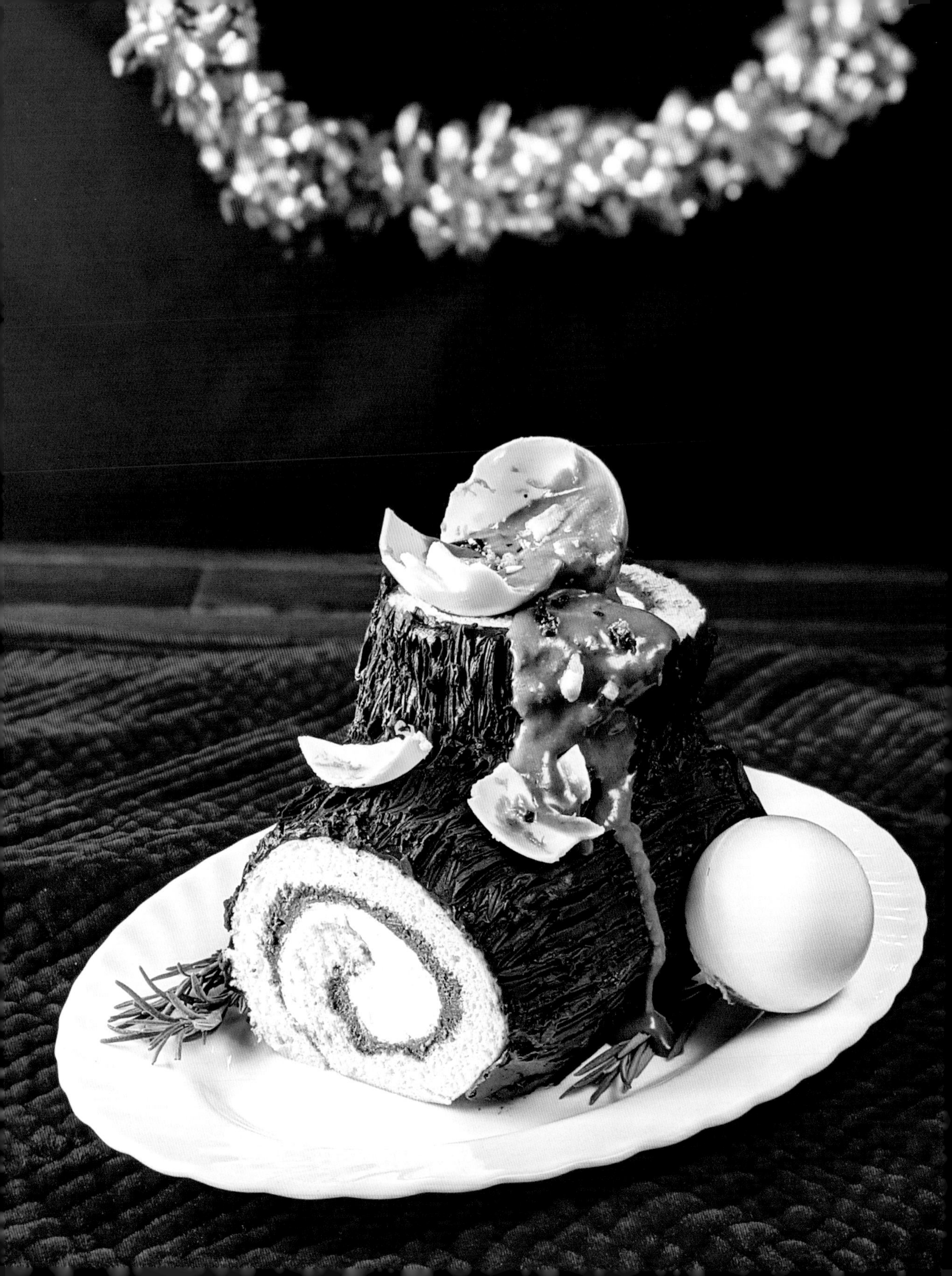

1. Make the Swiss roll cake: Preheat the oven to 350°F. Spray a jelly-roll pan with nonstick spray and line it with parchment paper, pressing it into the corners of the pan.

2. Separate the eggs into two medium bowls and set the egg yolks aside. Using an electric mixer, beat the egg whites until they start to foam, then add the granulated sugar spoonful by spoonful until it's all incorporated. Keep beating until you achieved stiff peaks, 5 to 8 minutes, then set the egg whites aside.

3. Use the mixer to break up the egg yolks, then beat in the vanilla. Sift the baking powder and flour over the yolks and mix to combine.

4. Add a scoop of the egg whites to the yolk mixture and mix until no visible streaks of white remain. Repeat with another scoop of egg white, then pour the lightened yolk mixture into the bowl with the remaining egg whites. Use a spatula to gently scrape around the bowl and fold the two mixtures together until they're fully incorporated and no white lumps remain. Stop folding immediately once this stage is reached.

5. Pour the batter into the prepared pan, then smooth the top and spread the batter into the corners of the pan. Tap the pan briskly on the counter to release any air bubbles, then bake for 10 to 12 minutes, until a toothpick inserted into the center comes out clean.

6. Remove the pan from the oven and immediately tip the cake out onto a cutting board. Orient the cake vertically so that one shorter side is facing you. Peel the parchment paper off the cake, then use a serrated knife to trim the short edge of the cake farthest from you so it tapers into a triangle.

7. While the cake is still warm, drape a clean dish towel over the top and begin tightly rolling up the cake and towel together. Drape a second dish towel over the rolled cake to protect the exterior, then allow the cake to cool completely.

8. Make the whipped cream fillings: Split the cream evenly between two medium bowls. Whip each until the soft-peak stage, then add 2 tablespoons of the confectioners' sugar to each bowl. To one bowl, add the orange zest. To the other, add the cocoa powder. Beat each until you achieve stiff peaks (clean the beaters in between so you don't combine the colors and flavors), then refrigerate until chilled.

9. Fill the cake: When the cake has completely cooled, unroll it, remove the dish towel, and place it on a sheet of parchment. Spoon all but 3 tablespoons of the chocolate whipped cream onto the cake and spread it over the cake so it's thicker toward the short edge that will be rolled into the cake and thinner toward the tapered edge, leaving about ½ inch uncovered on either long edge of the cake. Repeat with the orange zest cream, reserving 3 tablespoons for later. Take care not to mix the two creams, as we want distinctive lines of separation.

10. Use the edge of the parchment paper under the inner roll of the cake to start curling inward. Be gentle here. Guide the cake into a tight roll (but unlike before, don't roll the parchment in with the cake). Wrap the cake in parchment or plastic wrap, then freeze for at least an hour.

11. Make the white chocolate ornaments: Place 3 ounces of the white chocolate in a microwave-safe bowl and microwave in 30-second intervals, stirring after each, until the chocolate is melted. Stir the chocolate until it cools to 100°F. Portion out 1 ounce more unmelted white chocolate and add a few chips of this to the melted chocolate. Stir until the

Continued

RECIPE TIP:
Most American jelly-roll pans are larger (15.5 x 10.5 inches) than the one I used (my oven in Japan wouldn't fit a bigger one!). If you can't find a jelly-roll pan that's the same size as mine, don't fret. You can modify the shape of your pan by using some aluminum foil to create a new edge. Or you can spread the batter out across the pan to make a very thin cake that will give you more swirls (just watch the time as it bakes—it'll cook faster). Alternatively, you could shop for a Swiss roll pan or quarter sheet pan, which measure 9 x 13 inches. As a last resort, simply double the recipe above for a 15.5 x 10.5-inch pan, knowing that you'll have some leftover batter.

chocolate cools to 87°F. If the additional chocolate melts completely before it hits 87°F, add more chips and keep stirring.

12. Lay a sheet of parchment on your work surface. Spoon some melted chocolate into 4 sphere molds (4 halves will equal 2 ornaments, so make an extra pair of half spheres if you're worried about breaking a set). Tip the chocolate around the molds so that the insides are evenly coated, then tip the excess chocolate back into the bowl or onto the parchment paper and clean the edges of the molds. Set the molds upside down on the parchment so they can continue to drain and develop a thick edge. Allow to set, about 15 minutes.

13. When the first layer of chocolate has set, repeat step 13 and let set for 10 minutes. (If the melted white chocolate has hardened, repeat step 11 to temper it again before pouring it into the molds.) The second coat of chocolate adds strength to the ornament so we can handle it later.

14. After the second chocolate layer has set for 10 minutes, turn the molds right side up and sprinkle the interior of the molds with the orange zest, pressing the zest gently into the soft chocolate. Leave the molds right side up and allow the chocolate to finish setting. Chop the granola finely, then mix it together with the coffee beans in a small bowl.

15. Combine the reserved 3 tablespoons cocoa whipped cream and 3 tablespoons orange zest whipped cream in a small microwave-safe bowl and stir together. Add ¼ cup of the heavy cream, then stir to combine. Microwave the mixture for 45 seconds or until hot, then add the remaining 2 ounces of white chocolate and the caramels. Allow this to sit for 5 to 10 minutes, then stir until everything is thoroughly combined. Add more heavy cream as necessary to thin the sauce to your liking, then conduct a taste test and add more cocoa powder or caramel, depending on what you prefer. Set aside.

16. When the chocolate shells have completely set, unmold them carefully and and set them rounded side down on the parchment. You can leave fingerprints on these baubles, so handle them with a paper towel.

17. Pour a tablespoon of the prepared granola mixture into half of the half spheres. Heat a skillet over high heat until it's hot to the touch (don't burn yourself), then turn the heat off. Working with one at a time, take an unfilled half sphere and carefully set it flat edge down on the surface of the pan. Keep it there for a second or two, just long enough to melt the edge the tiniest bit. Moving quickly, lift the half sphere from the pan and match it with a filled half sphere, holding them together to let the seam set and fuse them into a whole sphere. Use your finger to smooth away any melted white chocolate. Repeat to make a second (and third, if you made an extra) sphere.

18. Holding a metal skewer with an oven mitt, heat the metal briefly over the stove, then hold it on top of the chocolate sphere to melt through and create a hole in the top of the sphere. Repeat with the remaining spheres.

19. Use a syringe to suck up some of the sauce, then squeeze the sauce into the hole in each ornament; reserve the remaining sauce for serving. Trim 1 inch from each end of the vanilla bean and place one in the hole in each ornament to make the ornament "fuse" or hook. Set the ornaments aside in a cool, dry spot.

20. Make the ganache frosting: Put the heavy cream in a microwave-safe bowl and microwave until it's hot, about 30 seconds. Add the chocolate and let stand for 10 minutes, then whisk until the chocolate has melted and the ganache is glossy and smooth. Chill the ganache in the refrigerator for 10 to 20 minutes.

21. Assemble and decorate the cake: Pull the cake out of the freezer, bring over a serving platter, and get a cutting board out. Twirl a serrated knife around expertly (just kidding, please don't do this, I'm not responsible for any hospital visits) and strike a pose. We're DOING THIS.

22. Unwrap the cake and place it on the cutting board. Trim a 2-inch piece from one end—this will become the small stump on top of the cake. From the other end, only trim as needed to even the cake and expose the beautiful swirl inside. Place the cake on the platter.

23. Pull the ganache out of the refrigerator and whisk it briefly. Using an offset spatula, spread the ganache over the exterior of the cake, taking care not to get any on the exposed cut ends. When the cake has been covered, pop the stump piece on top with the swirl (not the rough cut side) facing up. Cover the sides of the stump with ganache, avoiding the cut surface on top and blending the ganache into the ganache covering the cake below.

24. Soma used a broken wooden ice cream spoon to texturize the ganache in the anime. I like to use a combination of a fork and the broken top of a disposable chopstick. With the fork, make lines all over the ganache to mimic bark. Have them go horizontally along the length of the cake and shift the fork so the lines on the stump on top run perpendicular to the bottom log. Don't worry about the lines being straight or perfect—the more natural-looking, the better. While the fork usually gets the job done nicely, you can go in and add finer detail with the broken top of the chopstick.

25. Position your baubles—one on top of the stump and one (or two) alongside the cake. Garnish with rosemary (to give it that Christmas look). To serve, crack the baubles open with a spoon or the back of a knife and give everyone a few pieces of chocolate. Use the excess sauce to top off anyone's slice.

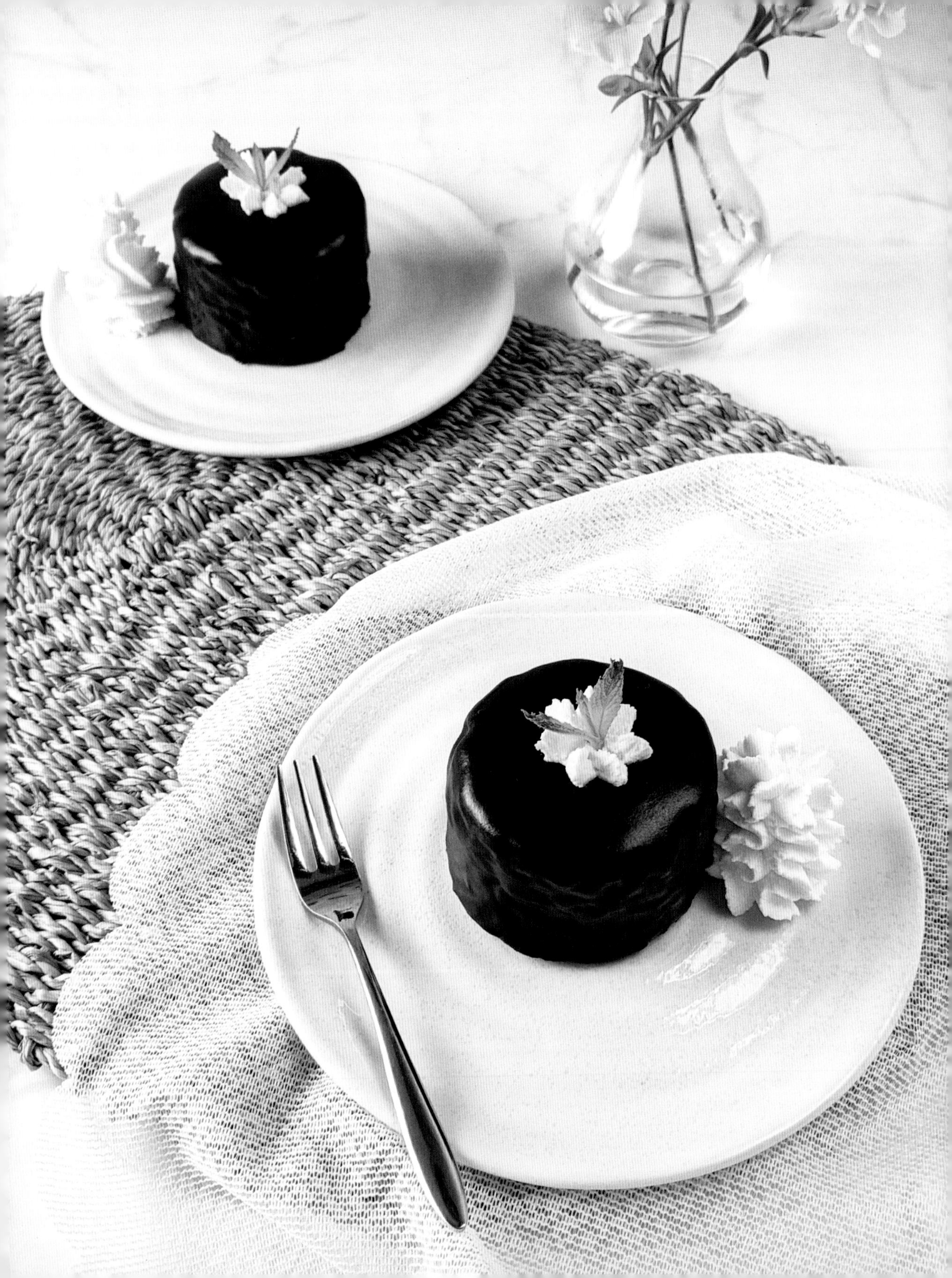

MINI SACHER TORTES

Takeo's not cool or suave like his best friend Suna, and his large presence and plain features inspire fear. This comes in handy, however, when one day, Takeo uses his frightening demeanor to save a girl named Yamato from being groped. Yamato is both impressed and grateful for Takeo's intervention, and falls for him instantly.

In thanks for his help, she bakes him a selection of Sacher tortes. A Sacher torte is lovely and sweet; the chocolate-glazed exterior is bright and shiny and cloaks a light and airy chocolate sponge layered with apricot marmalade. Whether you're in or out of love, these little cakes will be the perfect addition to your day.

1 HOUR 30 MINUTES

MAKES 9 MINI CAKES

SPECIAL EQUIPMENT: ROUND COOKIE CUTTERS

NUT-FREE

RECIPE TIP: Let's say you don't want to go to all this trouble for a bunch of mini cakes and would rather do one big one and get it over with. Fine! Butter and flour an 8-inch round cake pan, then pour in the batter. Bake for 50 minutes, or until a toothpick inserted into the center comes out clean. Allow to cool in the pan, then turn the cake out of the pan, cut it in half horizontally, and complete steps 8 to 10.

FOR THE CAKE
4½ ounces dark chocolate

6 large eggs at room temperature

¾ cup granulated sugar

11 tablespoons (1⅓ sticks) unsalted butter, at room temperature

¾ cup confectioners' sugar

2 teaspoons vanilla extract

1 cup all-purpose flour

1 cup apricot jam

FOR THE CHOCOLATE GLAZE
1 cup granulated sugar

½ cup water

2 tablespoons corn syrup

7½ ounces dark chocolate, chopped

FOR GARNISH (OPTIONAL)
Whipped cream

Fresh mint leaves

1. Make the cake: Preheat the oven to 350°F. Line the bottom of an 8-inch square cake pan with parchment paper cut to fit.

2. Place the chocolate in a microwave-safe bowl and microwave for 30 seconds, then stir and repeat. My chocolate was melted at this point, but if yours isn't, microwave in 10-second intervals, stirring after each, until completely melted. Set aside to cool.

3. Separate the eggs, placing the egg whites in a medium bowl and the yolks in a small bowl; set the egg yolks aside. Using an electric mixer, beat the egg whites until they've started to fluff, then add the granulated sugar a spoonful at a time and beat until fully incorporated. Keep beating until you've achieved stiff peaks, 5 to 8 minutes. Set aside.

4. In a large bowl, beat the butter on high speed for 2 minutes, or until light and fluffy. Beat in the confectioners' sugar until fully incorporated, then add the egg yolks one at a time, beating well after each addition. Pour in the vanilla and the melted chocolate, then mix until just combined. Sift in the flour and mix again until you no longer see white patches of flour.

Continued

5. Add a generous scoop of the egg whites to the mixture and whisk to combine. Add another large scoop of egg white to further lighten the mixture, whisking again to combine. Tip the chocolate mixture into the bowl with the remaining egg whites. Fold together with the whisk until there are no remaining lumps or ribbons of egg white and the batter is uniform.

6. Pour the batter into the prepared cake pan and bake for 45 to 50 minutes, until a toothpick inserted into the center of the cake comes out clean. Allow to cool completely in the pan, then unmold the cake by running a palette knife around the edges to loosen it, then turning the cake out onto a cutting board.

7. With a round cutter about 2.5 inches in diameter, cut out 9 cake rounds. With a serrated knife, level the tops of the cake rounds, then split each in half horizontally.

8. Place a teaspoon of the apricot jam onto one half of each cake round, then sandwich with the other half. Heat the remaining jam in the microwave until it's thinner, then use a pastry brush to dab the jam onto the outside of each cake. Set the cakes on a wire rack and set the rack on a baking sheet.

9. Make the chocolate glaze: Combine the granulated sugar, water, and corn syrup in a pot and stir until the sugar has dissolved completely and the mixture comes to a boil, about 5 minutes. Remove from the heat and immediately stir in the chocolate until a thick, shiny glaze forms.

10. Pour the glaze over the mini cakes, pausing to spread the glaze over each cake with a palette knife before moving on to the next once. Reheat the glaze gently as needed to maintain the right consistency for pouring. Garnish the cakes with whipped cream and a mint leaf, if desired, and serve.

FOUR-LAYER SEMIFREDDO

Takumi Aldini and his brother, the resident Japanese Italians at Totsuki Culinary Academy, engage in frequent food battles with their classmates. It's during one of these famous shokugeki that Takumi learns his prized mezzaluna is up for grabs. If he can't win the challenge, he'll forfeit it to his competitor Subaru.

Takumi makes an incredible four-layer semifreddo, and it's a true masterpiece—a bitter-caramel praline layer lacquers the top, under which lies a creamy frozen whipped lemon layer, bright lemon curd, and a cushion of plush limoncello-soaked genoise. Tragically, he loses to Subaru. Nonetheless, Takumi's recipe is nothing to turn your nose up at—it's bright, lemony, fresh, and absolutely luscious, a beautiful tribute to his Italian heritage and just the thing to make one hot summer day.

3 HOURS, PLUS CHILLING OVERNIGHT

SERVES 8 TO 10

SPECIAL EQUIPMENT: INFRARED THERMOMETER

RECIPE TIP: This recipe has a lot of steps, so feel free to split up the work. You can make the praline and semifreddo layer one day, the lemon curd layer the next, and finally the genoise layer on the last day, making sure to freeze the layers solid between each step. The candied lemon garnish is easily made on the day you choose to serve it. I made mine over the course of a week.

VARIATION TIP: Okay, so you're convinced Subaru's version would taste better. To get a similar taste, finely chop up some preserved lemon and toss this into the frozen lemon layer as one of the last steps.

FOR THE PRALINE LAYER

1 cup sliced almonds

Grated zest of 1 lemon

½ cup sugar

2 tablespoons water

3 tablespoons heavy cream

FOR THE SEMIFREDDO LAYER

½ cup sliced almonds

1 cup heavy cream

2 large eggs, separated

¾ cup sugar

Juice of 2 lemons

¼ teaspoon kosher salt

FOR THE LEMON CURD LAYER

2 large eggs

½ cup sugar

Grated zest and juice of 1 lemon

2 tablespoons limoncello

3 tablespoons olive oil

Pinch of kosher salt

FOR THE GENOISE LAYER

4 large eggs

½ cup sugar

½ cup cake flour, sifted

¼ cup limoncello

FOR THE CANDIED LEMON GARNISH

½ cup water

½ cup sugar

Juice of ½ lemon

1 lemon, thinly sliced and seeded

1. Make the praline layer: Line a standard 8 x 4-inch loaf pan with parchment paper. For the cleanest cake removal, line the bottom and sides, making sure to leave some overhanging paper on the long edges. Use tape to secure the parchment to the pan. Though it might be tempting to use butter to stick down the parchment, we'll be freezing the pan later, which will make unsticking the final dessert messier than it needs to be.

Continued

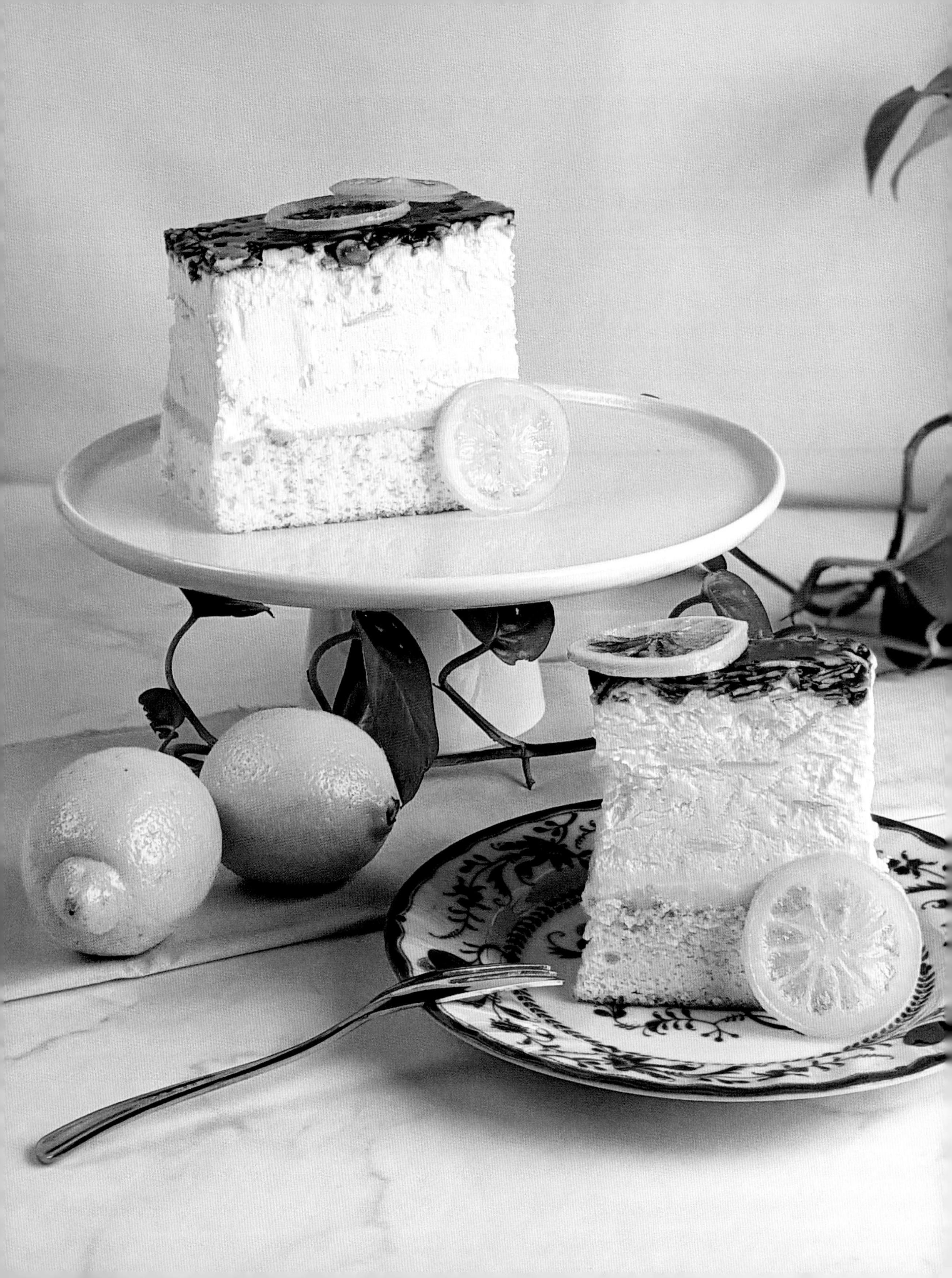

2. Toss the sliced almonds and lemon zest in a bowl, then set aside. Put the sugar in a small heavy-bottomed pot. Drizzle the water over the sugar and set the pan over medium heat. Don't stir—let the sugar dissolve in the water and begin caramelizing on its own. When it starts to go brown, drizzle in the cream while stirring, then cook, stirring, until the caramel reaches a color you like; keep in mind that it'll continue to darken off the heat. Remove from the heat and toss in the almonds and zest. Stir thoroughly to combine.

3. Pour the warm praline over the bottom of the prepared loaf pan and smooth it into an even layer. Set aside to cool completely.

4. Make the semifreddo layer: Preheat the oven to 350°F. Lay the almonds in a single layer on a baking sheet. Bake for 3 to 4 minutes, then shake the pan a little to flip the almonds over and bake until the desired toastiness is achieved, checking on the nuts each minute.

5. Using an electric mixer, whip the cream in a large bowl on a low speed for 1 minute, then raise the speed to high and whip until you achieve medium peaks. Set aside.

6. Fill a pot with 3 inches of water and bring to a boil over high heat. Combine the egg yolks, ¼ cup of sugar, lemon juice, and salt in a tempered glass or metal bowl. Place the bowl over the pot to make a bain-marie (make sure the bottom of the bowl does not touch the water), reduce the heat to medium, and cook, whisking continuously, for 5 minutes, or until the sugar has dissolved and the temperature reaches 160°F. Remove the bowl from the pot (keep the water simmering) and beat with an electric mixer on high speed until the egg mixture has doubled in size. Set aside.

7. Clean the beaters. Combine ½ cup of the sugar and the egg whites in a separate heatproof bowl and place it over the pot of water. Cook, whisking continuously, for 5 minutes, or until the sugar has dissolved and the temperature reaches 160°F. Remove the bowl from the pot and beat with the electric mixer (make sure the beaters are clean!) on high speed until the egg whites are glossy and ribbony and the bowl and mixture have cooled to room temperature. You won't be getting stiff peaks, but when you drizzle or dollop egg white from the beaters, it should slowly pile up on itself rather than sink back into the mixture. You can overbeat this, so stop once you reach this stage.

8. Add a dollop or two of the egg white mixture to the egg yolk mixture, whisking to combine. This will lighten the yolk mixture and make it easier to mix with the whites. Pour the yolk mixture into the bowl with the remaining egg white mixture and use a whisk in circular up-and-down motions to combine the two. Fold the egg mixture into the whipped cream mixture in the same manner until the two are completely combined. If you find that the batter is too aerated, switch to using a spatula to fold each component together. Fold in the toasted almonds, then pour the semifreddo into the loaf pan on top of the cooled praline layer. Cover with plastic wrap, pressing it directly against the surface of the semifreddo to prevent a skin from forming, and freeze for an hour.

9. Make the lemon curd layer: Combine the eggs and sugar into a small heavy-bottomed pot and whisk briefly in combine. Set over medium heat. Whisk in the lemon zest, lemon juice, and limoncello, then cook, whising continuously, for 5 minutes, or until the curd thickens. It's done when you're able to run your finger through the curd on the back of a spoon and leave a clear line behind. Remove the pot from the heat.

Continued

10. Add the olive oil and salt and whisk vigorously to incorporate. Strain the curd through a fine-mesh sieve into a bowl. Allow to cool, then spread the curd in an even layer over the semifreddo layer in the loaf pan. Cover with plastic wrap and freeze until solid.

11. Make the genoise layer: Preheat the oven to 350°F. Line the bottom of an 8-inch square baking pan with parchment paper cut to fit.

12. Add more water to the saucepan you used for your bain-marie earlier, if needed, and bring the water to a boil over high heat. Place the eggs and sugar in a clean heatproof bowl and set the bowl over the pot, making sure the bottom of the bowl doesn't touch the water. Cook, using an electric mixer to beat the mixture in the bowl, for 5 minutes, or until the temperature of the eggs reaches 110°F to 120°F. Remove the bowl from the pot and beat until the mixture is fluffy and has cooled completely.

13. Sprinkle the cake flour over the egg mixture and fold it through with a whisk, taking care to get down into the bottom of the bowl. Don't overwhisk—stop once you no longer see pockets of flour. Pour the batter into the prepared pan and tap the pan lightly on the counter to release any air bubbles. Bake for 25 minutes, or until a toothpick inserted into the center comes out clean. Remove from the oven and allow the cake to cool completely in the pan.

14. When the cake is cool, remove it from the pan and trim the caramelization from the top, bottom, and sides. Cut the cake into a rectangle that will fit into the loaf pan and place it in the pan over the lemon curd layer. Use a pastry brush to coat the cake with limoncello. Cover with plastic wrap and freeze for 12 to 24 hours.

15. Make the candied lemon garnish: Combine the sugar, water, and lemon juice in a skillet and bring to a simmer over medium-low heat. Place the lemon slices in a single layer in the pan. Cook for 8 to 10 minutes on each side, then set the slices aside on parchment paper to cool and harden.

16. Remove the frozen semifreddo from the loaf pan and place it praline side down on a cutting board. Trim the sides so that all the layers are flush, then cut slices. (Cutting upside down is much easier than cutting right side up—the praline is quite hard, and you're more likely to make a mess and squish the semifreddo everywhere if you try to cut from the top down.) Plate the slices praline side up and garnish with the candied lemon slices. Enjoy immediately!

YUMEIRO PATISSIERE

AT-HOME BAUMKUCHEN CAKE ROLLS

St. Marie Academy student Ichigo didn't mean to wake up late! When she misses her alarm in one episode, she has to rush to get to her first cooking class of the day. Whereas most folks would grab a piece of toast to eat on the go, Ichigo instead grabs a slice of baumkuchen, a sweet and mild ring cake with German origins.

In *Yumeiro Patissiere*, Ichigo has the most professional equipment available to her. She learns how to cook baumkuchen using a special oven and a cake spit in one of her daily classes, but that's not really available in the average kitchen. This recipe describes my favorite method for getting that iconic layered appearance and details how to achieve a (mostly) round ring cake with just a crepe or tortilla pan, a rolling pin, and a loaf pan. Try this recipe for yourself and see how fun (and easy) it is!

65 MINUTES, PLUS 1 HOUR COOLING TIME

SERVES 6

SPECIAL EQUIPMENT: **1-INCH DIAMETER ROLLING PIN**

NUT-FREE

RECIPE TIP: This recipe can be tricky because you're eyeballing the shape of the cake layers and it's difficult to get them perfectly even or rectangular. Make sure you scoop the same amount of batter into the pan each time to help lessen this problem. When rolling each layer, try to line up the corners as best as you can and always try to overlap the seam of the previous layer.

⅔ cup cake flour

1 teaspoon baking powder

⅓ cup whole milk

2 tablespoons unsalted butter

1 tablespoon honey

3 large eggs, separated, at room temperature

¾ cup confectioners' sugar

Neutral oil, such as vegetable or canola, for greasing the pan

1. Sift the cake flour and baking powder together into a small bowl. Set aside.

2. Combine the milk, butter, and honey in a microwave-safe bowl and microwave in 30-second bursts, stirring after each, until everything is warm, smooth, and liquidy.

3. Using an electric mixer, beat the egg whites in a large bowl on low speed for 2 to 3 minutes, until foamy but not holding shape. With the mixer running, add the confectioners' sugar a spoonful at a time, mixing until each spoonful is incorporated before adding the next. Raise the speed to medium and beat until the meringue is shiny and holds stiff peaks. Pop the egg yolks into the bowl and beat to combine. Add the flour mixture and fold it in with a whisk or spatula to combine. Keep folding until you no longer see streaks or pockets of flour.

4. Take a large scoop of the egg white mixture and add it to the butter mixture. Whisk to combine, then pour the mixture into the bowl with the remaining egg white mixture. Fold the two together until evenly combined.

5. Wrap a 1-inch-diameter rolling pin with parchment paper and tape it in place, set this near the stove. Grease a nonstick skillet with oil and heat over low heat. If your first pancake doesn't turn out like you want it to, trash it—for some reason, the first pancake is always the worst. Add a scoop of batter, about ⅓ cup, spread it into a thin rectangle, then cover the pan with a lid and steam the top of the pancake for 1 to 2 minutes. When the top of the pancake looks

Continued

dry (but isn't necessarily dry if you touch it), ease one short edge up with a spatula and place the rolling pin down onto the pancake. Flip the loose edge of the pancake over the rolling pin and use your hands to carefully pull the pancake over the top of the pin. When the pancake is anchored, carefully lift the whole pancake off the pan. Settle the covered rolling pin on a flat work surface, then roll the pancake over the pin, taking care to keep the pancake tight as you roll. The residual heat will continue to cook the side that didn't touch the pan and the sticky residue of the uncooked side will help glue the upcoming layers together.

6. Rest in a loaf pan—the edges of the rolling pin should rest on the sides of the loaf pan so the circular shape of the pancake can dangle and cool in the air. Repeat with the rest of the batter, steadily rolling each layer on top of the previous layer until the cake is complete around the pin.

7. Allow to cool completely before sliding the round cake off the rolling pin. Remove the parchment paper from the inside of the cake and then slice the cake into pieces. Dust with a little confectioners' sugar and serve with tea or coffee.

FOOD FACT:
Baumkuchen roughly means "tree cake" in German, a reference to the fact that the cake is baked in thin layers that look like the rings of a tree when the cake is sliced. In Japan, baumkuchen are made on cake spits in special ovens that rotate the cakes as they bake, a little like a rotisserie chicken.

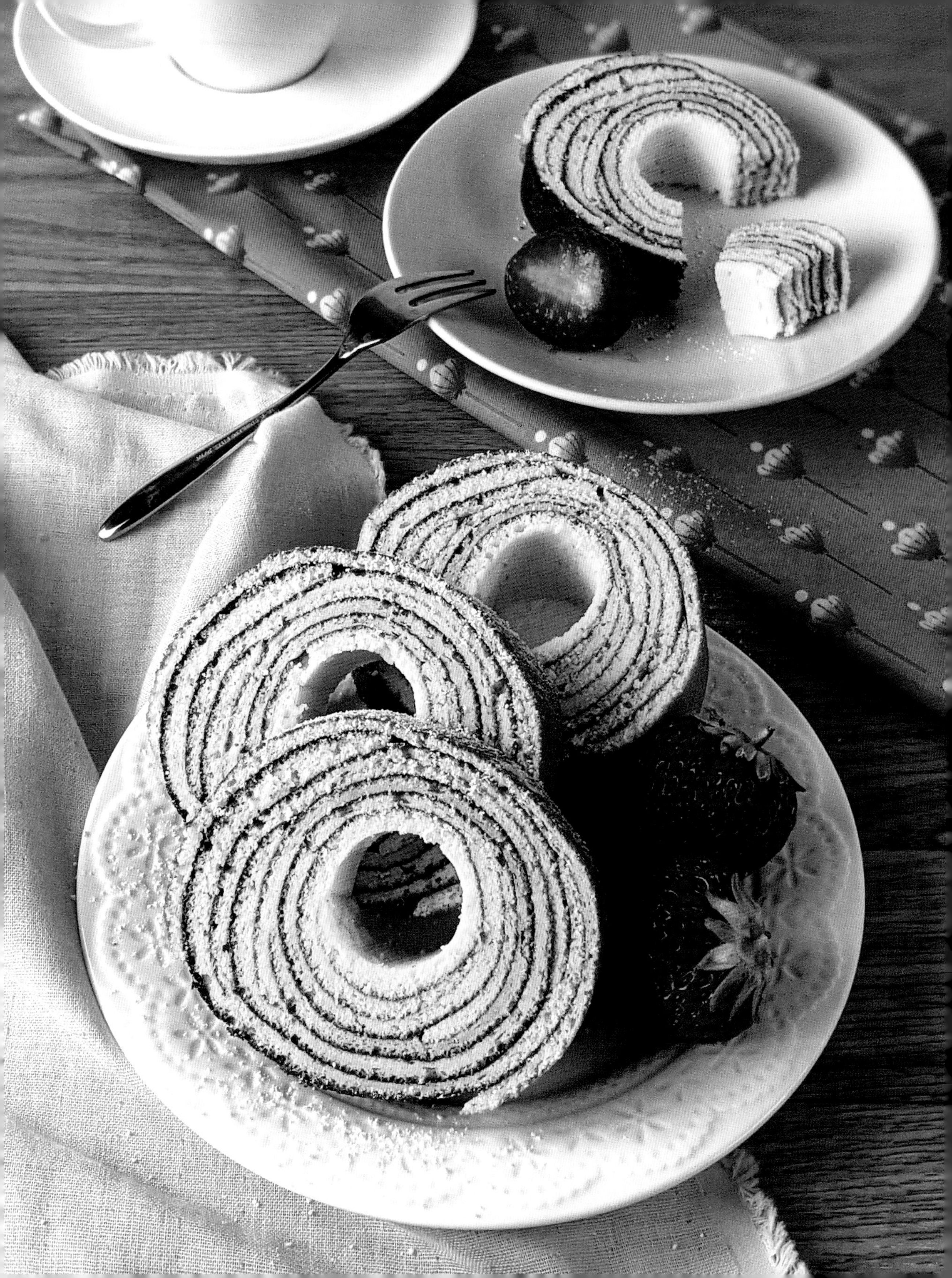

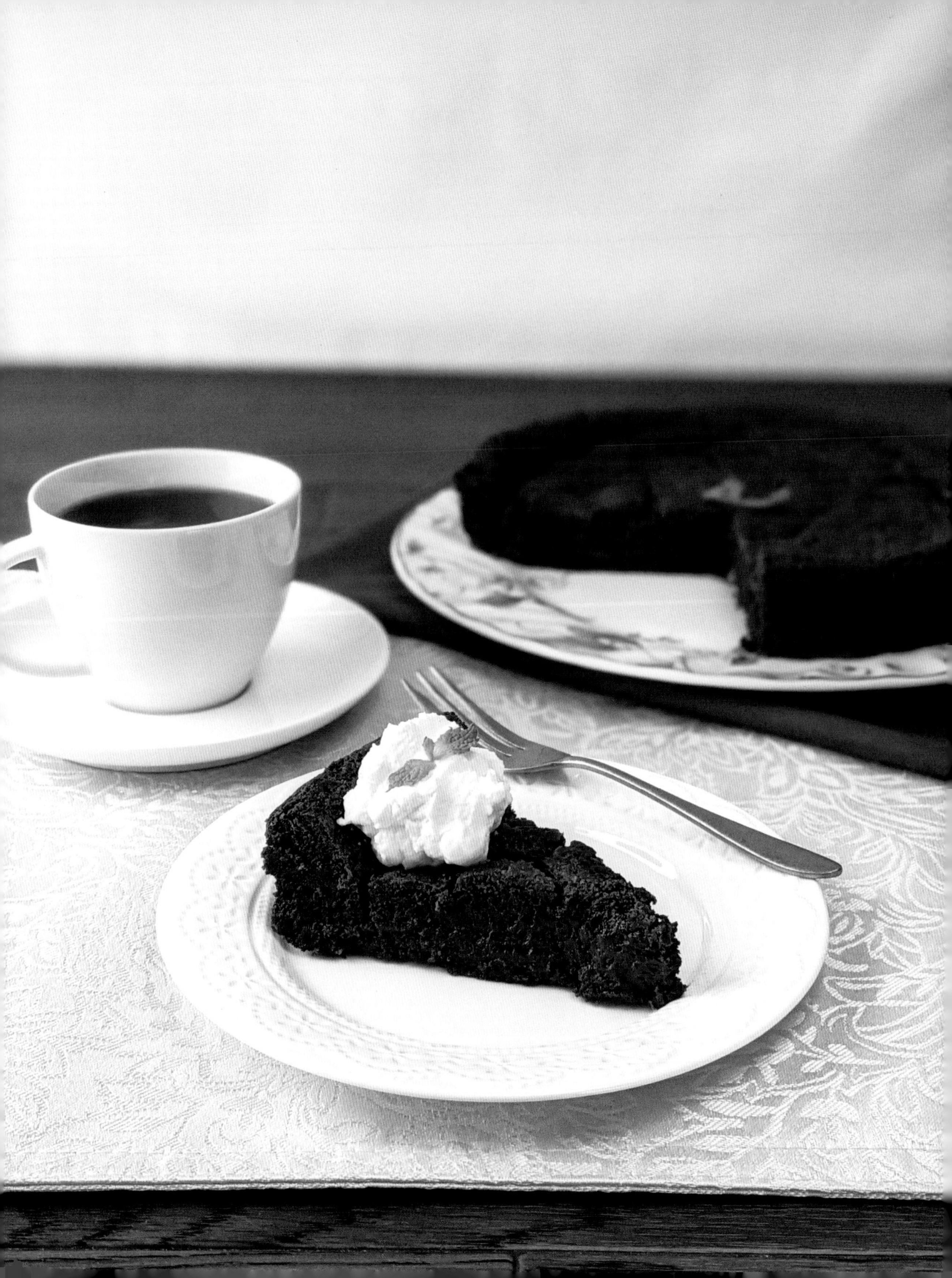

BLACK BUTLER

CHOCOLATE GATEAU

Ciel Phantomhive's life is cruelly taken from him when his parents are killed in a mysterious house fire. Soon after, he's sold into slavery to a demon-worshipping cult! However, Ciel outsmarts them all. He makes a deal with the demon, who agrees to kill the cultists in exchange for Ciel's soul later on. The demon, whom Ciel names Sebastian, goes to live in England with Ciel, who's attempting to uncover what happened that fateful night.

Sebastian assumes the guise of Ciel's butler and lives up to the job in every way. A particular talent of his is cooking. In one episode, Sebastian offers Ciel a slice of luxurious, decadent chocolate gâteau, a cake made nearly almost entirely of chocolate. Know that if *you* make this recipe, you don't have to sign your soul away to get a slice.

1 HOUR 30 MINUTES

SERVES 8

GLUTEN-FREE (WITH USE OF GLUTEN-FREE FLOUR), NUT-FREE

16 ounces good-quality dark chocolate, chopped

10 tablespoons (1¼ sticks) unsalted butter, at room temperature

1 tablespoon all-purpose flour (or a 1-for-1 gluten-free replacement)

1½ tablespoons sugar

1 teaspoon instant coffee granules

¼ teaspoon kosher salt

4 large eggs, at room temperature, separated

1 cup heavy cream

Fresh mint sprig, for garnish

1. Preheat the oven to 425°F. Line the bottom of an 8-inch springform pan with parchment paper cut to fit.

2. Fill a pot with 3 inches of water and bring to a boil over high heat. Put the chocolate in a tempered glass or metal bowl. Place the bowl over the pot to make a bain-marie (make sure the bottom of the bowl does not touch the water) and stir the chocolate until just melted. Remove the bowl from the heat and scrape the chocolate into a new bowl to halt carryover cooking. Immediately whisk in the butter, flour, sugar, instant coffee, and salt. Add the egg yolks one at a time, whisking until completely incorporated after each addition. Set aside.

3. Place the egg whites in a clean bowl and beat with an electric mixer until you achieve soft peaks. Scrape the egg whites into the chocolate mixture and fold through until the two are just combined and no streaks of egg white remain.

4. Pour the batter into the prepared pan and bake for 15 minutes, then turn the oven off and leave the cake in the oven to bake in the residual heat for 1 hour. Remove the cake from the oven and allow it to cool to room temperature.

5. While you wait for the cake to cool, quickly make some whipped cream: Using an electric mixer, beat the cream in a large bowl until you achieve soft peaks, 3 to 4 minutes. Keep chilled until ready to use.

6. Unfasten the springform ring and remove it from the cake, then place the cake on a serving platter. Serve garnished with a healthy dollop of whipped cream and a sprig of mint.

REHEATING TIP: This cake tastes fresh after a 30-second rejuvenation period in the microwave.

SERVING TIP: The whipped cream adds the right amount of lightness to take the edge off such a heavy, chocolaty cake. Don't skip it!

ANIME FACT:
In America, the name Jeeves is synonymous with "butler," but in Japan, the name Sebastian is more commonly associated with this position—hence the name of the butler in the show.

BLACK BUTLER

MIXED BERRY VICTORIA SPONGE CAKE

Ciel spends his time solving detective cases for Queen Victoria, with Sebastian's aid. During one case, Sebastian brings Ciel a slice of Victoria sponge cake for afternoon tea. The dessert was developed to suit the tastes of the queen, who preferred cake with her afternoon tea.

Typically made of a sponge filled with a layer of jam and a layer of cream, the cake can be topped with confectioners' sugar or fruit. The hallmark of this cake is that it looks impressive, but in practice it's rather simple. Funnily enough, even though it's called a sponge cake, Victoria sponge cake isn't made in the typical style of a genoise, chiffon cake, or angel food cake. Instead, the batter bakes into a crumbly cake that's as delicious as it is unique.

1 HOUR 30 MINUTES

SERVES 8

NUT-FREE

RECIPE TIP: If you don't feel like tackling the strawberry shortcake, this is a great alternative and in fact tastes quite a lot like an overgrown scone with jam and cream. Very tasty! Very British!

SUBSTITUTION TIP: A more traditional Victoria sponge cake is made with a simple strawberry jam, so go for that if you're feeling classic. Or shake things up and replace the jam filling with something totally different, if you're in a more adventurous mood.

1 cup (2 sticks) unsalted butter

1 cup granulated sugar

4 large eggs

1 teaspoon vanilla extract

1½ cups all-purpose flour

2 teaspoons baking powder

1 cup mixed berry jam

1 cup heavy cream

2 tablespoons confectioners' sugar, plus more for dusting

Handful of strawberries, for garnish

Handful of blueberries, for garnish

1. Preheat the oven to 350°F. Line the bottoms of two 8-inch round cake pans with parchment paper cut to fit.

2. Using an electric mixer, cream the butter and granulated sugar together in a large bowl for about 2 minutes, until light and fluffy. Scrape down the sides of the bowl with a rubber spatula. Add the eggs one at a time, beating until each is fully incorporated before adding the next, then beat in the vanilla. Add the flour and baking powder and mix until just incorporated and no lumps or streaks of flour remain.

3. Divide the batter between the prepared pans. (You can use a scale to get it perfectly equal, if you'd like.) Bake for 25 to 30 minutes, until the cake is springy to the touch and a toothpick inserted into the center comes out clean. Allow to cool in the pans on a wire rack for 10 minutes, then run a knife around the edge of the pans to loosen the cakes and turn the cakes out onto the rack to cool completely.

4. Using an electric mixer, whip the cream in a large bowl on medium-low speed until soft peaks form, then add the confectioners' sugar and whip on medium speed for another 30 seconds or so, just until medium peaks form.

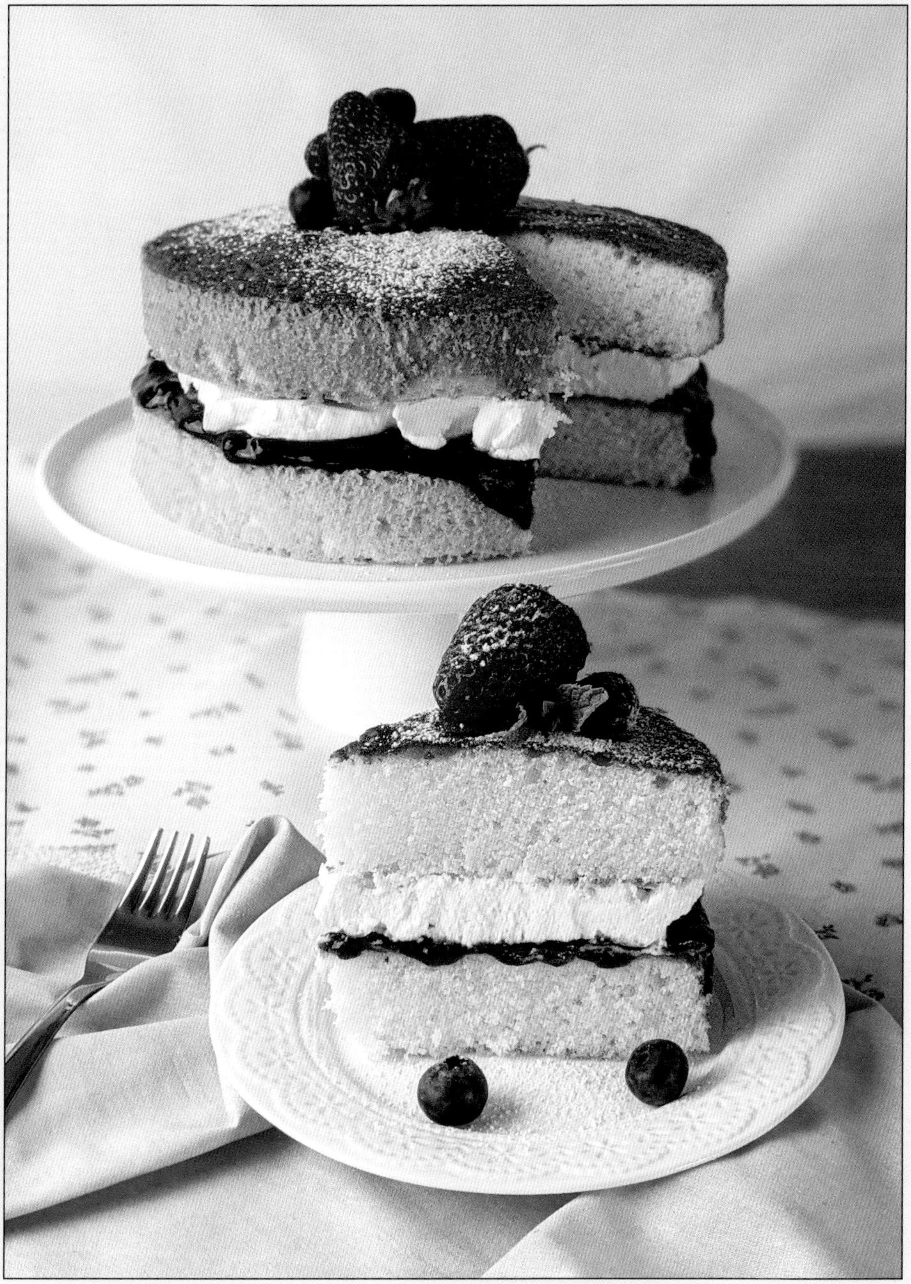

5. Assemble the cake: Place one cake layer on a serving platter. Spread the jam on the top of the cake, keeping it thicker toward the center and thinner on the edges. Dollop the whipped cream on top of the jam and spread it to the edges of the cake. Place the second cake layer gently on top of the whipped cream.

6. Place the fresh berries on top of the cake, garnish with a generous dusting of confectioners' sugar, and serve.

ANOHANA: THE FLOWER WE SAW THAT DAY

MUFFIN BREAD

When high school dropout Jintan wakes one morning to see the ghost of his childhood friend Menma, he thinks he's imagining things. When she starts talking to him, he thinks he's delusional. But when she starts making steamed muffin bread, a recipe Jintan's mother taught her, he starts to believe her ghost really is there. Menma reveals that he needs to fulfill her last wish so she can move on. The only problem? She doesn't remember what that last wish is.

Anohana is a story about how a group of old friends are brought together to discover this wish. Menma's haunting is a reminder that the honesty, love, and freedom we have as kids are important to keep as we grow older. Menma's muffin bread is a humble embodiment of that idea: a recipe from Jintan's mother, it's executed with all the fun (and grace) of an elementary schooler and made easy by its simple ingredients and cooking methods. This recipe gives room to experiment (want chocolate chips? Add some! Not a fan of raisins? Add blueberries!) and tastes good no matter what.

40 MINUTES

MAKES **10 TO 12 MUFFINS**

SPECIAL EQUIPMENT: **STEAMER BASKET**

NUT-FREE

RECIPE TIP: Menma's muffins are definitely homemade, and that's part of their charm—don't worry about making them perfect.

2½ cups pancake mix

4 tablespoons (½ stick) unsalted butter, melted

1 large egg

1 cup whole milk

½ cup granulated sugar

2 teaspoons ground cinnamon

1 cup dark raisins

1. Fill a large pot with a few inches of water and bring it to a simmer.

2. Combine the pancake mix, melted butter, egg, milk, sugar, and cinnamon in a large bowl. Mix until there are no lumps and the batter is sticky, then stir in the raisins (reserve a few to top the muffins before baking, if you like). The batter should be thicker and drier than a typical muffin batter.

3. Arrange several cupcake liners in a steamer basket, placing them so each has a little wiggle room, about ½ inch. Spoon batter equally among your muffin cases, about ¼ cup per liner. If you set some raisins aside, arrange a few nicely on top to make sure they pop in the final product. Wrap the top of the steamer basket with a dish towel and place the basket in the pot. Cover with the lid and steam the muffin breads for 15 minutes. Remove the steamer basket from the pot. Use tongs to pluck out the muffin breads and allow to cool on a wire rack. Repeat with the remaining batter.

RASCAL DOES NOT DREAM OF BUNNY GIRL SENPAI

CREAM PAN

Sakuta is taken aback when he sees teenage actress Mai Sakurajima wandering around the library dressed in a bunny outfit. Even more curious is the fact that Sakuta is the only person who's able to see her. Mai takes this in stride, however, and tells him to forget everything. Of course, that doesn't stick for long! When Sakuta runs into her again at the train station, he watches Mai try to buy a cream pan from a vendor who doesn't seem to see or hear her.

Cream pan is another Western-inspired Japanese snack: a half-moon-shaped bun with notched edges reminiscent of a bear claw donut but stuffed with vanilla custard instead of pasty filling. It's the perfect handheld treat; when it's fresh out of the oven, it smells a bit like a donut shop—the vanilla custard mingles with the soft, milky dough to result in a tempting snack. If you're feeling particularly invisible, like Mai, this will be the perfect pick-me-up for your afternoon.

3 HOURS

MAKES 8 BUNS

SPECIAL EQUIPMENT: INFRARED THERMOMETER

NUT-FREE

RECIPE TIPS: When you're cutting the "claws" on the cream pan, take care not to cut into the custard-filled cavity, or it'll melt out onto the baking sheet as they bake.

To tell if the dough is kneaded enough, use the windowpane test: pinch off a piece the size of a Ping-Pong ball and stretch it between your thumbs and pointer fingers while holding it up to the light. If you can see light through the dough *without* the dough tearing, it's ready.

FOR THE DOUGH

2/3 cup whole milk, warmed (110°F to 115°F)

1 teaspoon active dry yeast

2 cups bread flour, plus more for dusting

1/4 cup sugar

1 teaspoon kosher salt

2 tablespoons unsalted butter, at room temperature

1 large egg, whisked

FOR THE CUSTARD FILLING

1/2 vanilla bean, split lengthwise and seeds scraped out

3/4 cup whole milk

2 large egg yolks

3 1/2 tablespoons sugar

2 tablespoons all-purpose flour

1 tablespoon unsalted butter

1. Make the dough: Place the milk in a small bowl. Add the yeast and stir to combine. Set aside for 10 minutes, until bubbles form and the mixture smells yeasty.

2. Whisk together the flour, sugar, and salt in a large bowl. Pour the yeast mixture directly into the flour mixture. Add the butter and half the egg (set the remaining egg aside—you'll use it as an egg wash later). Use a rubber spatula to combine until everything is evenly incorporated.

3. Turn the dough out onto a floured counter and knead well for 10 minutes, or until the dough passes the windowpane test (see Tip). If the dough is too sticky, knead in more bread flour as needed, but don't go overboard.

4. Form the dough into a ball and place it in a clean bowl. Wet a finger under the kitchen faucet and swipe it along the inner rim of the bowl to add some moisture, then cover the bowl with plastic wrap. Place somewhere warm to rise for an hour, or until the dough has doubled in size.

5. Make the custard filling: Line a baking sheet with parchment paper.

Continued

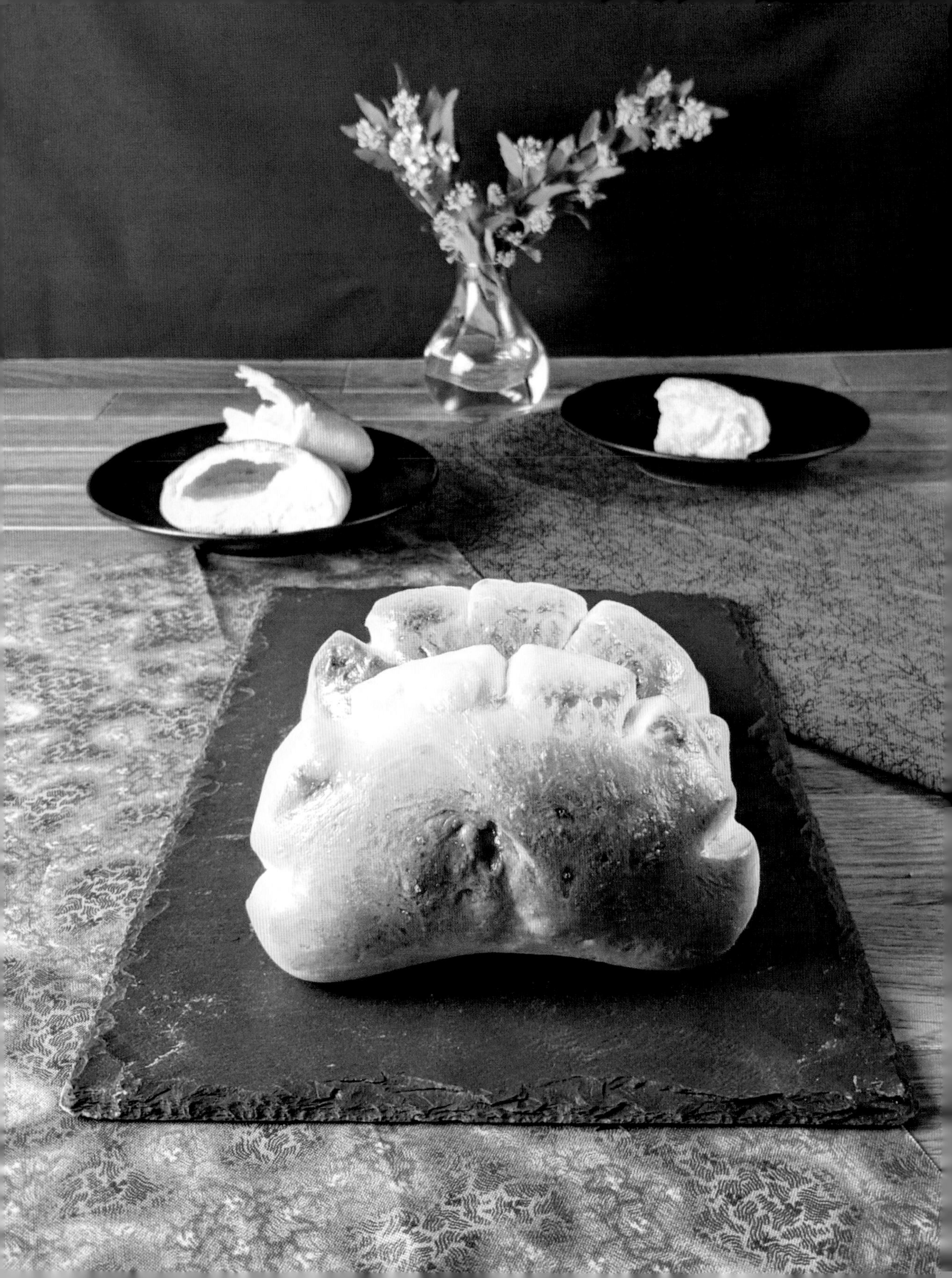

6. Combine the vanilla seeds, vanilla pod, and milk in a heavy-bottomed saucepan. Warm the milk over medium heat until it simmers at the edges, then remove the pot from the heat. Remove the vanilla pod.

7. In a measuring cup, whisk together the egg yolks, sugar, and flour. While whisking vigorously, slowly pour in ¼ cup of the hot milk mixture and whisk to combine. (This is called tempering—it slowly heats the eggs so they don't curdle when they come in contact with the hot liquid.) Strain the egg mixture into the pot with the remaining milk mixture, whisking vigorously until combined.

8. Place the pot over medium heat and cook, stirring continuously with a rubber spatula. After a minute or so, bubbles should ooze up through the mixture if you pause stirring. Cook for another minute, or until the temperature reaches 170°F and the mixture is thick. Remove it from the heat, add the butter, and stir until it's mixed in. Pour the custard onto the prepared baking sheet and spread it into a rectangular layer. Cover with plastic wrap, pressing it directly against the surface of the custard to prevent a skin from forming, then allow it to set in the refrigerator.

9. Turn the dough out onto the counter and punch the air out. Split the dough into 8 even pieces and form each piece into a round, then cover with plastic wrap and let rest for 15 minutes.

10. Line a baking sheet with parchment paper. Lightly flour your work surface and roll out each round of dough into an oval. Cut the custard into 8 pieces and place one piece on one half of each oval of dough. Fold the other half over and pinch the edges shut to create crescent buns. Tighten the dough around the custard by rolling and pinching the edges in the same direction to create tension. Arrange the buns on the prepared baking sheet. With a bench scraper or a knife, make 4 or 5 evenly spaced cuts around the rounded edge of the bun, similar to a bear claw pastry. Cover the baking sheet with plastic wrap and allow the buns to rise in a warm spot until doubled in size, about an hour.

11. At the tail end of the rising time, preheat the oven to 350°F.

12. Remove the plastic wrap and brush the risen buns all over with the egg yolk you reserved from the dough stage. If you don't have quite enough, thin the egg yolk out with a tablespoon of water to make it stretch. Bake for 20 minutes, or until golden brown. Eat the same day for the freshest bite of cream pan!

TANAKA-KUN IS ALWAYS LISTLESS

STRAWBERRY MELON PAN

Tanaka spends high school wishing every day would be boring (so he can continue to be lazy, his favorite hobby). In one episode, Tanaka's friend Oota is hurt, so he asks Tanaka to grab lunch for him. He specifically requests a sweet, bready treat, and Tanaka is happy to indulge. However, unused to exerting so much energy, Tanaka mindlessly devours the very food he set out to acquire and returns empty-handed. Luckily, another classmate offers their strawberry melon pan snack, which Oota accepts gratefully.

So-called because they're shaped to look like cut melon, melon pan don't actually taste like melons. In fact, the usual flavor for melon pan is vanilla, so this strawberry recipe is a little different from what you'd find in an average convenience store. A perfect way to celebrate strawberries when they're in season, this bread is especially tasty when warm from the oven. If you're listless just like Tanaka, give this a go.

3 HOURS

MAKES 8 BUNS

SPECIAL EQUIPMENT: 2-INCH ROUND COOKIE CUTTER

NUT-FREE

RECIPE TIP: When it comes to allowing the dough to rise, don't always rely on the clock. Dough can take sometimes 2 or even 3 hours to rise, depending on the temperature of the resting space. (And hotter isn't always better—I once tried letting some pizza dough rise on our rooftop, as I thought it would be warmest under the burning sun. Alas, after an unfortunate battle with the sloped roof and gravity, my dough ended up in the pool, and my mother's favorite metal prep bowl was irreparably dented for the rest of its life.) Be patient, leave the dough somewhere safe and warm, and wait until it has doubled in size.

FOR THE DOUGH

¼ cup whole milk, warmed (110°F to 115°F)

1 teaspoon active dry yeast

8 ounces strawberries, diced

¼ cup sugar

2 cups bread flour

1 teaspoon kosher salt

2 tablespoons unsalted butter, at room temperature

1 large egg, whisked

FOR THE COOKIE CRUST

1 cup cake flour

¼ cup sugar, plus more if needed

¼ cup powdered freeze-dried strawberries

3 tablespoons unsalted butter, at room temperature

1. Make the dough: Place the milk in a small bowl. Addd the yeast and stir to combine. Set aside for 10 minutes, until bubbles form and the mixture smells yeasty.

2. Stir together the strawberries and sugar in a small bowl, then set aside.

3. Whisk together the flour and salt in a large bowl. Pour the yeast mixture directly into the flour. Add the strawberries, butter, and half the egg (reserve the remaining egg for the cookie crust). Use a whisk or an electric mixer to combine until everything is evenly incorporated.

4. Turn the dough out onto a floured counter and knead well for 10 minutes, or until the dough passes the windowpane test (see Tip, page 97). If the dough is too sticky, knead in more bread flour as needed, but don't go overboard.

5. Form the dough into a ball and place it in a clean bowl. Wet a finger under the kitchen faucet and swipe it along the inner rim of the bowl to add moisture, then cover the bowl with plastic wrap. Place somewhere warm to rise for an hour, or until the dough has doubled in size.

Continued

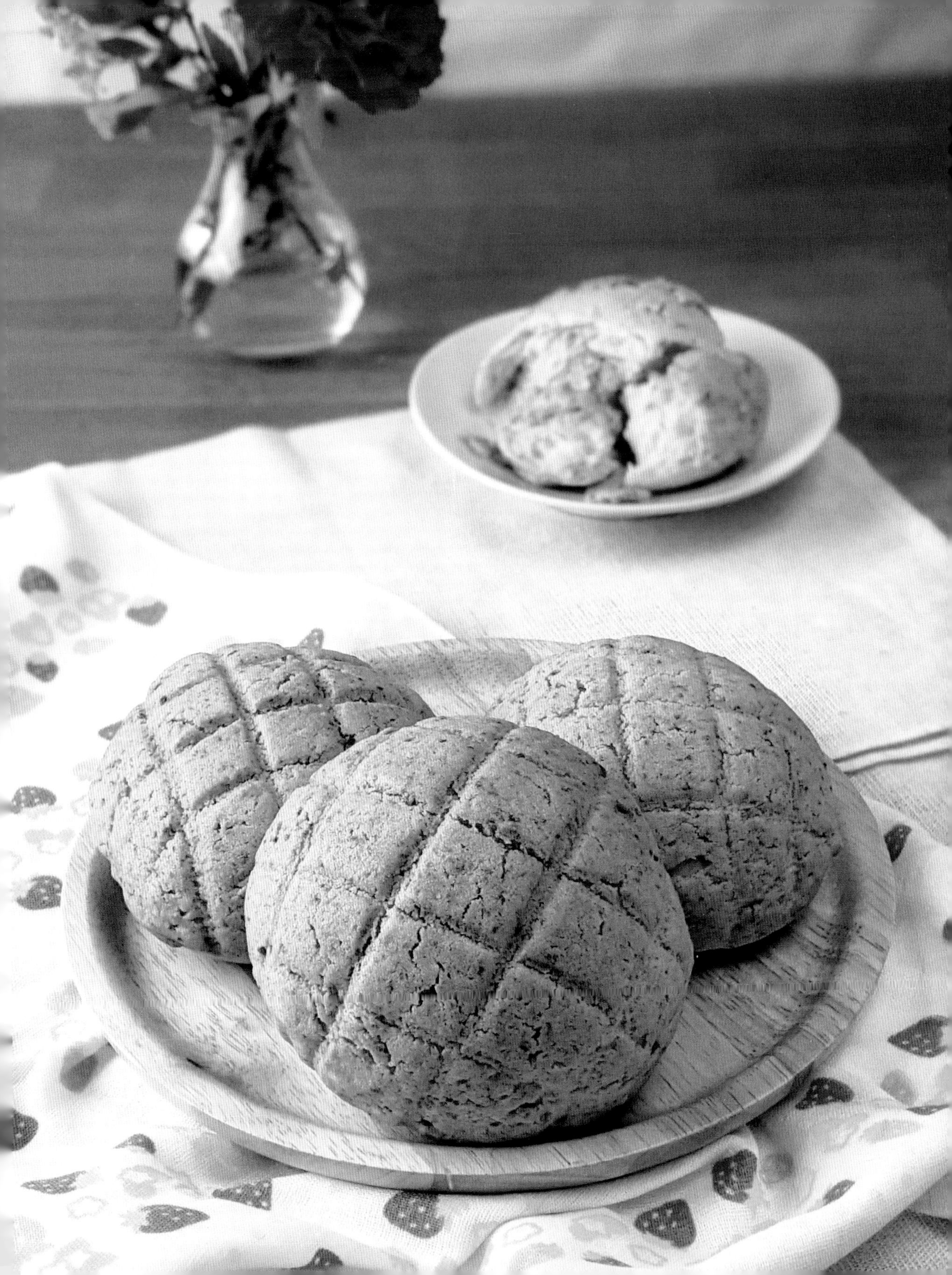

6. Make the cookie crust: Combine the cake flour, sugar, freeze-dried strawberries, and butter in a bowl, add the ½ egg reserved from making the dough, and use an electric mixer or rubber spatula to mix the ingredients together into a paste. The cookie crust should be sticky and soft, but not so sticky that it's gluing itself to your hands. If that's happening, add more flour by the teaspoon as needed. If you're finding the dough is crumbly, add water by the teaspoon to relax the dough.

7. Scrape the cookie crust out onto a sheet of plastic wrap and roll it into a log. Place the log in the freezer to firm up a bit.

8. Line a baking sheet with parchment paper. Turn the dough out onto the counter and punch the air out of it. Split the dough into 8 even pieces and form each piece into a round. Twist the dough at the bottom of the round tightly and pull the sides down and under to create tension across the top. Set the rounds of dough aside on the prepared baking sheet.

9. Remove the log of cookie crust from the freezer and cut it crosswise into 8 equal pieces. Roll each piece between two sheets of parchment paper until it's just under half an inch thick and about 2½ inches in diameter, and then use a round cutter to cut each piece into a uniform circle. It should be big enough to cover the top and sides of the bun. Gently place one round of cookie crust over the top of each bun and use your fingers to smooth it down along the edges.

10. Using the back of a knife, carefully make impressions in the cookie crust first one way, then the other, forming a crosshatched design on top. Cover the baking sheet with plastic wrap and allow the buns to rise in a warm spot until doubled in size, about an hour. Be careful not to put the buns directly under a heating lamp or anything of the sort, or the cookie crust will melt.

11. At the tail end of the rising time, preheat the oven to 350°F.

12. Remove the plastic wrap and pop the buns in the oven for 25 minutes. Toward the last 10 minutes, lay a sheet of aluminum foil loosely over the buns to prevent them from browning. Eat the melon pan the same day to enjoy them at their yummiest!

CHOCOLATE CORNET

Which way do you eat a chocolate cornet—from the pointy end, or from the wide end? And which end is the top? Konata, one of the central figures of *Lucky Star*, debates these very questions with her friend Tsukasa. *Lucky Star* follows the day-to-day life of four girls at a high school in Saitama, a working-family prefecture just outside Tokyo. This comedy homes in on the everyday questions that come up among bored teenage girls. This show is one for the ages, and the chocolate cornet is one of the most well-known food jokes from the series.

Though this cornet looks complicated, the most difficult thing about it is wrapping the dough around the pastry cones. Despite the challenges with the pastry, nearly all sins are forgiven when they bake, because the cone shape is so cute. Also, the chocolate filling is sinfully delicious. Make these for yourself and find your own answer to the question of how to eat them!

3 HOURS

MAKES 6 CORNETS

SPECIAL EQUIPMENT: CONE MOLDS, INFRARED THERMOMETER

NUT-FREE

FOOD FACT: While these treats are called chocolate cornets in Japan, they're called chocolate cream horns elsewhere in the world.

FOR THE CORNET DOUGH

1/3 cup warm water

1 teaspoon active dry yeast

1 tablespoon sugar

2/3 cup bread flour

1/2 teaspoon kosher salt

1 large egg, whisked

FOR THE CHOCOLATE CUSTARD

2 large egg yolks

2½ tablespoons sugar

1½ tablespoons cornstarch

1 tablespoon cake flour

1 tablespoon unsweetened cocoa powder

¾ cup whole milk

1½ ounces dark chocolate

1 tablespoon unsalted butter, plus more for greasing the molds

1. Make the cornet dough: Pour the warm water into a small bowl, add the yeast and sugar, and stir to combine. Let stand for 10 minutes, or until the water is bubbling, foamy, and smells yeasty.

2. Combine the flour and salt in a bowl. Add 1 tablespoon of the egg to the yeast mixture, then pour the yeast mixture into the flour mixture and stir until the dough comes together (reserve the remaining egg to use as an egg wash before baking the cornets).

3. Turn the dough out onto the counter and knead it until it forms a ball that's a little sticky and passes the windowpane test (see Tip, page 97). Shape the dough into a ball and put it in a bowl. Cover the bowl with plastic wrap and set it in a warm place to rise for about an hour, until the dough is doubled in size.

4. Make the chocolate custard: Whisk together the egg yolks, sugar, cornstarch, flour, and cocoa powder in a large bowl.

Continued

5. Heat the milk in a heavy-bottomed saucepan over medium heat until it begins to steam. While whisking continuously, slowly pour ¼ cup of the hot milk into the egg mixture and whisk to combine. While whisking, pour the egg mixture into the pot with the remaining milk. The custard will thicken suddenly—cook, stirring, for a minute longer, or until it hits 175°F.

6. Remove the custard from the heat and strain it through a fine-mesh sieve into a bowl. Add the chocolate and butter and stir until both are melted and combined. Cover the custard with plastic wrap, pressing it directly against the surface of the custard to prevent a skin from forming, and immediately place in the freezer to chill until cool to the touch and set nicely.

7. The dough is ready when you can poke a finger into it and the hole that's made doesn't close back up. Turn the dough out onto a lightly floured surface and cut it into 6 equal pieces. (Use a scale to ensure each piece is the same size.) Shape each piece into a ball, drape a damp paper towel over the top, and let rest for 15 minutes.

8. Grease the cone molds with the butter and line a baking sheet with parchment paper. Roll one ball of dough into a 12-inch-long strip that tapers at one end. Starting with the thin, pointy end of the cone, wrap the dough around the mold. Stretch the dough lightly to create tension as you wrap, but not so much that you lose definition of the swirls. Place the finished cone on the prepared baking sheet, with the end of the dough strip down. Repeat with the remaining dough. Place plastic wrap lightly over the baking sheet and allow the cones to rise one final time, 30 to 40 minutes. Toward the end of the rising time, preheat the oven to 400°F.

9. Brush the cones with the egg reserved from making the dough and bake for 12 to 14 minutes, until golden brown. Allow the cones to cool on a wire rack to room temperature. To remove the molds, gently twist and pull them loose.

10. Place the custard in a pastry bag and snip off the tip. Put the pastry bag inside one of the cones and use gentle pressure to fill the cone with custard. Gently swirl the tip of the pastry bag around when the custard reaches the opening of the cone to avoid a chocolate point popping out of the cone. Enjoy!

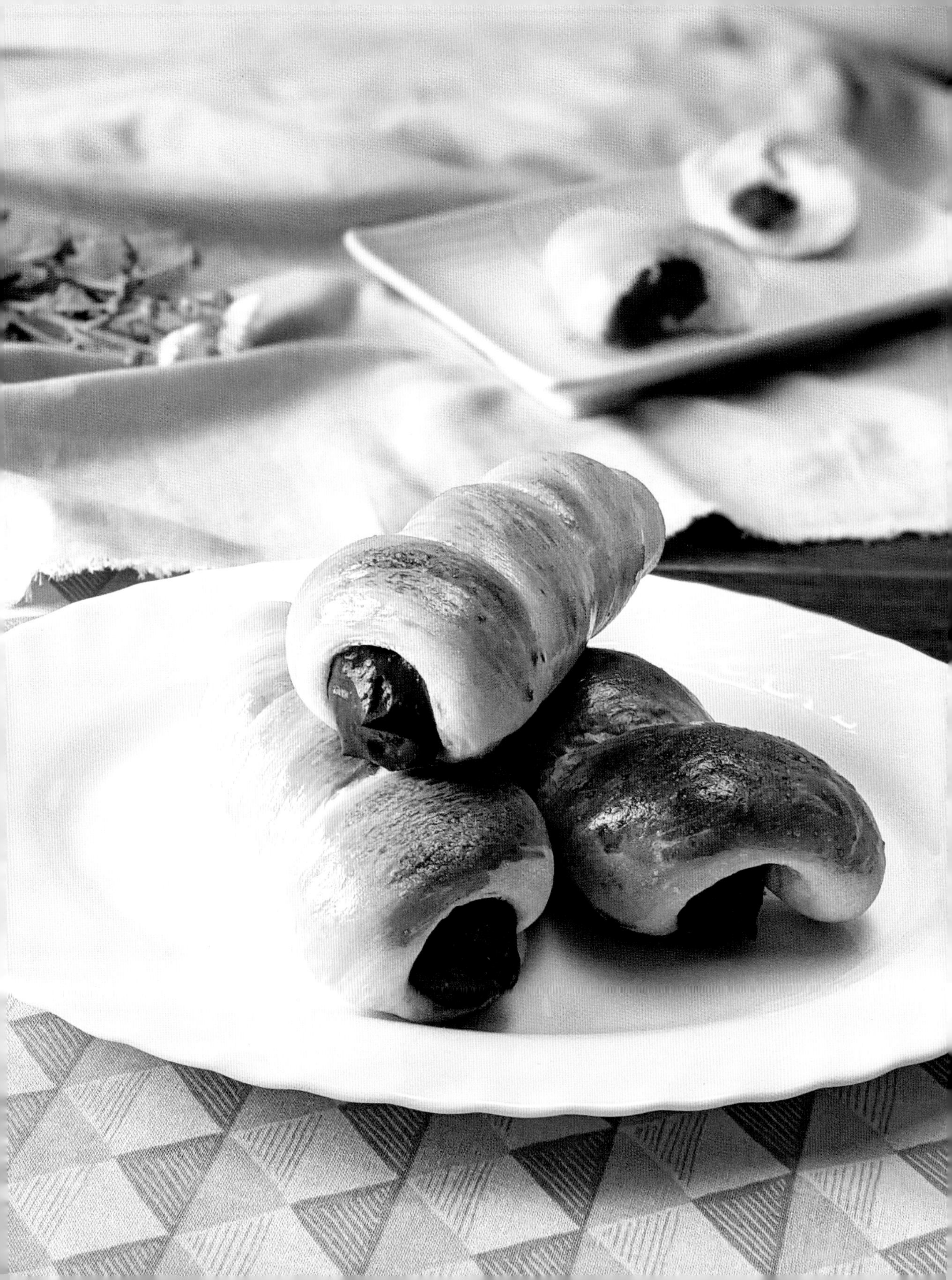

AKASHIC RECORDS OF BASTARD MAGIC INSTRUCTOR

SCONES

At the Alzano Imperial Magic Academy, being top of the class is the number one priority. The teachers are among the very best, and the students come prepared to dominate. When Glenn Radars comes in to replace everyone's favorite teacher, his arrival is met with trepidation, and tensions rise when it seems like he doesn't particularly care about magic, teaching, or the students. Students Sistine and Rumia take it upon themselves to learn more about him, but when dark forces arise at the academy, the students and their teacher are unexpectedly thrust together.

While Glenn Radars isn't the best teacher, the students at least have quality food to enjoy. Since the academy is set in a vaguely European fantasy world, most of the food featured is Western in origin. Characters eat lunch in the dining hall, and they can also help themselves to a small tea service. One of my favorite things is afternoon tea, so I figured that if these students can eat scones and tea for lunch, so can we.

30 MINUTES

MAKES 16 SMALL SCONES

SPECIAL EQUIPMENT: 2-INCH ROUND COOKIE CUTTER (OPTIONAL)

NUT-FREE

4 cups all-purpose flour, plus more for dusting

¼ cup sugar

2½ tablespoons baking powder

1 teaspoon kosher salt

6 tablespoons unsalted butter, cubed and chilled

1½ cups whole milk

1 large egg, whisked, for egg wash

Clotted cream, for serving

Jam, for serving

1. Preheat the oven to 425°F. Line a baking sheet with parchment paper.

2. Whisk together the flour, sugar, baking powder, and salt in a large bowl to combine.

3. Massage the butter into the flour mixture with your fingers until the butter is spread throughout the mixture in flaky pieces and the flour has a crumblike texture. Move fast so the butter doesn't melt too much.

4. Pour in the milk and use a spatula to stir, stopping as soon as the milk is incorporated. At this point, the dough will be sticky and a little wet.

5. Dust a clean work surface generously with flour and turn the dough out onto it. Sprinkle the top of the dough with more flour and knead a few times to bring it together. Pat the dough into a round that's 1 inch high. Use a 2-inch round cutter or the rim of a glass to cut scones, pressing it down cleanly into the dough without twisting (twisting as you push can impact the rise on the scones) and dusting the cutter generously with flour if it gets overly sticky. Plop the scones on the prepared baking sheet.

6. Brush the tops of the scones with the egg wash. Pop the baking sheet in the oven for 12 minutes, or until the tops of the scones are golden and the bottoms are browned.

RECIPE TIP: Adding lemon or orange zest can impart a fun kick that transforms your typical scone. Feeling indulgent? Add chocolate chips with the zest. Feeling fruity? Dried fruits hold up well in this recipe; just add them after you add butter. Fresh fruit is also acceptable (berries are best): Add the fruit after the milk, with as little fuss as possible, being careful not to smash the fruit, and keep an eye on the baking time, as you may need to cook the scones slightly longer.

7. While the first batch of scones is baking, gather the remaining scraps of dough and gently pat and knead them back into a 1-inch round. Be gentle and don't overwork the dough. Cut out more scones from the dough. You can press the remaining scraps together to get the most out of the dough, but avoid kneading them this time.

8. Shimmy the scones onto a wire rack to cool. Brush the tops of your next batch with egg wash, then place them in the oven. Since the baking sheet is hot, the second batch might need a minute less in the oven.

9. Enjoy warm, with clotted cream and jam of your choice!

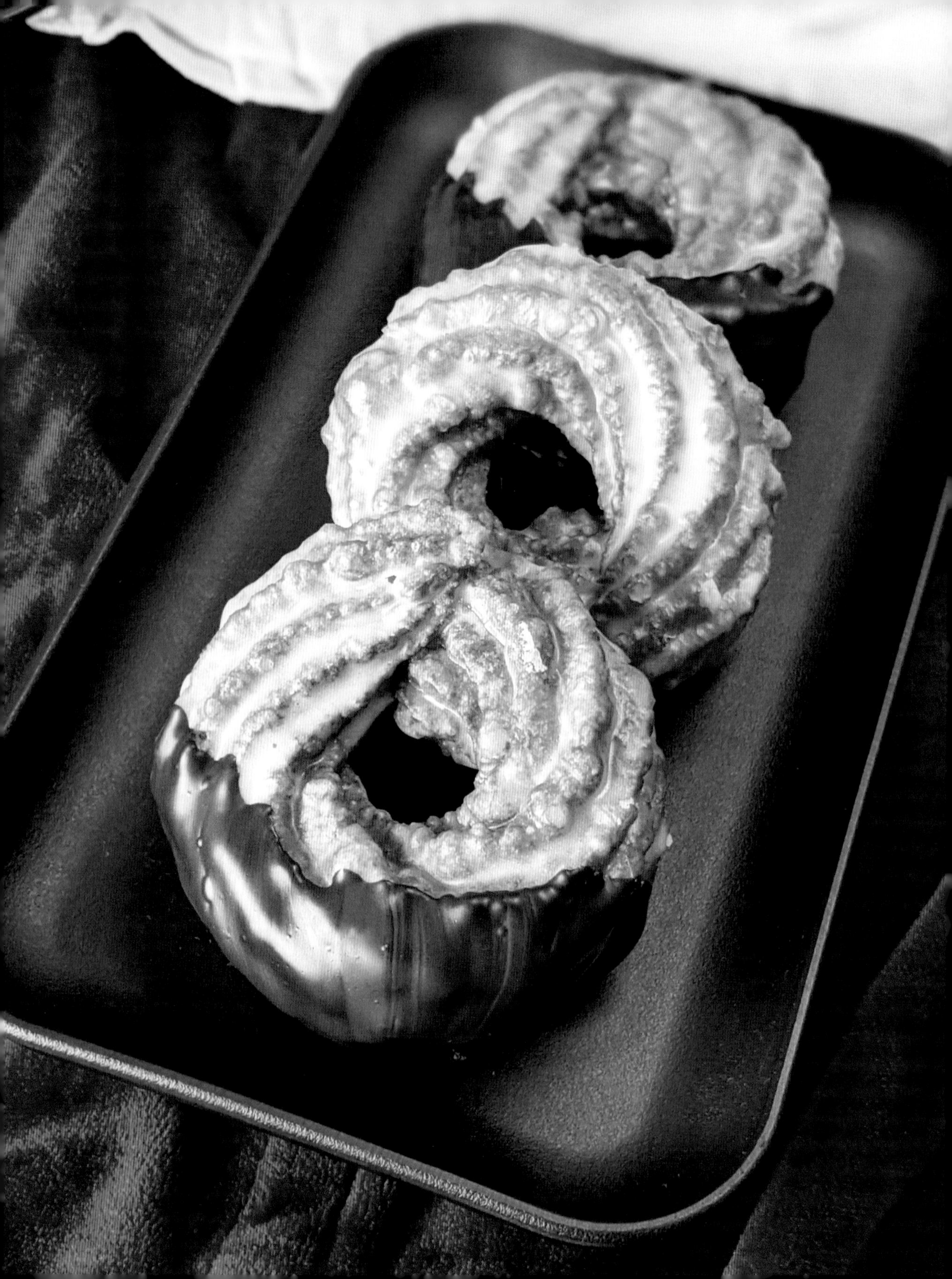

CRULLERS

Koyomi is a peculiar high schooler with an even more peculiar secret: a vampire girl named Shinobu lives in his shadow. This vampire isn't afraid to take what she thinks is rightfully hers, be it your blood or . . . your donuts? Throughout the series, the two solve mysteries that arise when everyday people bump into supernatural forces, often with harmful or even deadly consequences.

Living in the current age isn't all bad for Shinobu. Among the many modern delights she partakes in are donuts. She's a frequent patron of Mister Donut (a real Japanese chain), where her usual choice is a chocolate-dipped French cruller, a donut made with choux pastry. What I love best about these donuts is that the ridges in the dough trap the glaze, making each bite mouth-wateringly delicious.

2 HOURS

MAKES 12 DONUTS

SPECIAL EQUIPMENT: PASTRY BAG AND LARGE STAR PIPING TIP, INFRARED THERMOMETER

NUT-FREE

RECIPE TIPS: The inside of a good cruller should be pocked with large air bubbles and dry to the touch.

If you're having trouble keeping the temperature of the oil steady, reduce the number of donuts you cook in each batch. The more donuts in the oil, the faster it will cool off, and the longer it will take to heat back up.

FOR THE CHOUX PASTRY
½ cup whole milk

½ cup water

½ cup (1 stick) unsalted butter

1 cup all-purpose flour

1 tablespoon granulated sugar

1 teaspoon kosher salt

3 to 4 large eggs

Vegetable oil, for frying

FOR TOPPING
2 cups confectioners' sugar

2 to 3 tablespoons whole milk

1 teaspoon vanilla extract

2 ounces dark chocolate

1. Make the choux pastry: Combine the milk, water, and butter in a nonstick pot (no need to stir). Bring to a boil over high heat.

2. Meanwhile, whisk together the flour, granulated sugar, and salt in a bowl.

3. When the liquids come to a boil, dump the dry ingredients into the pot and stir vigorously. Keeping the heat on, beat the batter with a rubber spatula for 2 to 3 minutes, until the dough sticks to the sides of the pot.

4. Remove the pot from the heat and transfer the dough to a bowl. Using an electric mixer, beat the dough for a minute or so to cool it slightly, then, with the mixer running, add 3 eggs, one at a time, beating well and stopping to scrape down the sides of the bowl with a rubber spatula after each addition before adding the next. We're looking for a smooth, sticky dough that drips from the spatula in thick ribbons: when you hold the spatula straight down over the bowl, the batter should slouch off in a triangle. If you're finding the dough to be particularly thick and clumpy, whisk the remaining egg and add it to the dough 1 tablespoon at a time until you're happy with the consistency.

5. Spoon the dough into a pastry bag fitted with a large star piping tip and set aside.

Continued

6. Fill a large heavy-bottomed pot with oil to a depth of 4 inches and heat the oil to 370°F. Prepare a resting spot for the crullers by setting a wire rack over a layer of paper towels.

7. Lay a sheet of parchment paper on your work surface and cut into roughly 4 x 4-inch squares. As you wait for the oil to come to temperature, pipe rings of dough as big or as small as you like onto the parchment squares, leaving some room on the edges for easy handling. Keep the tip ½ inch above the parchment as you pipe. Squeeze gently, then trace a ring of dough onto the paper. As you near the start of the circle, lighten the pressure and swipe the tip across the beginning of the ring to connect the dough.

8. For the most control, I prefer to cook my crullers one at a time, but you can cook them in batches. Whatever method you choose, lower your donuts into the hot oil with the parchment facing up. Using tongs to protect your fingers, peel off the parchment, then cook the donuts on the first side for 3 minutes. As you cook, monitor the temperature of the oil; you want to keep it between 360°F and 380°F as much as possible. The donuts are ready to flip when the bottoms (what you see on top) have puffed up so much that the donuts have cracked. When you flip it, you want the dough to be cooked enough that it won't crack on the piping-tip-patterned side. Flip the donuts and cook for 3 minutes more, or until the bottom of the donuts match the coloring of the top half. Transfer the donuts to the wire rack to cool completely. Repeat with the remaining donuts.

9. Make the vanilla glaze: Whisk together the confectioners' sugar, milk, and vanilla in a bowl until smooth. Place the cooked donuts in the bowl, top side down, and press them into the glaze. Hook them through the middle and remove from the glaze, placing them back on the rack, icing side up. Allow the glaze to set.

10. Make the dark chocolate dip: Lay a piece of parchment paper on your work surface. Place all but a few squares of the dark chocolate in a microwave-safe bowl. Microwave for 30 seconds, stir thoroughly, then microwave for another 15 seconds and stir again. If needed, microwave again in 10-second stints, stirring well after each, until the chocolate is melted and smooth. Remove the chocolate from the microwave and stir until it cools to 100°F, then add the reserved dark chocolate squares. While stirring, add more chips of dark chocolate until the chocolate cools to 90°F.

11. Quickly dip the donuts in the chocolate to coat, dunking one side in for the right effect. Allow to harden on the parchment, then enjoy.

CANELÉS

After the death of his mother, prodigy Kosei Arima resigns himself to giving up the piano. Everything changes, however, when he meets Kaori, a girl who plays a melodica so freely and with so much joy, it stops Kosei in his tracks. Over time, the two strike up a friendship and Kosei learns that Kaori is also a gifted violinist. She persuades him to try the piano again, and together, they make beautiful music. But when Kosei collaspes suddenly following a transcendent duet, Kosei is forced to reckon with his own past. What follows is a journey of beauty, pain, and the importance of committing to your passion with everything you have.

As it turns out, canelés are Kaori's favorite treat, and it's understandable why she'd want them. Canelés are a French pastry usually baked in a special beeswax-lined copper mold. In order to achieve their glossy exterior, a mixture of beeswax and butter is used to coat the canelé pans (if you don't want to buy beeswax, using nonstick cooking spray or just butter will be fine). The treat has a custardy interior flavored with rum and vanilla. Kaori had to wait for Kosei to bring her these treats, but you can easily make them yourself!

FOR THE CANELÉS

2 vanilla beans, split lengthwise and seeds scraped

2 cups whole milk

1¼ cups sugar

⅔ cup all-purpose flour

4 tablespoons (½ stick) unsalted butter, melted

2 large eggs

2 large egg yolks

¼ cup dark rum

FOR THE MOLD COATING

⅓ cup beeswax (see Tip, page 112)

4 tablespoons (½ stick) unsalted butter

1. Make the canelés: Combine the vanilla seeds, vanilla pods, and milk in a pot. Bring to a simmer over medium heat, cook for a minute or so, then turn off the heat.

2. Whisk together the sugar, flour, melted butter, eggs, and egg yolks in a large bowl.

3. While whisking continuously, ladle ¼ cup of the warm milk into the egg mixture and whisk to combine. It's crucial that you whisk as you add the milk to cool the egg mixture as you stir. While whisking, pour the egg mixture into the pot with the milk and whisk until everything is combined.

4. Strain the batter through a fine-mesh sieve and discard the vanilla pods. Pour in the rum and give the batter a final stir. Cover and refrigerate for at least 24 hours, but ideally 48 hours.

5. Make the mold coating: Put the canelé molds in a warm spot so they take on a little heat before you coat them (this will later help the wax slide out so you don't get too thick of a coating). Place beeswax and butter into a heatproof measuring cup, then place the measuring cup in a pan. Fill the pan with water so it comes up to the height of the mixure in the measuring cup, then heat over high heat and allow the butter and beeswax to melt fully, about 5 minutes. Carefully remove the measuring cup from the pot and wipe down the exterior.

Continued

3 DAYS

MAKES 16 PIECES

SPECIAL EQUIPMENT: **CANELÉ MOLDS (PREFERABLY COPPER)**

NUT-FREE

RECIPE TIP: Avoid silicone molds, as they won't produce the same bronze color on the outside, and look for individual molds rather than molds set in a tray. Traditionally, copper molds are used to ensure even heat distribution, but I have had success with heavy aluminum molds as well, which are cheaper. You can find options online if you can't find any physical stores that carry the molds. When you're done using them, *don't* wash them. Simply wipe out any excess drips of butter, stack the molds, and set aside for the next project.

6. Remove the molds from their warm spot and line them up on a sheet of parchment paper. Pour some of the beeswax mixture into the first mold, then immediately tip the contents into the next mold. Repeat to coat all the molds, tipping the wax from one to the next, topping off the wax in the molds with what's left in the measuring cup as needed. Move quickly here—the wax will harden fast. Tidy up the rims of the canelé molds so you don't have clumps of wax pooled around the edges, then set aside in a cool spot until you're ready to bake the canelés.

7. Preheat the oven to 550°F. Line a baking sheet with aluminum foil.

8. Fill the canelé molds three-quarters full with the batter, leaving room at the top to allow the canelés to rise. Place the filled molds on the prepared baking sheet (to catch any beeswax overflow) and bake for 15 minutes. Without opening the oven door, reduce the oven temperature to 375°F and bake for 45 to 50 minutes more, until browned.

9. Remove the molds from the oven and immediately turn the canelés out onto a wire rack so the wax doesn't reharden, trapping the canelés inside the molds. Use oven mitts for this and move carefully. If they don't come out of the molds, tap them on a hard surface to release them. Allow the canelés to cool and their beeswax coating to harden, about 2 hours, then serve.

RECIPE TIPS: If you don't want to bother with the special coating, you can use just butter or nonstick cooking spray to grease the pan instead. Why bother with the beeswax coating at all if I can use cooking spray? The beeswax-butter mixture gives the final product a beautifully shiny exterior.

The baking sequence of canelés is two-pronged: The first temperature is designed to set and brown the outer shell so it has the strength to support the custard center. It's important to give it time at 550°F to do this, but after your first batch you may find that the canelés wilt when they come out of the pan. This is a sign that you need to either reduce the amount of batter in the mold (resulting in shorter canelés), or increase the baking time at 550°F to provide more structure. The second wave of baking takes place at 375°F and lasts much longer—this cooks the custard interior of the canelés.

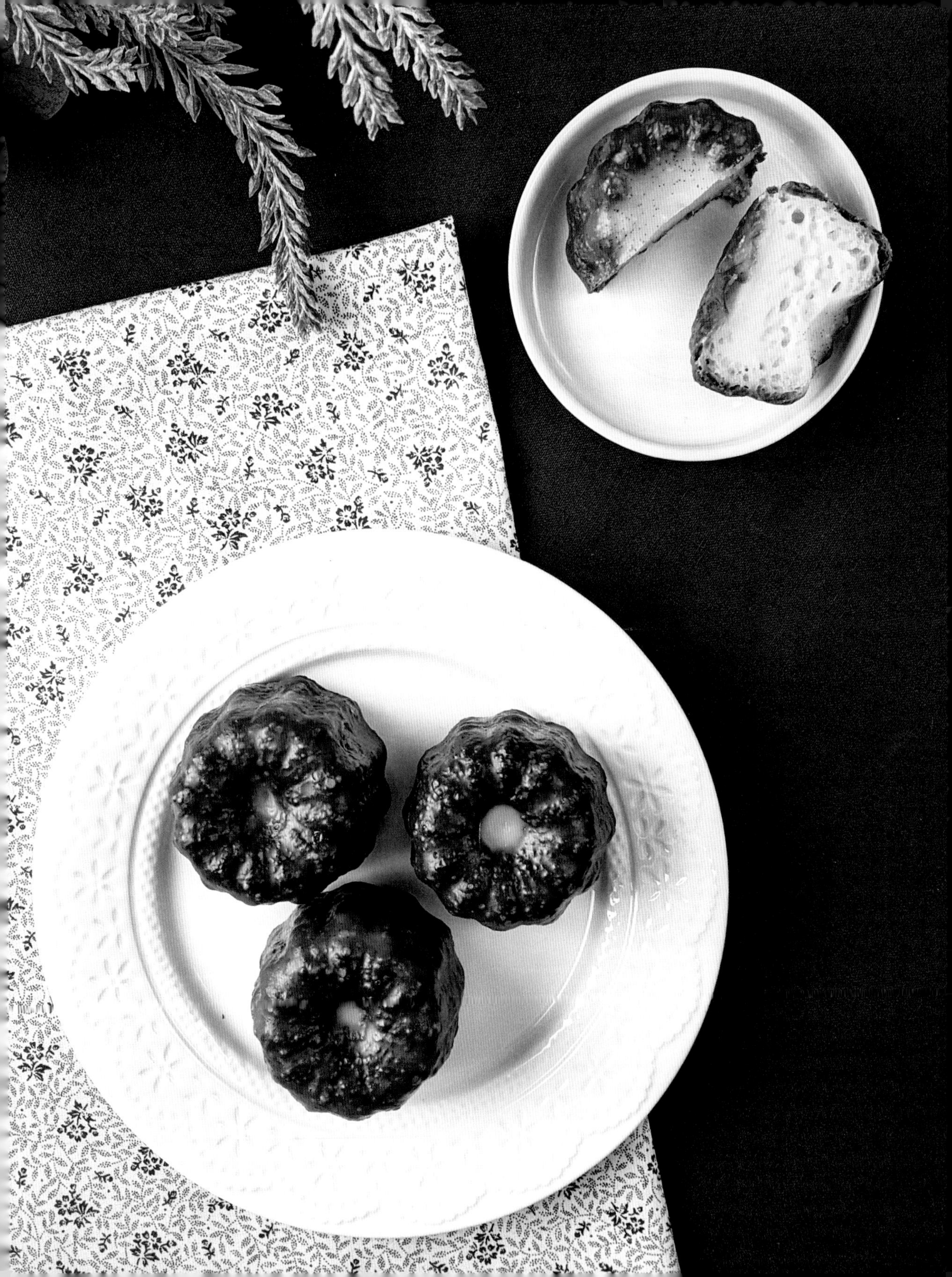

YAKITATE!! JAPAN

INVERSE PUFF PASTRY LOQUAT TART

Kazuma Azuma has a dream: make a type of bread so unique, it'll come to be known as the signature bread of Japan. To achieve his goal, he works at a prestigious bakery, Pantasia, where he discovers his own special talent: Solar Hands. Kazuma is blessed with unusually warm hands, which helps him make fermented breads and gives him a leg up in his new bakery.

In one episode, Kazuma goes head-to-head with a baker named Yukino in a fruit tart competition. Yukino also possesses a special ability—Blizzard Hands—which makes it easy for her to make butter-rich doughs that must be kept cold. Yukino is cold and cruel to her fellow competitors; she even goes so far as to beat up a man who makes preserved loquats, a town specialty. In this competition, she makes a tart crust using the inverse puff pastry method, which allows the butter to extend all the way through each layer. Meanwhile, Kazuma makes a tart that uses preserved loquats to help the man Yukino beat up, and ultimately ends up winning the whole thing! To combine the best of both worlds, this recipe uses Yukino's dough technique, but with loquats as the topping.

2 DAYS

SERVES 8

SPECIAL EQUIPMENT: **9-INCH TART PAN WITH REMOVEABLE BOTTOM**

NUT-FREE

FOR THE OUTSIDE BUTTER PACKET

1 cup (2 sticks) unsalted butter, at room temperature

6 tablespoons all-purpose flour

FOR THE INSIDE DOUGH PACKET

4½ tablespoons unsalted butter, at room temperature

½ cup plus 2½ tablespoons all-purpose flour

½ cup plus 2½ tablespoons cake flour

¾ tablespoon granulated sugar

½ teaspoon kosher salt

½ teaspoon distilled white vinegar

⅓ cup ice water

FOR TOPPINGS

½ cup heavy cream

8 ounces mascarpone cheese, at room temperature

¼ cup confectioners' sugar

½ teaspoon vanilla extract

18 loquats

½ cup apricot jam or preserves

Fresh mint, for garnish

RECIPE TIP: A key thing to remember as you roll out the dough is that you're trying to roll out two layers simultaneously while keeping them separate but intact. If you feel resistance under the rolling pin from the dough layer, or see the butter layer cracking all over the place, take a step back and try to repair as you go. Being careful and taking your time will pay off—do not rush it, or you run the risk of ruining the dough.

SUBSTITUTION TIP: Can't find loquats? Substitute apricots or strawberries instead!

1. Make the outside butter packet: Using a stand mixer or working by hand, whip the butter and flour together in a bowl until just combined. Spread the butter into a 5-inch square between two sheets of parchment paper. Use a rolling pin to make the square the same thickness all the way through and use a bench scraper to even out the sides. The cleaner you are with these lines, the easier the folding will be in the future. Refrigerate while you make the dough.

2. Make the inside dough packet: Combine the butter, all-purpose flour, cake flour, granulated sugar, and salt in a bowl and blitz with an electric mixer until the dough comes together into shaggy crumbs. Add the vinegar to the water and pour it into the center of the dough. Mix until a dough forms again. Turn the contents of the bowl out onto the counter and knead everything until no dry bits remain. If you're having trouble getting all the dry spots moistened, dip your hand in ice water and tap it on the dough where needed.

3. Set the dough on a sheet of plastic wrap and roll or press it into a 3-inch square. Again, make sure the thickness of the dough is uniform and the edges are straight. Wrap the dough in the plastic wrap and refrigerate for 30 minutes.

4. Generously flour your work surface. Take the butter packet out of the refrigerator about 5 minutes before the dough has finished chilling and set it on the flour-dusted surface so one edge is parallel to you. Unwrap the dough and put it on top of the butter so that it looks like a diamond on the square of butter and each corner of the diamond is situated in the middle of one side of the square.

5. Fold the edges of the butter up and around the dough (like closing an envelope flap) to enclose it. If you notice the butter starts to break, step away from the dough for a minute to allow the butter to soften until you can fold the edges without breaking them. Seal the edges of the butter by pinching and pressing the butter in on itself.

6. Roll the packet out until it's 9 inches long by 4 inches wide, aiming to keep the edges as sharp as possible. Make your first fold like you'd fold a letter: pull one third of the dough toward the middle, then pull the opposite third over the first third of dough. Line up all the edges then press down on the folds, sealing everything together. Repeat this once more—roll, fold, and press—then wrap the dough in plastic wrap and chill for 30 minutes. The goal here is to work quickly so that the butter doesn't melt. The minute you feel the dough getting too soft, quickly finish up and get it in the fridge.

7. Perform two more sets of folds, refrigerating the dough for 30 minutes after each set. If you find the dough is pulling back or shrinking after you roll it out, refrigerate it for an additional 10 minutes to give the dough time to relax. On your final set after the last roll out, fold the dough again and finish by wrapping it in plastic wrap. Refrigerate for at least 2 hours or preferably overnight.

8. Flour your work surface lightly to prevent stick. Unwrap the dough and roll it out to 9 x 13 inches. Roll until the dough is ¼ inch thick and wide and round enough to cover a 9-inch tart pan (with a removeable bottom). Roll the dough onto the rolling pin and transfer it to the tart pan. Press it into the edges of the pan, making sure it's flush with the sides. Use a rolling pin to trim the excess dough from the edges of the tart shell, rolling it over to top of the pan to cut off the excess pastry. Chill the tart shell in the refrigerator for at least 30 minutes and up to 3 days before baking.

9. Preheat the oven to 375°F.

10. Prick the bottom of the tart shell all over with a fork to allow steam to escape as it cooks. Bake for 30 to 40 minutes, until golden brown. Remove from the oven and allow to cool completely.

11. Prepare the tart toppings: Using an electric mixer, whip the heavy cream in a large bowl to soft peaks. In a separate large bowl, combine the mascarpone, confectioners' sugar, and vanilla and whip until combined. Using a rubber spatula, fold the whipped cream into the mascarpone mixture until everything is light and fluffy and there are no visible streaks of whipped cream.

Continued

12. With your fingers, peel off the fuzzy skin of the loquats. Start by pinching the nib where the stem would be and tug down. It'll come off in strips, or even as one intact skin. Cut the loquats in half, then use a small spoon to scoop out the seeds on the inside, preserving as much flesh as possible.

13. Place the cooled tart shell on a serving platter. Scoop the mascarpone filling into the tart shell and use a spatula to spread it over the bottom, nudging it out toward the edges but leaving a small gap between the edge and the cream. Decorate with the loquats. You can take two different approaches: you can slump the loquat halves together on the cream, or you can lay the halves cut side down on top of the cream.

14. When the fruit is where you want it, thin the apricot spread with a tablespoon of water, then brush it over the surface of the fruit. If you have gaps between the fruit and cream, douse them with the apricot spread. Garnish with mint sprigs and enjoy the same day.

QUEEN'S TART

Momo, the dessert specialist of the elite Totsuki Culinary Academy, battles Megumi, a chef specializing in hospitality, for control of the school. They must use a random ingredient to craft a dish that embodies the very soul of their selected food. Their choice? Apples. While Megumi displays a modernized dorayaki with an apple filling (see page 37), Momo is ultimately declared the winner. Her dish is elaborate—mini apple tarts shaped to look like roses, presented in a hand-woven basket made of bread.

Momo's dish is quite involved. The apples are soaked in rose water and dyed red with apple peel. The tart itself is flaky and buttery, which perfectly complements the floral aromas. Ie experimented with making her recipe to the letter, but immediately found shortcuts that will simplify cooking it at home. This dessert tastes and looks identical to the anime version as the characters describe it, but this recipe makes cooking it that much simpler!

4 HOURS

MAKES 8 SMALL TARTS

SPECIAL EQUIPMENT: ROUND COOKIE CUTTERS

NUT-FREE

RECIPE TIP: Make the tart shells a day in advance to break things up if this recipe seems too hefty to do in one day. Can't eat them all in one day? Store them in an airtight container in the fridge for up to a day.

FOR THE TART SHELLS

1½ cup all-purpose flour

½ cup sugar

¼ teaspoon kosher salt

½ cup (1 stick) unsalted butter, cubed and chilled

1 large egg yolk, whisked

2 to 4 tablespoons ice water

FOR THE ROSE WATER SYRUP

½ cup water

2 cups sugar

½ cup rose water

Red food coloring (optional)

3 or 4 large red apples

1. Make the tart shells: Whisk together the flour, sugar, and salt in a bowl. Toss in the butter and work it into the dry ingredients with your fingers, rubbing until you've created a sandy mixture with butter pieces no bigger than peas.

2. Sprinkle the egg yolk over the dough. Mix quickly with your hands and sprinkle in the ice water a tablespoon at a time until the dough comes together and holds its shape when you squeeze it. Turn the dough out onto your work surface and form it into a disc. Wrap the disc in plastic wrap and chill it in the refrigerator for an hour.

3. Prepare the rose water syrup: Combine the water, sugar, and rose water in a pan and bring to a boil over high heat. As soon as the sugar has completely dissolved, turn the heat off but leave the pan on the stove. Add 2 drops of red food coloring. (If you really want to bring color to the apples, you'll need a lot of dye. My photo of the apple tarts is the result of just 2 drops of dye.

4. Halve the apples, then quarter and core them. If you have a mandoline, use it to create thin slices. If using a knife, cut slices as thinly (and as safely) as possible. By the time you're done, the rose water syrup will have cooled so it's warm to the touch. Add the apple slices to the syrup and let them soak for at least 2 hours.

5. Preheat the oven to 400°F.

Continued

6. Unwrap the dough, leaving it on the plastic wrap, and knead it a few times to bring it together. Add another tablespoon of chilled water if you still feel it's crumbly, then knead it through.

7. Flour your work surface, then roll out the dough so it's about ¼ inch thick. Cut out rounds that are bigger than the cupcake wells, then press each round of dough into an open cupcake mold. Use your fingers to squish the dough into the cup so the tops are level and uniformly thick, then press the dough into the corners of the cups. The tart should rest about halfway up the sides of the pan.

8. Scrunch pieces of parchment paper into balls and fit them inside the tart shells. Bake the tart shells for 10 minutes, then pull the parchment out and bake for 10 minutes more, or until the bottoms are dry and golden. Take the tart shells out of the oven and allow them to cool slightly; keep the oven on.

9. Lay down 5 apple slices lengthwise so the edge of each apple slice overlaps the one next to it. Starting on one end, roll the slices horizontally into a rosette. Layer more slices around the rosette to build the rose out until it's big enough for the tart shell, and then nestle it snugly into the pastry cups. Flare the edges out and drizzle with some of the leftover rose water syrup. Repeat to fill the remaining tart shells.

10. Put the tarts back in the oven for 15 minutes, but cover them with aluminum foil to prevent browning. Meanwhile, bring the remaining rose water syrup to a boil, then reduce until it thickens. When the tarts are out of the oven, glaze the tops one final time with the syrup. Serve the same day, with a scoop of vanilla ice cream if you're feeling especially sweet.

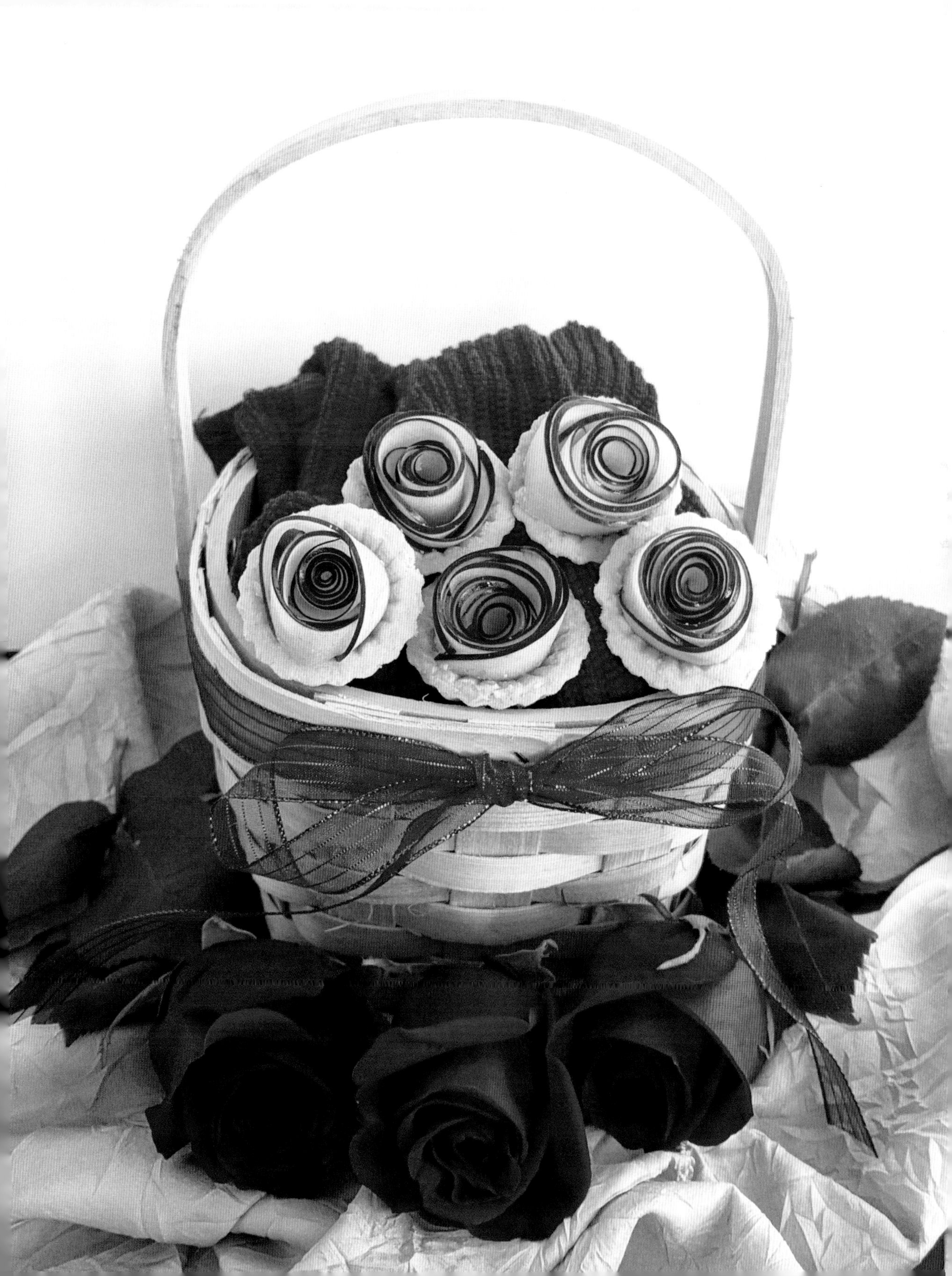

RASPBERRY & ROSE WATER CROISSANTS

Set just before the French Revolution, *The Rose of Versailles* invites us into the life of Marie Antoinette. Oscar was born a daughter to a father who wanted a son. She's raised as a boy with the hopes that one day she'll fill the role of commander of the Royal Guard to the French royal family. To her father's pleasure, everything goes as planned—until she finishes training and is tasked with guarding Marie Antoinette herself! Oscar quickly becomes friends with her charge and soon becomes wrapped up in politics, forbidden romance, and the decadence of court life.

So how do we avoid these problems? Eat, of course! There are many ostentatious feasts and celebrations in this anime, but I wanted to take a quintessential French pastry—the croissant—and turn it into something outrageously good. Stuffed with cream cheese and fruit and drizzled with a rose water glaze, this croissant is buttery, flaky and indulgent. As the girls fight for their happiness, you'll find your happiness in your first bite of this fragrant treat.

2 DAYS

MAKES 14 CROISSANTS

NUT-FREE

RECIPE TIP: Consider baking just half the dough now and saving the rest for another project. Wrap the dough in plastic wrap, place it in a zip-top bag, and store in the freezer for up to a month.

FOR THE INNER BUTTER PACKET

1½ cups (3 sticks) unsalted butter, at room temperature

FOR THE OUTSIDE DOUGH PACKET

1½ cups whole milk, lukewarm

¼ cup packed light brown sugar

3¼ teaspoons active dry yeast

3¼ cups all-purpose flour, plus more for dusting

1 tablespoon kosher salt

FOR THE FILLING

6 ounces cream cheese, at room temperature

½ cup packed dark brown sugar

1 teaspoon rose water

14 fresh raspberries, rinsed and dried

1 large egg, whisked, for egg wash

FOR THE ROSE WATER GLAZE

1 cup confectioners' sugar

1 to 2 teaspoons rose water

1 teaspoon water, if needed

Crushed freeze-dried strawberries or raspberries, for garnish (optional)

1. Make the inner butter packet: Put the butter in a bowl and use a rubber spatula to combine it into a cohesive lump. Plop the butter onto a piece of parchment paper and place another piece on top. Use a rolling pin to spread the butter into a 6-inch square, making sure the butter is the same thickness all the way through, and use a bench scraper to make the sides even. Place the butter and parchment paper in the refrigerator to firm up while you make the dough.

2. Make the outside dough packet: Stir together the milk, brown sugar, and yeast in a measuring cup to combine and set aside for 10 minutes or so, until you notice frothy bubbles on top of the milk and a strong yeasty smell. If these signs are missing after 10 minutes, it may be that the yeast has expired—get new yeast and repeat this step until the yeast is activated.

3. In the same bowl you used for the butter, stir together the flour and salt. Pour the yeast mixture into the bowl and mix until the dough comes together. Turn out the dough onto a flat surface and knead it until all the dry bits are incorporated. Place the dough on a piece of parchment and roll it into a 10-inch square, making sure it's a uniform thickness throughout. Chill in the refrigerator for at least an hour.

4. Generously dust your work surface with flour. Take the butter packet out of the fridge about 5 minutes before the dough has finished chilling to allow it to become elastic. Unwrap the dough and set it on the flour-dusted surface so one edge is parallel to you. When the butter is bendable but still cold, place it on top of the dough square so it looks like a diamond and each corner of the diamond is situation in the middle of one side of the square.

5. Wrap the dough around the butter like you're closing the flap of an envelope and pinch the dough together to enclose the butter.

6. Roll out the packet until it's 18 inches long and 7 inches wide, keeping an eye on the edges to ensure they're straight and the thickness of the dough is uniform. Since the butter is harder than the dough, move gently and be sure you're rolling the butter *with* the dough. Use the rolling pin to gently push down on the butter to help create grooves that can provide friction if you're struggling.

7. Fold the top third of the dough down and the bottom third up like you're folding a letter. Make sure the edges are even and the folds are uniform before pressing down and pinching the edges together. Wrap the dough in plastic wrap and refrigerate for 30 minutes to 1 hour. Repeat these folds four more times for a total of five folds, refrigerating the dough after each set of folds to preserve the layers of butter as much as possible (croissants with large, flaky layers are best) and make sure the butter is intact and isn't melting into the dough. Finally, wrap the dough in plastic wrap and refrigerate overnight.

8. The next day, prepare the cream cheese filling: Using an electric mixer, beat the cream cheese, brown sugar, and rose water in a bowl until smooth, and set aside in the fridge.

9. When you're ready to assemble the croissants, line a baking sheet with parchment paper. Generously flour your work surface, then cut the chilled dough in half. Return one half to the refrigerator to stay cool while you work on the other piece. Roll the dough out until it's 9 x 13 inches (make sure the corners and edges are sharp and the thickness of the dough is uniform).

10. Cut the dough in half again crosswise so that you have two 4.5 x 6.5-inch sections, and put one half in the fridge. Roll the dough that's left into a thin rectangle, about ⅛ inch thick. Trim the edges of the dough with a knife and cut it into long triangles, about 4 inches wide at the base and 7 inches long. Take each piece of dough and, holding by the base of the triangle, gently stretch the point of the triangle out so that it lengthens slightly.

11. On the widest part of one triangle, place a teaspoon of the cream cheese. Split one raspberry so that it lies flat, then press the raspberry into the cheese. Starting at the base of

Continued

the triangle, roll up the dough, tightly enclosing the filling. Continue rolling up the dough and then stretch the point of the triangle around and over the croissant to create tension across the top. Set the filled croissant on the prepared baking sheet, making sure the pointy end is tucked well under the croissant so it doesn't unfurl during baking. Repeat with the remaining dough, including what's in the fridge.

12. Place a sheet of plastic wrap over the croissants and stick them in a warm spot (around 90°F to 100°F) to rise for about 2 hours. If you wiggle the baking sheet and the croissants have an airy jiggle to them and have grown in size, they're ready to bake.

13. Preheat the oven to 400°F.

14. Brush the tops of the croissants with the egg wash. Pop them in the oven and bake for 10 minutes, then reduce the oven temperature to 375°F and bake for 10 minutes more, until golden brown. Allow them to cool completely on a wire rack before glazing.

15. Prepare the rose water glaze: Stir together the confectioners' sugar and rose water in a bowl. If you find the consistency of the glaze to be too thick, add the water a little at a time to thin it out. When the croissants are cool, drizzle the tops with the glaze. While they're still wet, sprinkle them with freeze-dried strawberries or raspberries for that wow factor, if desired.

YUMEIRO PATISSIERE

MADELEINES

As a new student at St. Marie's Academy, Ichigo is looking for friends. As someone with no particular baking ability, Ichigo leaves her classmates scratching their heads as to why she was admitted. When she's paired up with the three most talented students in her class, her other classmates become jealous, making it even harder for her to make friends. Luckily, madeleines seem to be Ichigo's good-luck charm. She offers them as a small token to the spirits of the school, who then help her along in her classes. Madeleines strike again as a unifying force when her teammates share them with each other and finally start to bond.

Madeleines are a French treat known for their shell-like shape and humped backs, and their crispy exteriors cradle a soft, lemon-flavored interior. Having a warm madeleine fresh from the oven alongside tea or coffee has got to be one of life's greatest pleasures. These are actually small cakes, though people often confuse them with cookies. While they might look tricky to make, the shell mold is easier to work with than you'd think!

1 DAY

MAKES 18 PIECES

SPECIAL EQUIPMENT: MADELEINE PAN

NUT-FREE

2 large eggs, at room temperature

½ cup granulated sugar

1 teaspoon vanilla extract

Grated zest of 1 lemon

1 cup all-purpose flour

½ teaspoon baking powder

½ teaspoon kosher salt

½ cup (1 stick) unsalted butter

Confectioners' sugar, for garnish

1. Using an electric mixer, beat the eggs and sugar in a bowl on high speed until the mixture has grown in size and the batter makes distinct ribbons when allowed to drip back into the bowl. Those ribbons should linger for a few seconds on top of the batter before slowly melding. Add the vanilla and lemon zest to the batter and give it a quick blitz to mix.

2. Sift the flour, baking powder, and salt on top of the batter. Use a rubber spatula to fold the dry ingredients in, scooping down along one side of the bowl, across the bottom, and up through the middle of the batter. Fold until you no longer see pockets of flour, taking care not to overmix. Cover with plastic wrap, pressing it directly against the surface of the batter so it isn't exposed to the air, and refrigerate overnight.

3. The next morning, preheat the oven to 400°F. Place a baking sheet in the oven to preheat as well. Melt the butter in a microwave-safe bowl. Brush the madeleine mold with the melted butter and chill the mold in the refrigerator for 10 to 15 minutes.

4. Remove the madeleine mold and the batter from the refrigerator and dollop a tablespoon of batter into each well of the mold. Don't spread the batter out—it'll relax in the oven. Place the mold in the oven on top of the hot baking sheet and bake for 12 to 15 minutes, until the madeleines are golden brown and spring back when you tap them with a finger.

5. Turn them out onto a wire rack to cool slightly. When ready to serve, sprinkle with a little confectioners' sugar to finish, and enjoy warm.

EQUIPMENT TIP: I'd recommend a metal madeleine pan for even heat distribution. If you can only find silicone options, place the silicone tray on a metal cooling rack before putting it on top of the baking sheet in the oven to prevent the shells from getting brown where the silicone touches the cookie sheet.

RECIPE TIP: You might wonder why you need room-temp eggs if you're chilling the batter later—this is to help denature the proteins in the eggs, which makes it easier for them to form air bubbles that will add lightness to the batter.

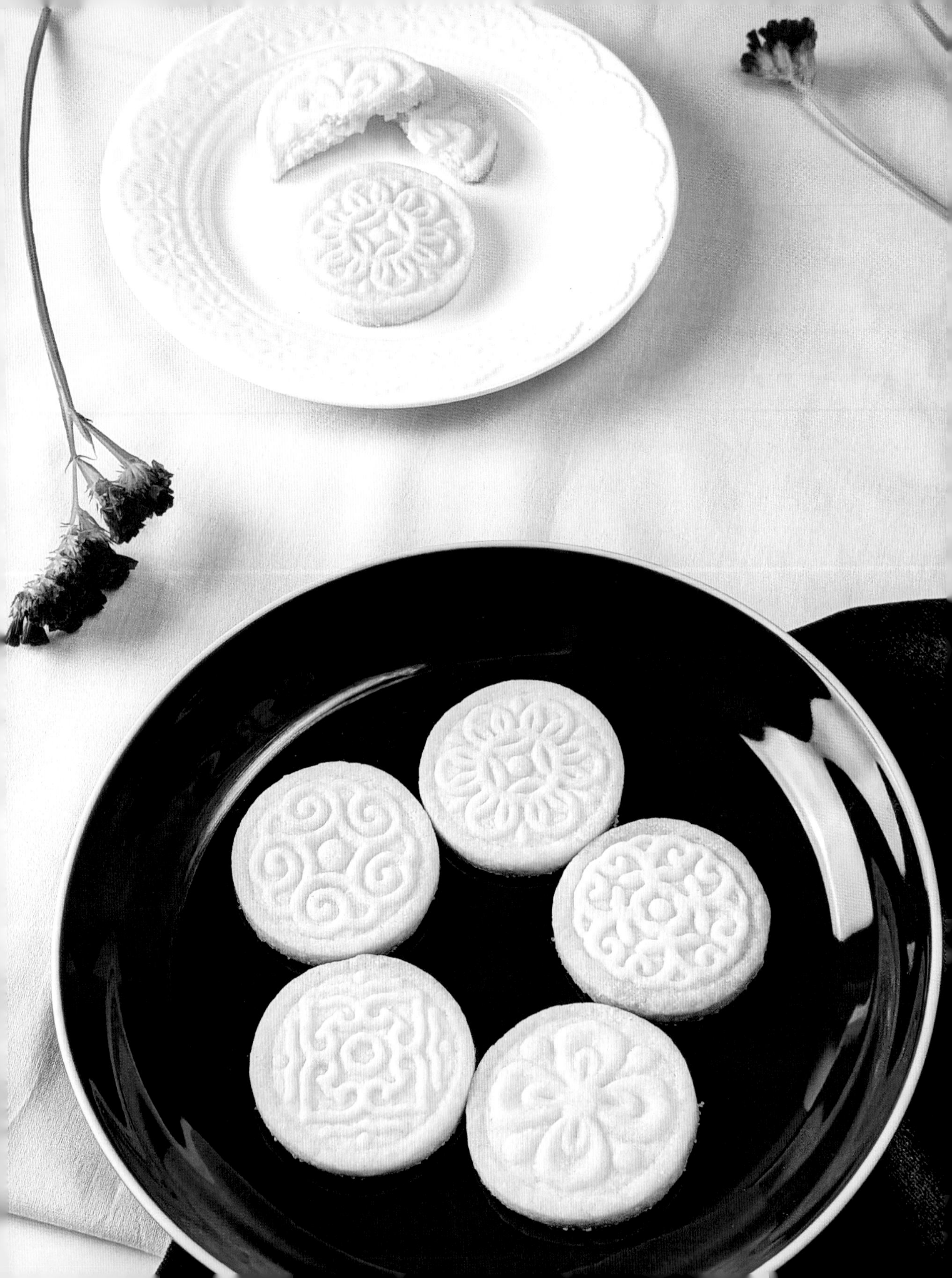

SAILOR MOON SUPERS: THE MOVIE

STAMPED COOKIES

Usagi is an average middle schooler who one day finds a talking cat named Luna. Luna gives her a beautiful brooch that allows her to transform into a magical girl, and so Usagi's alter ego, Sailor Moon, is born! Usagi soon assembles a dream team of Sailor Scouts, who help protect the earth from evil.

When the girls aren't working together to save the day, they like to hang out and have fun. On one such occasion, the Sailor Scouts bake cookies. While Usagi and Chibiusa compete to make the best heart- and bunny-shaped cookies, Ami teaches the girls how to make stamped cookies. By using the bottom of a patterned glass, she's able to stamp designs into the cookie dough. You can use regular rubber stamps to press unique designs into your cookies, but I like the impressions moon cake stamps leave. Whatever you choose, this cookie dough is strong enough to stand up to the force of the stamp without losing its shape in the oven.

2 HOURS

MAKES 24 COOKIES

SPECIAL EQUIPMENT: **ROUND COOKIE CUTTER, MOON CAKE STAMPS OR RUBBER STAMPS**

NUT-FREE

1 cup (2 sticks) unsalted butter, at room temperature

1 cup sugar

1 large egg

1 teaspoon vanilla extract

2⅔ cups all-purpose flour

2 tablespoons cornstarch

½ teaspoon kosher salt

1. Using an electric mixer, cream the butter and sugar in a bowl until light and fluffy. Add the egg and vanilla and mix just until the egg is fully incorporated.

2. Pour in the flour, cornstarch, and salt all at once and use the mixer to blend them into the butter mixture, stopping as soon as the dry ingredients have been incorporated.

3. Divide the dough in half. Place one half between two sheets of parchment paper and roll it out to ¼ inch thick. Place the dough (still between the parchment) on a baking sheet and repeat with the remaining dough. Refrigerate the sheets of dough for an hour.

4. Preheat the oven to 350°F.

5. Working with one sheet of dough at a time, set the dough on your work surface and remove the top sheet of parchment. For each cookie, press a moon cake stamp or clean rubber stamp firmly into the dough, making sure to apply even pressure, then, with the stamped impression centered, use a round cutter to cut out the cookie. When you've stamped and cut all the cookies, peel away the excess dough (you can reroll and cut from the scraps later), leaving the cookies on the parchment. Slide the parchment onto a baking sheet and repeat with the second sheet of dough, then chill the cookies in the refrigerator for 10 minutes.

6. Bake for 10 to 12 minutes, until the cookies have browned on the bottom and edges turn golden. Then enjoy!

RECIPE TIPS: If you find that the stamps are sticking to the dough, dust them in a little flour.

Chilling the dough helps to both ensure the stamp comes out cleanly and help the cookies retain their shape in the oven. Don't skip this step!

THE SECRET WORLD OF ARRIETTY

THUMBPRINT JAM COOKIES

Arrietty and her family are Borrowers, tiny people who secretly live in human homes and borrow easily misplaced things like sugar cubes, tissues, and hair clips from the houses they live in to use as upcycled home goods. Arrietty's family lives in the floorboards of a house belonging to Shō. One day, Shō finds this secret family; while Shō is overjoyed to discover them, Arrietty's parents don't feel the same, and promptly make preparations to move to another room in the house. For Arrietty, the trek to their new home is a journey. A run-in with a crow or a cat is deadly, and the family's escape vehicle is a teapot floating in a rivulet of water.

Despite their size, the Borrowers are similar to humans, and just like us, they appreciate the finer things in life . . . like these cookies. The cookies Arrietty eats are teeny-tiny, but I've scaled up the size of this recipe to work with your human-size thumbs.

1 HOUR 30 MINUTES

MAKES **24 COOKIES**

SPECIAL EQUIPMENT: **½-OUNCE COOKIE SCOOP**

NUT-FREE

RECIPE TIP:
If you notice the dough is cracking around the edges when you make indents, it might be too firm. Dampen your fingertips, tap a little water into the dough balls, mix it in, and try again.

- **1 cup (2 sticks) unsalted butter, at room temperature**
- **⅔ cup sugar**
- **1 large egg yolk**
- **1 teaspoon vanilla extract**
- **2¼ cups all-purpose flour**
- **2 teaspoons cornstarch**
- **½ teaspoon kosher salt**
- **1 cup jam (I like raspberry or blueberry), for filling**

1. Using an electric mixer, cream the butter and sugar together in a bowl until smooth. Add the egg yolk and vanilla and mix until the egg is completely incorporated. Pour in the flour, cornstarch, and salt all at once, then beat with the mixer until you have a thick, crumbly dough.

2. Use your hands to pat the dough into a ball, kneading to work out any dry spots. With a cookie scoop, portion all the dough into balls, then knead each dough ball between your fingers to make them cohesive and set them on a plate. Use your thumb to make a circular indentation in the center of each cookie, then chill in the refrigerator for 30 minutes.

3. Preheat the oven to 375°F. Line a baking sheet with parchment paper.

4. Set the chilled cookies on the prepared baking sheet, spacing them 2 inches apart. Spoon jam into the indentation in each cookie. Bake for 11 minutes, or until the bottoms are lightly browned. Allow the cookies to cool completely in the pan, then enjoy!

SHORTBREAD COOKIES

Karen, who goes by the handle LLENN in the virtual reality game *Gun Gale Online*, has only ever wanted to be short. In real life, she towers above everyone, and her height complex makes her shy and reclusive. She turns to video games for comfort, looking for a virtual world where she can spawn as the cute, short girl she's always wanted to be. When this finally happens, she realizes the one game that gives her the avatar she wants happens to be a tough-as-nails shooting adventure that amounts to a deadly (virtual) game of laser tag.

The virtual reality game is all-encompassing: she can eat, drink, run, and fight in the game—and it feels as though she's doing these things in real life. Even in the midst of a game, Karen takes time for tea and cookie breaks, during which she eats these buttery shortbread cookies. She luxuriates in her small treat, even with gunfire sounding in the background.

2½ HOURS

MAKES 12 COOKIES

NUT-FREE

RECIPE TIP:
Chilling the dough is essential; if you don't chill it thoroughly, the shortbread won't hold its shape in the oven.

1 cup all-purpose flour	¼ teaspoon kosher salt
¼ cup sugar	½ cup (1 stick) unsalted butter, at room temperature

1. Combine the flour, sugar, salt, and butter in a large bowl and beat with an electric mixer until you have a smooth, thick dough.

2. Turn the dough out onto a piece of plastic wrap and use the plastic wrap to shape the dough into a log. Gently roll the dough along the counter to form an even cylinder, then twist the ends of the plastic wrap closed and chill in the refrigerator for 2 hours.

3. Preheat the oven to 300°F. Line a baking sheet with parchment paper.

4. Slice the chilled cookie dough crosswise into ¼-inch-thick rounds. If you'd like perfectly circular edges, use a round cutter to trim the cookies. Place the cookies on the prepared baking sheet 2 inches apart. Use a toothpick to punch one hole in the middle and five more holes around the edge of each cookie.

5. Bake for 10 to 12 minutes, until the bottoms become golden. Remove the cookies from the oven and allow them to cool on the pan. Enjoy alongside a nice cup of tea!

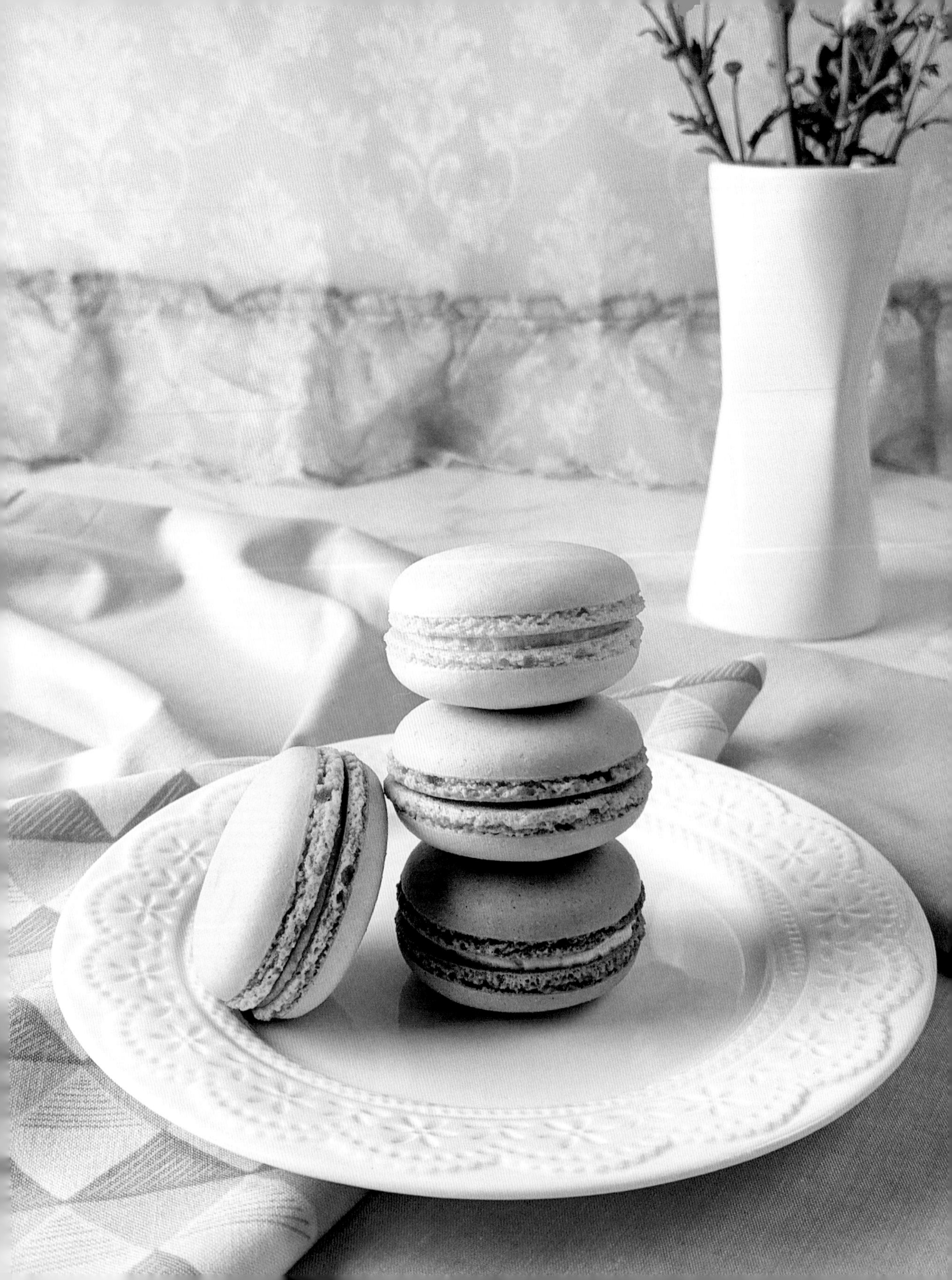

MY LOVE STORY!!

MACARONS

High school student Rinko Yamato is minding her own business on a crowded train one day when a molester makes his move! Using the crowd they're in as an excuse, he tries to get close. Luckily for Rinko, Takeo steps in to save the day. Rinko gratefully bakes him a selection of macarons, the first of many baked goods she makes to convey her thanks.

Macarons are a French sandwich cookie filled with buttercream, jam, or ganache. While the almond flour shells can be a little tricky to make, I've done my best to make it foolproof. Trust me, the effort is worth the reward!

FOR THE MACARON SHELLS

3 large eggs, at room temperature

1½ cups almond flour

1 cup confectioners' sugar

1 teaspoon cream of tartar

½ cup granulated sugar

1 teaspoon vanilla extract

Food coloring of choice

FOR THE BUTTERCREAM FILLING

1 cup (2 sticks) unsalted butter, at room temperature

3 cups confectioners' sugar

2 to 3 tablespoons whole milk

Flavoring of choice (1 teaspoon vanilla extract, 1 tablespoon matcha, ½ cup powdered dehydrated strawberries, or 1 teaspoon vanilla extract plus ½ teaspoon caramel sauce per cookie)

Food coloring of choice

1. Make the cookies: Separate the eggs into two bowls; reserve the yolks for another use. Cover the egg whites with plastic wrap and refrigerate for 24 hours; bring them to room temperature before using.

2. Blitz the almond flour in a food processor, then sift it and the confectioners' sugar into a bowl.

3. Using an electric mixer (remember, use *clean* beaters), whip the room-temperature egg whites in a glass or metal bowl on low speed for 2 minutes, or until foamy. Tap in the cream of tartar and blend in. With the mixer on medium speed, add the granulated sugar a tablespoon at a time until everything's incorporated. If using vanilla (for vanilla cookies, or for the caramel variation), beat that in now.

4. At this point, you should have soft peaks. Tint the mixture with food coloring to correspond with your flavor of choice (for example, green coloring for a matcha cookie, pink for strawberry, and so on), then kick the mixer speed up to high and beat until stiff peaks form.

Continued

2 HOURS

MAKES 18 MACARONS

SPECIAL EQUIPMENT: **PASTRY BAGS AND ROUND PIPING TIPS**

GLUTEN-FREE

RECIPE TIPS:

Macarons can be tricky to master. Some common things to look out for: make sure the oven temperature is correct, don't overmix the macaron batter or there's no saving it, and be careful that you don't add the sugar to the egg whites all at once in the initial mixing stage.

You can make a guide to help you pipe the macaron shells evenly. Draw a circle of the size you want the macarons to be on a piece of regular paper, then slide it under the parchment paper—it'll be visible through the parchment!

STORAGE TIP:

These macarons keep well in an airtight container in the refrigerator for a day or two.

5. Sprinkle half the dry ingredients across the surface of the egg whites and fold it in, scraping down along the side of the bowl, across the bottom, and up through the middle of the mixture, until only a few streaks of the dry ingredients remain. Sprinkle the rest of the dry ingredients over the top and continue to fold just until the dry ingredients are incorporated. Don't overmix—the final batter should fall from the spatula in a triangle shape and sit on the surface of the mix before eventually melding back in.

6. Line a baking sheet with parchment paper. Spoon the batter into a pastry bag fitted with a ½-inch round piping tip and pipe rounds of batter onto the baking sheet, holding the bag with the tip pointing straight down onto the parchment and squeezing the bag until you're happy with the size of the macaron shells. When you've filled the pan, go over the shells with a toothpick to neaten up any edges. Tap the baking sheet on the counter to release any large air bubbles, then allow the cookies to sit, uncovered, for 1 hour, or until their tops are dry to the touch.

7. Preheat the oven to 300°F.

8. Bake the cookies for 12 to 15 minutes, until the shells lift up easily from the parchment and sound hollow when tapped with a finger. Remove them from the oven and let them cool completely.

9. Make the buttercream filling: Using an electric mixer, beat the butter in a bowl for a minute or two. Add the confectioners' sugar and whip for 5 to 8 minutes, starting on low speed and moving to a higher speed after a few minutes of mixing. Add the milk as needed to thin the frosting and make it softer.

10. Flavor and tint the frosting: For vanilla frosting, beat in vanilla. For matcha, beat in the matcha and green food coloring to match the color of the macaron shells. For strawberry, beat in the powdered dehydrated strawberries and adjust the color with food coloring as needed. For caramel, you'll use caramel sauce in assembly, so simply make a vanilla buttercream.

11. When the macaron shells are cool, transfer the buttercream to a pastry bag and snip the tip off the bag. Pipe a generous dollop of frosting onto the flat side of half the shells. For caramel macarons, pipe a ring of vanilla frosting and fill the center with a bit of caramel sauce. Finish each cookie with a second macaron shell. Enjoy!

MY NEXT LIFE AS A VILLAINESS: ALL ROUTES LEAD TO DOOM!

VANILLA & CHOCOLATE HEARTS

After suffering a bump to the head, Katarina Claes recollects her memories and learns that in another life, she was a hard-core otaku. This *would* be fine—except she realizes she's been reincarnated as the villain from a video game she played in her past life! Even worse, she knows that every single ending ultimately leads to her death.

Using her knowledge of the game, Katarina tries to avoid all the red flags and ultimately change the outcome of her life. She befriends the game's protagonist, Maria Campbell, a character who has trouble standing up to her peers. As Katarina tries to rewrite her destiny, she speaks up for Maria, tutors her, and does her best to protect her from others. In thanks, Maria (who loves to bake) offers Katarina vanilla and chocolate heart-shaped cookies. They're simple and sweet, but also hint at a little mystery: Will Katarina get the happy vanilla ending she so desperately wants? Or will she fall victim to her dark, villainous archetype?

1 HOUR 30 MINUTES

MAKES 36 COOKIES

SPECIAL EQUIPMENT: **SMALL HEART-SHAPED COOKIE CUTTER**

NUT-FREE

SUBSTITUTION TIP: If you want something other than a vanilla heart, try grating some lemon or orange zest into the vanilla portion and adding a sprinkle of ground cardamom or a pinch of freshly grated nutmeg along with the ¼ cup flour.

1 cup (2 sticks) unsalted butter, at room temperature

1 teaspoon vanilla extract

2 cups all-purpose flour

½ cup sugar

½ teaspoon kosher salt

¼ cup unsweetened Dutch-process cocoa powder

1. Using an electric mixer, beat the butter and vanilla in a bowl for 30 seconds. Add 1¾ cups of the flour, the sugar, and the salt to the bowl and mix until the flour is incorporated.

2. Split the mixture in half and transfer one half to a separate bowl. Add the remaining ¼ cup flour to one bowl and the cocoa powder to the other. Mix in the dry ingredients in completely until you have two thick doughs. Wrap them separately in plastic wrap and refrigerate for an hour.

3. Preheat the oven to 350°F.

4. Unwrap one portion of the chilled dough and place it on a sheet of parchment paper. Roll it out to ¼-inch thickness, then do the same for the other batch of dough. Use a heart-shaped cookie cutter to cut out cookies from both doughs, then peel away the excess dough, leaving the cookies on the parchment. Slide the parchment onto baking sheets and chill the hearts in the refrigerator for 10 minutes.

5. Bake for 12 to 15 minutes, until the bottoms are golden brown and the cookies are nicely set.

STRAWBERRY PARFAIT

When the alien race Amanto takes over feudal Japan, the old rules go out the window. Samurai, once the glorious warriors of Japan, are forced to give up their katanas as the aliens become the dominating force. Gintoki, a famed samurai known as the White Demon, goes along with the new rules (more or less) willingly, until two Amanto customers spill the parfait he was eating in the local family restaurant. It's then that Gintoki reaches his breaking point. In defense of his sweet, sweet parfait, he pulls out his wooden sword and sends the Amanto packing, ultimately making them regret the day they first laid eyes on him.

Warned against eating sugar by his doctor, the biggest risk Gintoki takes is succumbing to his sugar addiction. In honor of his fierce passion for the treats, I've made his parfait. Parfaits are usually quite elaborate, and pretty much anything can be used as a parfait topping or filling. Have fun with the recipe if you aren't fond of any one element—play around with what you choose to layer and enjoy! Luckily for you, you don't have any pesky Amanto to worry about.

⅓ cup strawberry ice cream

6 to 10 fresh strawberries

¼ cup granola, chocolate cookie crumbles, or cornflakes

½ cup whipped cream

Vanilla cake of choice, or a brownie (you can also make a simple sponge cake)

1 vanilla wafer cookie

3 Pocky sticks

Chocolate syrup

1 maraschino cherry

1. Take the ice cream out of the freezer and allow it to soften. Hull and halve all but 2 strawberries; set the whole strawberries aside for garnish.

2. Sprinkle half the granola into the bottom of a parfait glass. Lay down a layer of whipped cream, then stack a layer of cake (cut to fit inside the glass) on top of that. Add another ring of whipped cream and then layer the strawberry halves in a ring around the glass, cut sides facing outward. Fill the space inside and on top of the strawberries with more whipped cream, then add a second layer of cake, another layer of whipped cream, and a final, liberal sprinkling of granola.

3. Stick the wafer cookie into the granola layer on one side of the glass. Using an ice cream scoop or a large spoon, place several portions of strawberry ice cream on top. Wiggle a few Pocky sticks into the parfait and decorate with the reserved whole strawberries, chocolate syrup, and a cherry. Eat immediately, before the ice cream melts, preferably with a friend.

15 MINUTES

MAKES 1 PARFAIT

SPECIAL EQUIPMENT: PARFAIT GLASS

NUT-FREE

RECIPE TIP:

Japanese parfaits are in a league of their own! Have fun with the process and feel free to experiment with your own ingredients for the different layers. The key thing to focus on is having a crunchy texture, a cakey texture, some kind of fresh fruit, and a creamy binding element to glue the parfait together. Toppings could include cookies, fruit, and ice cream!

FOOD FACT:

The typical Japanese parfait takes more closely after an American-style parfait than a French one. American parfaits are more sundae-like in nature, and a combination of ice cream, sauces, and crunchy cereal make the dessert special.

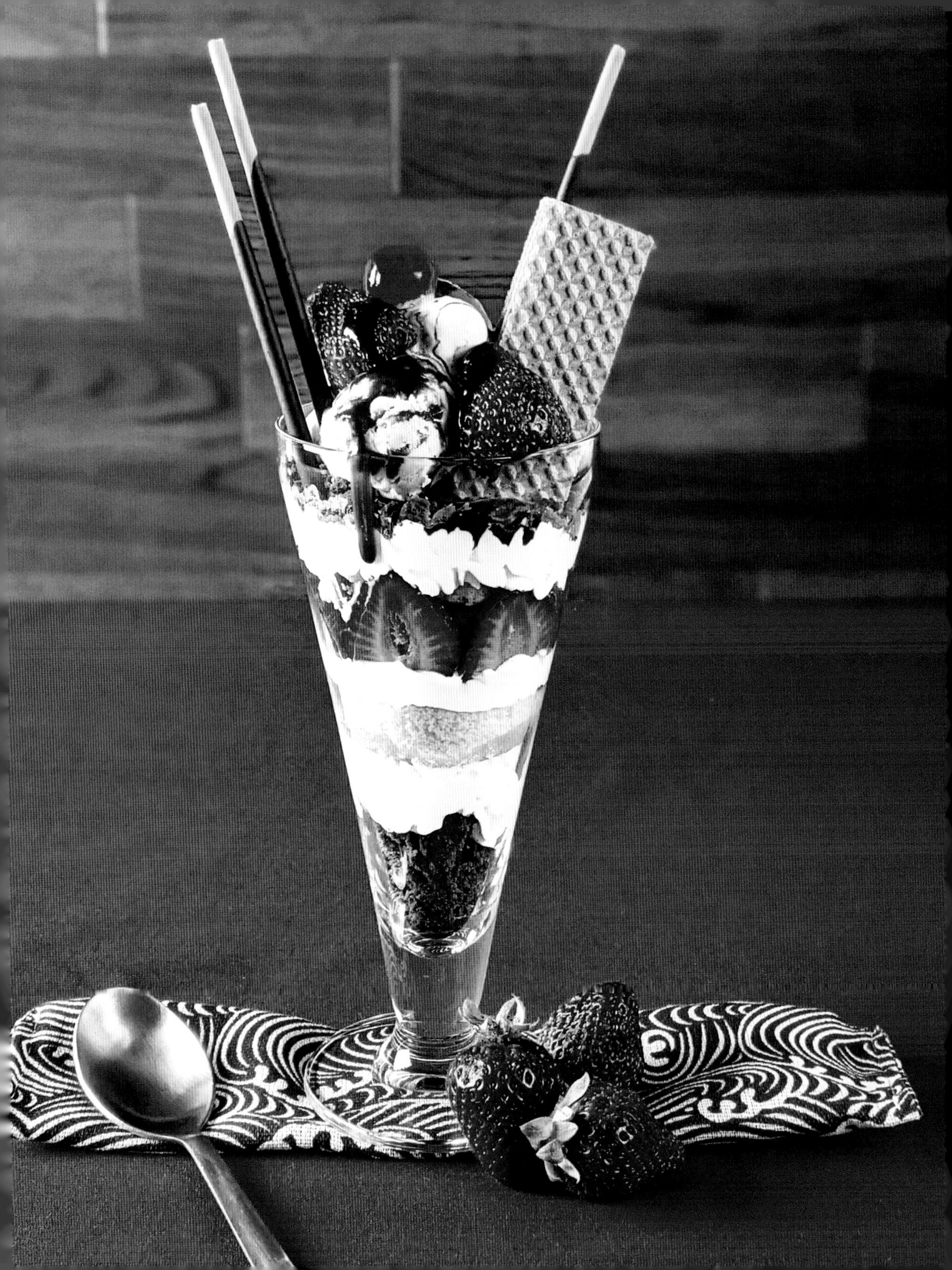

HIGURASHI: WHEN THEY CRY

BUTTER SWIRL COOKIES

Keiichi is your average transfer student. When he moves into the small town of Hinamizawa, everything seems perfectly normal. He makes friends and starts to fit in at school, but he soon notices unusual behavior from his new friends. It seems like they're keeping secrets, and the more he tries to unravel what's going on, the more he realizes what little control he has.

During a sleuthing session, Keiichi's father brings him tea and cookies to help keep his energy up. Among the cookies offered are butter cookies. Soft and moist, these cookies are both pretty to look at and easy to stuff into your face (I ate six before I realized what I was doing). Who says you have to solve eerie murder mysteries on an empty stomach?

1 HOUR

MAKES ABOUT 24 COOKIES

SPECIAL EQUIPMENT: PASTRY BAG AND STAR PIPING TIP

NUT-FREE

1 cup (2 sticks) unsalted butter, at room temperature

1 cup sugar

1 teaspoon vanilla extract

½ teaspoon kosher salt

1 large egg, at room temperature

2¼ cups all-purpose flour

1. To begin, start with the end: Line a baking sheet with parchment paper.

2. Using an electric mixer, cream the butter and sugar together in a bowl until light and fluffy. Add the vanilla, salt, and egg and whip until the egg is just incorporated. Scrape down the sides of the bowl with a rubber spatula while doing this to ensure you get everything mixed.

3. Add the flour all at once and mix until just incorporated. Scrape down the sides of the bowl and give it another blitz to make sure all the flour has been mixed.

4. Spoon the cookie dough into a pastry bag fitted with a star tip. (I used a ½-inch tip, but you can use whatever you have. Just know that a smaller tip will result in a smaller and finer cookie, and vice versa.) Pipe rings of dough onto the prepared baking sheet 1 to 2 inches apart. Start at the bottom of the ring and pipe over and around, keeping the tip pointing down toward the parchment. Lighten up the pressure on the pastry bag as you come to the start of the circle, but carry the motion through so the dough forms a full ring. Refrigerate the dough until it's hard to the touch, 15 to 20 minutes.

5. Preheat the oven to 350°F.

6. Bake the cookies for 12 to 14 minutes, until the bottoms are golden brown. Allow to cool on a wire rack and enjoy over the next few days!

RECIPE TIP: Ensuring all the ingredients are at room temperature before you make the dough will make it easier to pipe; don't chill it before piping, or it'll stiffen and be difficult to work with. If you're struggling to push the dough out of the pastry bag, you might need to thin it out a little with a tablespoon or two of milk.

CHRISTMAS PUDDING

Chise Hatori is one of the few people in her world with the Sight—the ability to see the supernatural around her—and for reasons she can't understand, these Neighbors (as they're known) seem drawn to her. Their constant presence destroys her family: her father runs away, taking her little brother with him, and her mother eventually takes her own life. A despairing Chise, effectively orphaned, struggles to find a place in the world as she's passed from one unloving family member to another—until she ultimately decides to auction herself to the highest bidder in the hope that someone will want her and give her a home. A cloaked man with an animal skull for a face buys her. The man, Elias, reveals she's a special type of mage. He also declares that she's to be his bride. With that, the two begin a tentative relationship focused on learning to control and use magic and finding self-acceptance. In this strange situation, Chise finds the home she so desperately sought. Before, she slept on the streets; now she has a clean bed, clean clothing, and all the food she could ever want.

Since Elias resides in Britain, the food in the series is European in origin. Perhaps the most special dessert she gets to try is Christmas pudding. This steamed cake is thick, rich, and brimming with jammy flavors from dried fruit, underscored by the bittersweet tang of brandy. It's warm, homey, and the perfect comfort dessert.

2 HOURS, PLUS RESTING FOR AT LEAST 36 HOURS

SERVES 8

SPECIAL EQUIPMENT: **2-QUART PUDDING BOWL, KITCHEN TWINE, INSTANT POT (OPTIONAL), STEAMER BASKET**

RECIPE TIP:
Christmas pudding is hard to overcook, so don't worry about that. However, it's quite easy to *undercook*, so don't skimp on the listed cooking times.

FOOD FACT:
Christmas pudding is traditionally made with the help of the whole family—everyone needs to take a turn stirring while making a Christmas wish. It's also usually left to age for several weeks before being eaten

- 2 cups dark raisins
- 1 cup packed dark brown sugar
- ½ cup brandy
- ½ cup (1 stick) unsalted butter, frozen, plus room-temperature butter for greasing
- ½ cup chopped prunes
- ½ cup blanched almonds
- ½ cup almond flour
- ½ cup fresh bread crumbs
- ⅓ cup all-purpose flour
- ½ teaspoon freshly grated nutmeg
- 1 teaspoon ground cinnamon
- ½ teaspoon ground ginger
- ½ teaspoon ground cloves
- ⅓ cup stout beer
- Heavy cream, for serving

1. Stir together the raisins, brown sugar, and brandy in a bowl. Cover the bowl with plastic wrap and leave on the counter to soak overnight.

2. When you're ready to make the pudding, grease a pressure cooker–safe 2-quart pudding bowl with butter and line the bottom of the bowl with a small round of parchment paper cut to fit.

3. Drain the soaked raisins, reserving the soaking liquid for serving. Grate the frozen butter into a large bowl and add the raisins, prunes, blanched almonds, almond flour, bread crumbs, all-purpose flour, nutmeg, cinnamon, ginger, cloves, and beer. Stir until thoroughly combined.

Continued

4. Pour the batter into the prepared pudding bowl and level off the top. Cut a round of parchment paper to fit over the pudding and place it on top of the batter, then cover the whole top of the pudding bowl with aluminum foil. Fold and crunch the edges of the foil until it rests securely just under the lip of the bowl.

5. Tie a ring of kitchen twine under the lip of the pudding bowl. Attach a second piece of twine to the first ring to make a handle. You need this to be able to lift the pudding bowl into and out of whatever pot you cook the pudding in.

6. If using an Instant Pot or pressure cooker to steam the pudding, place a metal steamer basket in the bottom of the inner pot and set the pudding bowl in it. Bring some water to a boil on the stove, then pour boiling water into the space around the pudding bowl until it comes to just under the foil lid. Activate the steam function and leave the sealing vent open. As soon as you hear steam hissing out of the vent, start a 15-minute timer. When it goes off, close the sealing vent, change the setting to Manual, and set the time to 45 minutes. When the cooking time is done, allow the pressure to release naturally for 15 minutes before quick-releasing the remaining pressure. A toothpick inserted into the pudding should come out completely clean.

7. If using a pot on the stovetop to steam the pudding, place a metal steamer basket in a large stockpot and set the pudding bowl in it. Boil some water in a separate pot, then pour boiling water into the space around the pudding bowl until it comes to just under the foil lid. Cover the top of the pot with a lid and bring the water back to a boil over high heat, then reduce the heat to maintain a simmer. Steam for 6 to 8 hours, until a toothpick inserted into the pudding comes out completely clean. Check the pot during the cooking process, about every hour or so, and top up with more boiling water as needed to keep it at the same level.

8. Remove the pudding from the pressure cooker or pot. Peel away the foil and parchment and turn the pudding out onto a clean plate. Allow it to cool completely. Clean out the pudding bowl and pop the pudding back into, then let it rest in a cool, dark place for at least 24 hours or up to 5 weeks to mature.

9. To serve, simply cut the pudding into slices, and when you're ready to eat, pour a little cream over the top to finish the dessert.

REHEATING TIP:
To reheat, microwave individual slices until warm, or steam again in the pudding basin for 2 hours (cover with parchment paper and a lid if you do this).

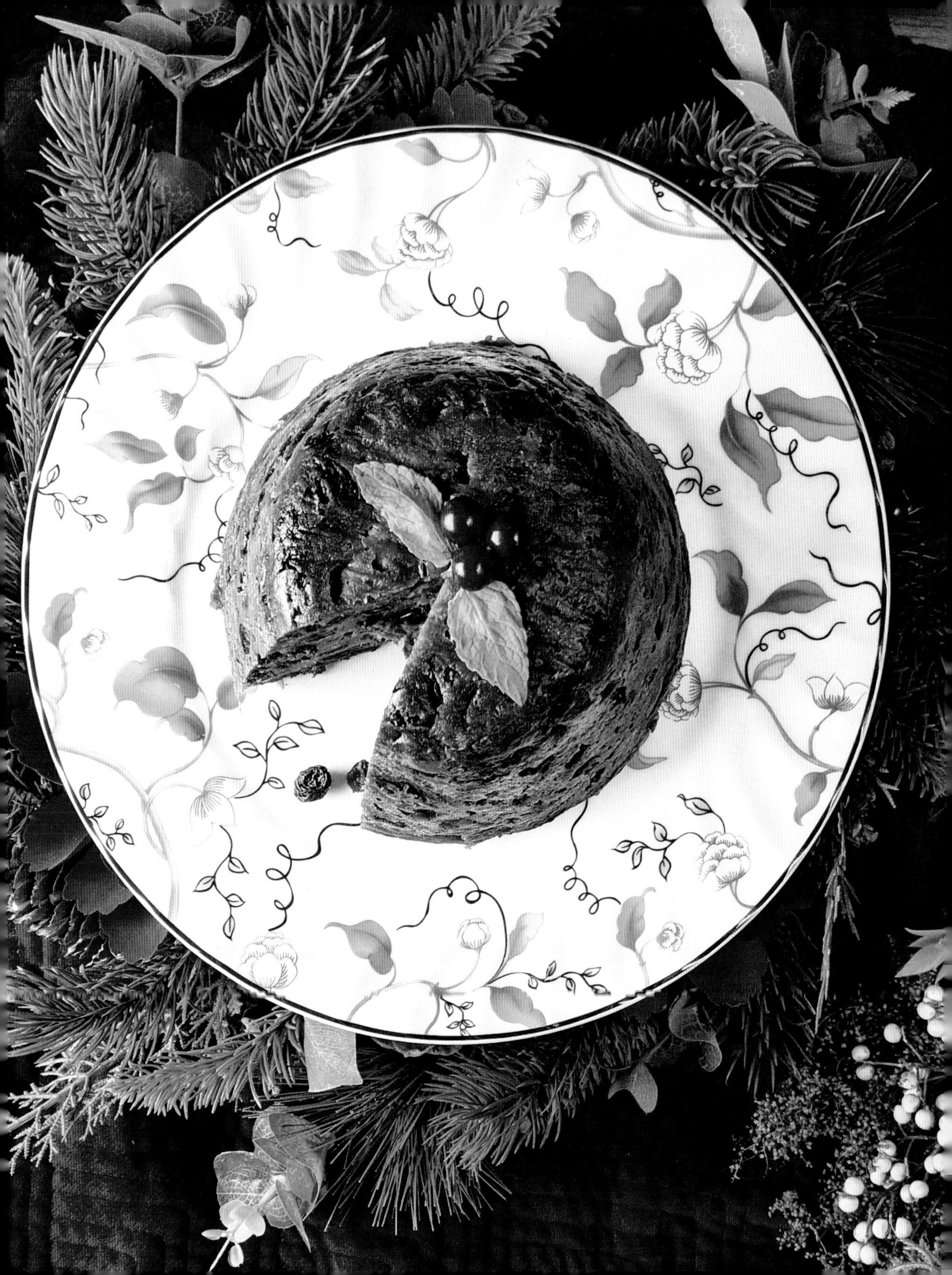

TADA NEVER FALLS IN LOVE

HOT CHOCOLATE SPOONS

Inspired by his late father, Mitsuyoshi Tada dreams of being a professional photographer. One day, he runs into an exchange student taking pictures, and they strike up a conversation. Mitsuyoshi is instantly smitten by the girl, Teresa, and invites her over to his family's coffee shop.

The show follow's Mitsuyoshi's day-to-day life as he slowly falls for Teresa. In one episode (which is told completely from the perspective of a cat), Teresa and her friend Alec come over to lend a hand when the shop is particularly short-staffed. At the end of the day, they come together to share a cup of coffee, complete with hot chocolate spoons. While trying out the different flavors, Teresa and Mitsuyoshi each drink from the same spot on the cup, which leads to an indirect kiss. Romance is in the air, so stir some into your coffee with one of these hot chocolate spoons!

2 HOURS

MAKES 8 CHOCOLATE SPOONS

SPECIAL EQUIPMENT: **8 DISPOSABLE SPOONS, 8 SMALL SILICONE BAKING CUPS, INFRARED THERMOMETER**

GLUTEN-FREE, NUT-FREE, VEGAN (DEPENDING ON CHOCOLATE OF CHOICE)

4 ounces dark chocolate

4 ounces milk chocolate

4 ounces pink/strawberry chocolate, or 4 ounces white chocolate plus ¼ cup crushed freeze-dried strawberries

4 ounces white chocolate

Hot chocolate or coffee, for serving

1. Set out 8 small silicone baking cups and get 8 plastic spoons ready.

2. Temper one chocolate layer at a time: Finely chop the dark chocolate except for 2 or 3 squares; set those aside. Place the chopped chocolate in a microwave-safe bowl and microwave in 15-second intervals, stirring after each, until the chocolate has melted completely.

3. Stir the melted chocolate continuously until it cools to around 100°F, then toss in one of the chocolate squares you set aside and stir it in. If the square of chocolate melts completely, toss in another of the squares and stir until the thermometer reads 90°F for dark chocolate.

4. Repeat to temper the other chocolates; stir until they cool to 88°F after adding the second reserved square of chocolate. If you're adding freeze-dried strawberries to white chocolate, stir them in now.

5. Pour the chocolate into the silicone cups in the patterns you like and gently tap the cups against the counter to release any air bubbles. (How you layer the chocolates in the cups is up to you—I made four patterns: 1 strawberry spoon, 1 dark/milk chocolate spoon, 1 dark/white/milk chocolate spoon, and 1 strawberry/dark chocolate spoon.) In the first layer for any of the molds, place the bowl of the spoon in the chocolate. Hold it in place by bracing the spoon on either side with Popsicle sticks or toothpicks. Wait until each layer has hardened before pouring the next layer. You may have to re-melt and re-temper the unpoured chocolate to make it pourable. Make sure to tap the cup to release air bubbles after adding each layer of chocolate.

6. When you've filled the silicone cups, allow them to set completely at room temperature, 30 minutes or so, then carefully peel the cups away from the chocolate. Serve cups of hot chocolate or coffee with the spoons alongside for stirring.

RECIPE TIP: As you work your way up the spoon with the chocolate, you may find a pastry bag to be helpful in getting perfect layers.

JOJO'S BIZARRE ADVENTURE: DIAMOND IS UNBREAKABLE

SENSATIONAL BOOZY CARAMELIZED PUDDING

Josuke and his friend Okuyasu have been traveling for a while; they're tired and looking for something good to eat, so they come into Tonio's restaurant for a meal. After Tonio serves Okuyasu food, Okuyasu is totally rejuvenated and his stiff shoulders and stomach problems disappear. This rouses Josuke's suspicions—the food can't be *that* good, so it must be a plot to kill the two of them! As he investigates, he finds that while Tonio is powerful, he only uses his powers for good.

As punishment for tearing up his kitchen, Tonio makes Josuke clean up the mess. In the meantime, he serves Okuyasu one last dish—a pudding that cures Okuyasu's bad case of athlete's foot. While I can't promise my recipe will do the same (there's a cream for that), this dessert is definitely good enough to lift your spirits. Japanese and Italian puddings are remarkably similar. As a result, this recipe is a Japanese pudding (pronounced *purin*) made with Italian flavors—a nuanced caramel pudding that will give you life.

1 HOUR, PLUS CHILLING OVERNIGHT

MAKES 8 PUDDING CUPS

SPECIAL EQUIPMENT: 8 JAPANESE PUDDING MOLDS (OR HEAT-SAFE CUPS WITH SLOPED SIDES THAT HOLD ⅔ CUP LIQUID EACH)

GLUTEN-FREE

RECIPE TIP: If you're having trouble getting the pudding out of the cup, remember that what you're really trying to do is break the airlock around the pudding. You need to get a bubble of air up by the caramel to help pop the pudding out.

FOR THE CARAMEL SAUCE

⅔ cup sugar

2 tablespoons water

1 tablespoon light corn syrup

2 tablespoons hot water

FOR THE PUDDING

2½ tablespoons unflavored powdered gelatin

¼ cup water

1¾ cups whole milk

1 vanilla bean, split and seeds scraped out

4 large egg yolks

⅓ cup sugar

1 cup mascarpone cheese

2 tablespoons amaretto liqueur

1. Set the pudding cups on a baking sheet.

2. Make the caramel sauce: Combine the sugar, water, and corn syrup in a pan. Don't stir together—turn on the heat and let it bubble, keeping an eye on the color. Allow the mixture to darken to a deep brown, then immediately remove it from the heat and add the hot water. The water will splash, so be careful and use oven mitts to protect yourself. Stir everything together with a rubber spatula, then pour the sauce into a measuring cup with a spout.

3. Quickly pour a layer of caramel into 8 pudding cups (just enough to cover the bottom). Set the cups to the side to allow the caramel to harden.

4. Make the pudding: Pour the gelatin into a bowl and stir in the water. Set aside for 3 to 5 minutes to allow the gelatin to bloom.

Continued

5. Combine the milk, vanilla seeds, and vanilla pod in a heavy-bottomed saucepan. Bring to a simmer over medium-low heat. When the milk is bubbling around the edges of the pan, turn off the heat.

6. Whisk together the egg yolks and sugar in a bowl. While whisking continuously, ladle ¼ cup of the hot milk into the egg mixture and whisk to combine. Repeat this until the egg yolks are tempered, then pour the egg yolk mixture into the pot with the remaining milk. Return the heat to medium-low and cook, whisking continuously, until the milk mixture is steaming.

7. Pour in the bloomed gelatin and whisk until it's melted into the milk mixture. Turn off the heat and strain the mixture through a fine-mesh sieve into a bowl. Add the mascarpone and amaretto and whisk until the mascarpone is melted in.

8. Divide the custard evenly among the prepared pudding cups, then cover the cups with plastic wrap. Chill in the refrigerator overnight.

9. To serve, run a knife around the edge of the pudding and tip each pudding out onto a plate.

FOOD FACT:
What you might notice is that Japanese purin is remarkably similar to crème caramel, otherwise known as flan. The Portuguese first introduced Japan to flan, and mentions of the sweet date back to 1872; but it didn't really take off until the 1970s, when premade versions became available in stores.

LEMON MERINGUE TART

Sebastian is a dedicated butler to Ciel Phantomhive. He cooks, cleans, and, on occasion, disposes of Ciel's enemies. It makes sense—once Ciel learns the truth about his parents' deaths, Sebastian gets to claim Ciel's soul as payment for services rendered. To Sebastian, the more corrupt he can make Ciel, the better his soul will taste.

This devious behavior is showcased in the first episode. The audience is treated to both Sebastian's charming side—his friendly attitude and delicious cooking—and his devilish side—his lack of morals regarding human lives. Within minutes, we see him lock a man in an oven to be cooked alive, only to turn around and serve a lemon meringue tart to the other servants. It's disturbing to think Sebastian cooked a man in the same oven he baked the tart in, but it can't be denied that the dessert looks absolutely scrumptious.

7 HOURS

SERVES 8

**SPECIAL EQUIPMENT:
9-INCH TART PAN,
PASTRY BAGS AND
TIPS**

NUT-FREE

RECIPE TIP: Adding a tablespoon of cornstarch to the egg whites along with the sugar can help prevent the meringue from weeping (creating a puddle of liquid on top of the curd, which can soak into the crust and look a bit unpleasant).

FOR THE TART CRUST

1 cup (2 sticks) unsalted butter, frozen

1 cup plus 1 tablespoon all-purpose flour

¼ cup confectioners' sugar

1 teaspoon kosher salt

1 tablespoon ice water

1 large egg yolk

FOR THE LEMON FILLING

¾ cup granulated sugar

½ teaspoon kosher salt

Juice of 6 lemons

4 large egg yolks

4 large eggs

¾ cup (1½ sticks) unsalted butter

FOR THE MERINGUE TOPPING

3 large egg whites, at room temperature

¼ cup granulated sugar

¼ teaspoon cream of tartar

1. Make the tart crust: Grate the frozen butter into a large bowl. Add the flour, confectioners' sugar, and salt and toss together with a rubber spatula. Using your hands or a pastry cutter, break up the butter and cut it into the flour until the butter is broken down into pea-size pearls and evenly distributed throughout.

2. Add the ice water and egg yolk, cutting it in with the spatula until a dough begins to form. When it's ready, the dough will look crumbly and shaggy and should stick together when you pinch some between your fingers.

3. Turn out the dough onto the countertop, kneading slightly to bring it all together, and gently pat it into a disc. Wrap the dough disc in plastic wrap and refrigerate for at least an hour and up to 3 days.

4. Preheat the oven to 400°F.

Continued

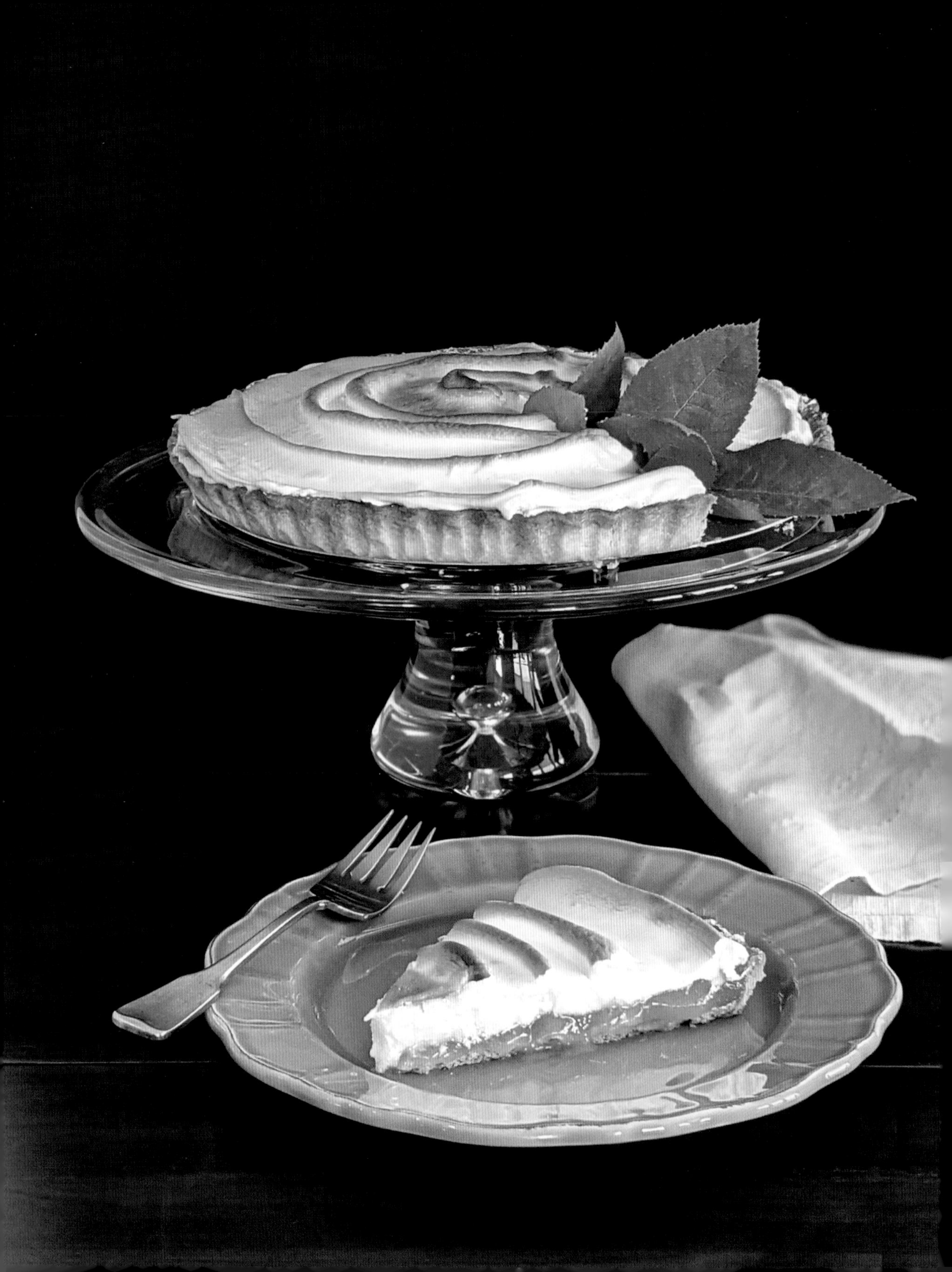

5. Plop the chilled dough onto a lightly floured surface and roll it into a round roughly 2 inches wider than the circumference of your tart pan. (If it's still too crumbly to roll, knead in a little water and refrigerate for 30 minutes more, then try again.) Gently roll the dough around the rolling pin and transfer it to the tart pan. Push the dough into the corners of the pan and up the sides, then trim the excess dough from the rim of the pan. Prick the bottom and sides of the dough with a fork.

6. Line the tart shell with aluminum foil and weigh it down with pie weights, dried beans, or uncooked rice. Bake for 12 minutes, then remove the foil and weights and bake for 12 to 15 minutes more, until the crust is golden brown.

7. Meanwhile, make the lemon filling: While the tart shell cooks, combine the granulated sugar, salt, lemon juice, egg yolks, eggs, and butter in a pan. Cook over low heat, stirring, until the butter melts. Raise the heat to medium-low and cook, still stirring, until the mixture reaches a pudding-like consistency, 15 to 20 minutes. The filling is done when it falls thickly from a spoon and mounds up in the pot.

8. Remove the tart shell from the oven and reduce the oven temperature to 350°F. Pour the hot filling into the hot tart shell and bake for 20 minutes, or until the tart is set around the edges and jiggles just a little in the center. Remove from the oven and allow to cool completely before topping. Switch the oven to broil.

9. Make the meringue topping: Using an electric mixer, beat the egg whites in a bowl on high speed until they become foamy, like bath bubbles. Beat in the granulated sugar one spoonful at a time until all the sugar has been mixed in. Add the cream of tartar and beat until you get stiff peaks.

10. Spoon all the meringue on top of the cooled tart and spread it out into a flat, even layer. Make sure the meringue goes all the way to the edges and completely covers the lemon filling. Make artful swirls in the top with a palette knife or the tip of a rubber spatula.

11. Set the tart on a baking sheet and slide it under the broiler. Leave the tart under the flame for a minute or so to get the meringue toasty brown. (But keep watch! It can turn black in the blink of an eye.) Serve fresh and enjoy! This tart is best the day it's made.

Anime-Inspired Desserts

Now that we've toured through Japanese and Western sweets in anime, there's only one frontier left to be explored: the collaboration-event desserts in Japan, where places like anime-themed cafés make food, both savory and sweet, to publicize and popularize anime. The desserts on these menus can be either Japanese or Western, but what sets them apart is the café's dedication to making these sweets as cute and photo-worthy as possible. This section takes cues from those Japanese cafés to make anime-inspired treats easily achieved in your home.

While all the recipes in the first two sections are focused on food that *appears* in anime, this section is dedicated to making desserts *inspired* by popular anime. I mean, take a look at Totoro, for example. He's so fluffy and squishy, he's basically the walking embodiment of a cookie-coated cream puff (stuffed with apple-flavored whipped cream, very tasty). Or how about Tanjiro's signature black-and-green-checked outfit, baked into a cake (very crisp, such clean lines, highly impressive)? In this section, we get a chance to combine Japanese and Western cooking techniques to make desserts that are tasty and totally unique. The best part is that these recipes are also great starting points for your own innovation. Playing with these elements will pave the way for your own creativity as you embark on your baking journey.

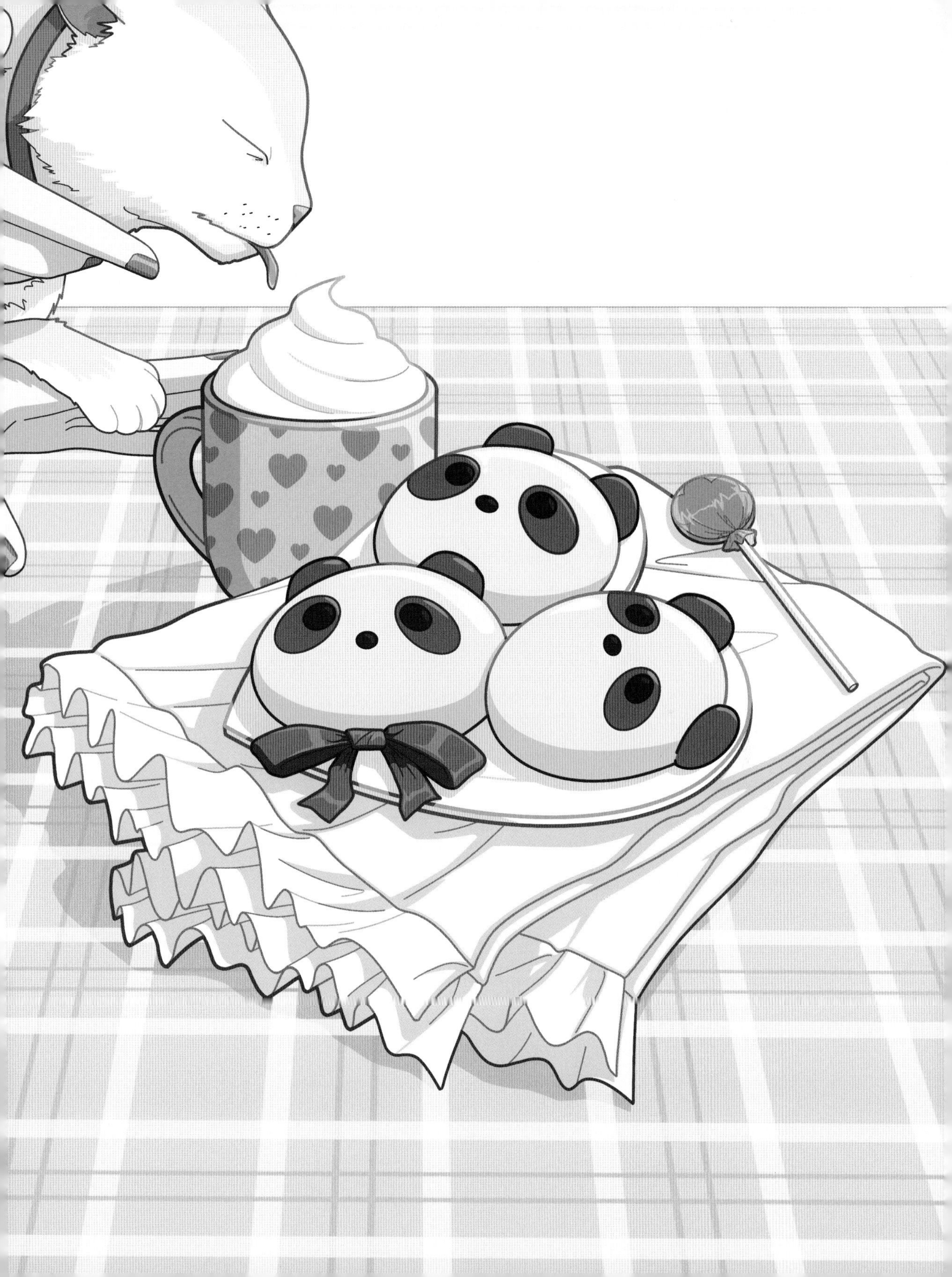

MY NEIGHBOR TOTORO

FOREST-KEEPER APPLE CREAM PUFFS

Mei, Satsuki, and their father move to the countryside to be closer to the hospital where their mom is staying. The girls are delighted by their new location, especially Mei, who notices little spirits living in and around their new house. During one play session, she follows the spirits into the forest and stumbles upon a slumbering creature she dubs "Totoro." It soon becomes clear to the girls that Totoro helps make the trees and plants grow.

Totoro assists the sisters in more ways than one—with the help of his friend the Cat Bus, he reunites the girls with their mother. It's a beautiful story that reinforces the importance and power of the local spirits believed to live all over Japan and the significance of relying on family and friends when times are tough. To celebrate Totoro, I made a cookie-covered cream puff filled with apple whipped cream to evoke a childlike flavor and feel. With a few decorations, you can make these puffs look just like Totoro and be transported back to your own childhood.

3 HOURS

MAKES 16 2-INCH PUFFS

SPECIAL EQUIPMENT: **FOOD COLORING MARKER (BLACK), PASTRY BAG AND ROUND PIPING TIP, 3-INCH ROUND COOKIE CUTTER**

NUT-FREE

FOR THE CRAQUELIN

- ½ cup sugar
- ½ cup (1 stick) unsalted butter, at room temperature
- 1 cup all-purpose flour
- Pinch of kosher salt
- Black food coloring

FOR THE CHOUX PASTRY

- ½ cup water
- ½ cup whole milk
- ½ cup (1 stick) unsalted butter
- 1 cup all-purpose flour
- 1 teaspoon sugar
- ¼ teaspoon kosher salt
- 3 to 4 large eggs, at room temperature

FOR THE FILLING

- 2 cups heavy cream
- ½ cup apple butter or apple jam

FOR THE DECORATIONS

- White fondant
- Black food coloring marker
- Corn syrup

1. Make the craquelin: Using an electric mixer, cream the sugar and butter together until light and fluffy. Add the flour and salt and mix until a loose dough forms. Add 1 to 2 drops of the black food coloring and mix until the dough is uniformly gray in color and very soft. Wrap the craquelin in plastic wrap and chill in the refrigerator until firm.

2. Make the choux pastry: Preheat the oven to 425°F. Line a baking sheet with parchment paper.

3. Combine the water, milk, and butter in a nonstick pot. Bring to a boil over high heat.

RECIPE TIP:
If you're having trouble getting the eyes to stick, you can also glue them on using chocolate candy coating wafers. Just melt the chocolate in the microwave and apply it to the back of the fondant eyes with a toothpick.

STORAGE TIP:
Unfilled, undecorated cream puffs can be stored in an airtight container at room temperature for up to 5 days.

Continued

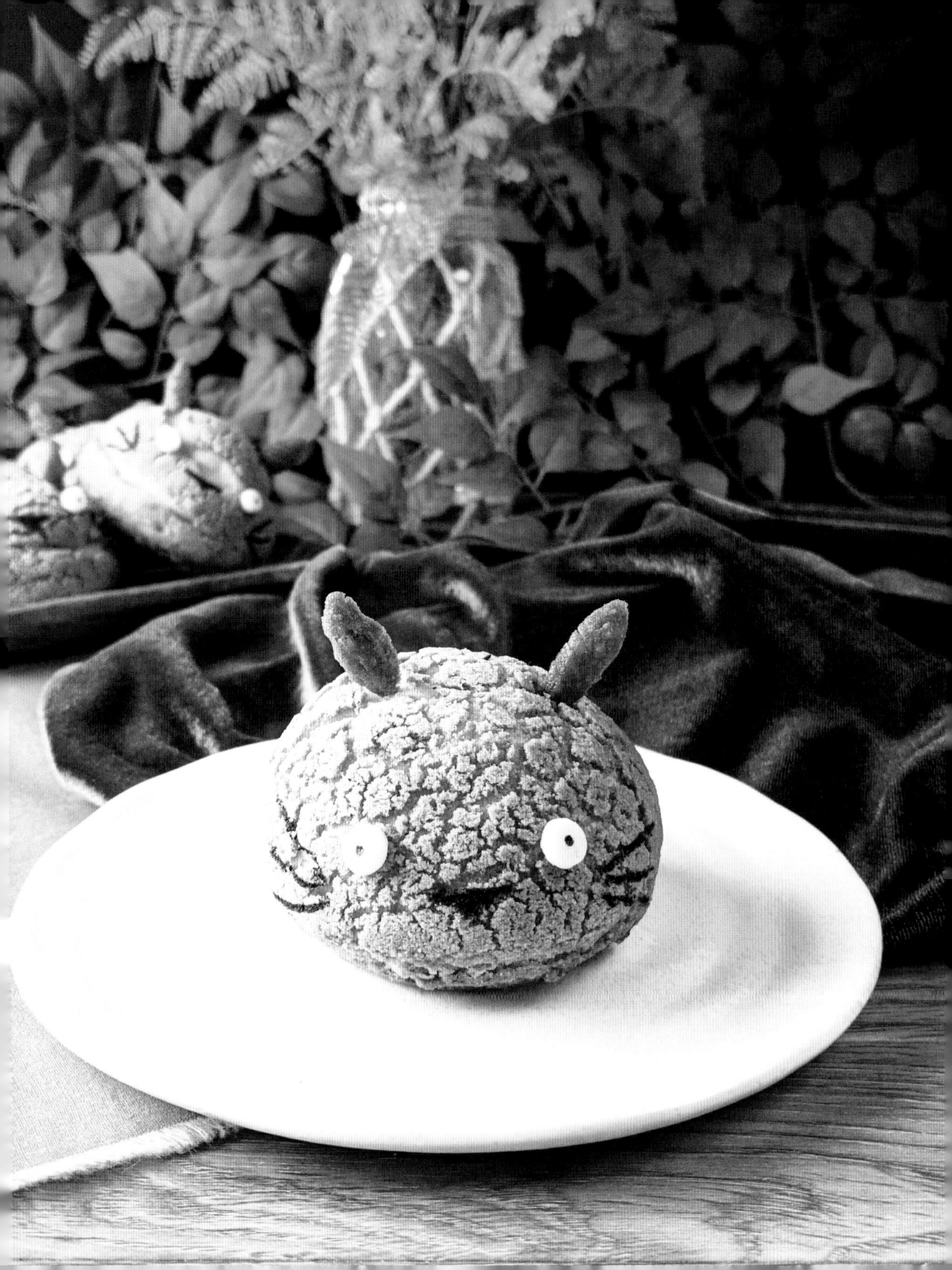

4. Whisk together the flour, sugar, and salt in a bowl. When the milk mixture is boiling, dump in the dry ingredients all at once and stir vigorously. Keeping the heat on, beat the batter with a rubber spatula for 2 to 3 minutes, until the dough sticks to the sides and bottom of the pot. Remove from the heat and transfer the dough to a bowl.

5. Using an electric mixer, beat the dough for a minute to cool it slightly. With the beaters running, add 3 eggs, one at a time, beating well and scraping down the sides of the bowl with a rubber spatula after each addition. You're looking for a smooth, sticky dough that drips from the spatula in thick ribbons. If you find the dough to be particularly thick and clumpy, whisk the remaining egg and add it to the dough 1 tablespoon at a time until you're happy with the consistency.

6. Spoon the batter into a pastry bag and snip ½ inch off the tip of the bag (no piping tip needed). Pipe rounds of dough 2 inches in diameter and 1 inch high onto the prepared baking sheet, leaving 2 inches between each. If there are any pointy bits on top of the rounds, wet a finger and gently tap them down.

7. On a floured surface or between two sheets of parchment paper, roll out the craquelin to about ⅛-inch thick. Cut out 3-inch rounds of craquelin and place one on top of each round of dough like a flat little hat. Place the craquelin scraps in the refrigerator for later.

8. Pop the puffs in the oven and bake for 10 minutes, then, without opening the oven, reduce the oven temperature to 325°F and bake for 30 minutes more. If the craquelin starts to brown too much during the last 5 minutes, cover with a sheet of aluminum foil.

9. When finished baking, turn off the oven and immediately remove the puffs. Use a knife or chopstick to pierce the bottom of each puff, creating a hole for the filling. Stick them back in the still-warm oven to dry out for about 15 minutes, then remove them from the oven and allow them to cool completely.

10. Make the filling: Using an electric mixer, whip the cream in a large bowl to soft peaks. Add the apple butter and beat until medium peaks form. If you're not filling the puffs right away, refrigerate the filling until you're ready to fill them. Otherwise, transfer the filling to a pastry bag fitted with a round tip. Press the pastry bag into the hole in each puff and gently squeeze in the filling. Stop when the puff gets full (you should feel the pastry bag start to push back out of the puff). Set the filled cream puffs aside.

11. Make the decorations: Preheat the oven to 425°F.

12. On a sheet of parchment paper, roll out the craquelin scraps so they are about ¼-inch thick. Use the tip of a knife to cut out oval ears (2 per cream puff), 1 inch long and ¼-inch wide at their widest point. Remove the excess craquelin, leaving the ears on the parchment, then slide the parchment onto a baking sheet. Bake for 3 minutes, then remove from the oven and allow to cool.

13. On a sheet of parchment paper, roll out the white fondant into a thin layer and use a straw or piping tip to cut out circles for eyes (2 per cream puff). Draw a pupil in the middle of each eye with a food coloring marker.

14. Decorate the cream puffs: Apply a dab of corn syrup to the back of the eyes and stick them onto the puffs, set fairly wide apart. Use the food coloring marker to sketch out a nose by drawing a short upside-down triangle. Draw 3 whiskers on each side, just outside the eyes and slightly under the nose. Finally, use a knife tip to cut 2 slits in the top of each puff. Slide the craquelin ears into the slits and serve.

FOOD FACT:
As of the time of writing, there's a café in Tokyo that sells adorable Totoro cream puffs—these are a riff on that idea, with my own personal twist.

CHOCOLATE TANUKI STEAMED BUNS

In *Monthly Girls' Nozaki-kun*, Nozaki is secretly a famous manga-ka who publishes under a pen name. When his classmate Chiyo tries to confess her love, he mistakes her for a fan and gives her an autograph! What follows isn't exactly a romantic relationship. Instead, Chiyo gets roped into being Nozaki's manga assistant, spending her days after school shading backgrounds and adding screen tones. Along the way, she makes friends with more odd characters and eventually forms a group centered around helping Nozaki-kun.

One such friend is Nozaki-kun's neighbor Yuraki Miyako, who also happens to be a famous manga-ka. Yuraki is known for writing tanuki into all the manga she makes. Why? Because her editor likes them. As a result, these cute creatures have a habit of popping up and become a running gag in the show. Whether they be from this anime or another (*Pom Poko*, *Eccentric Family*, *BNA: Brand New Animal*, and *Poco's Udon World*—I'm looking at you), tanuki are too cute not to food-ify. These buns, like tanuki themselves, are full of secrets: I stuffed mine with chocolate, but add whatever you want inside for a delicious and adorable treat!

3 HOURS

MAKES 12 BUNS

SPECIAL EQUIPMENT:
STEAMER BASKET

NUT-FREE

SUBSTITUTION TIP:
Opt for a flavored chocolate truffle to shake things up!

RECIPE TIP:
I used piping tips and a small cookie cutter to create my shapes for the tanuki faces, but boba straws and regular straws work well and can be manipulated into an oval shape by squeezing gently.

1¼ cups cake flour	Brown food coloring
⅓ cup whole milk	12 chocolate truffles
2 tablespoons sugar	Black food coloring
½ teaspoon instant yeast	

1. Combine the cake flour, milk, sugar, and yeast in the bowl of a stand mixer fitted with the dough hook and mix on a low speed for 10 minutes, or until the dough is soft, pliable, and stretchy. (Alternatively, combine the ingredients in a lare bowl and stir with a wooden spoon until a rough dough forms, then knead the dough by hand for 15 to 20 minutes, until it's soft, pliable, and stretchy.) The dough should be able to pass the windowpane test (see Tip, page 97).

2. Place a few drops of brown food coloring in the center of the dough and knead until the dough is uniformly tinted a light tan color. (If kneading by hand, return the dough to the bowl once you're done.) Cover the bowl with a damp paper towel and set aside for an hour.

3. Cut twelve 2-inch parchment paper squares to put under the buns.

4. Turn the dough out onto the counter and gently roll it into a log, pressing out any air that may have developed. Tear off a golf-ball-size chunk and set that aside. Split the remaining dough into 12 equal pieces and roll each piece into a ball. Cover the dough with a damp towel and allow to rest for 15 minutes.

5. Take one dough ball and squash it between your palms into a disc. Make an *O* with your thumb and index finger and place the dough disc on top of the *O*. Press a truffle into the center of the dough disc, then push down gently through the *O*, allowing the dough to stretch around

Continued

the truffle and enclose it. Pinch the dough together at the top to seal and roll away any wrinkles. Place the filled bun on top of a parchment square, cover with a damp paper towel, and set aside. Repeat to fill all the buns.

6. Divide the reserved chunk of dough into thirds. Add a few drops of black food coloring to the center of one portion and knead it through to tint the dough black. Tint the other two-thirds a shade of dark brown with the same method. Roll out each piece of dough into a thin layer and press out 24 small dark brown ovals for the eyes, 24 smaller circular black pupils, 12 small black circles for the noses, and 12 large brown circles for the ears. I like to use round piping tips and a small round cookie cutter to get the right sizes. Cut the circles for the ears in half with a knife.

7. Decorate the buns: Brush the surface of a bun lightly with water. Stick on 2 oval eye shapes at an upward angle, with the inner part of the oval near where the nose will be and the outer part sloping out and down the face. Add black pupils to the top edge of each eye. The nose goes right between the eyes. The ears are placed by pinching the sharp corners of each half circle together, then pressing them to the top of the head. Repeat to decorate all the buns.

8. Cover the buns with a damp paper towel and let rest in a warm spot for 30 minutes.

9. Fill a pot with a few inches of water and bring it to a boil over high heat. Place half the buns in a steamer basket, leaving room between them for them to grow, then place the steamer in the pot, cover, and steam for 11 minutes. If you're worried about steam dripping onto the buns, wrap a dish towel around the top of the steamer basket. Repeat to steam the remaining buns. When finished, allow the buns to cool slightly on a rack and then eat immediately.

GUDETAMA

INSIDE-OUT CRACKED EGG JELLY DONUTS

Gudetama is everyone's favorite lazy egg. He can't be bothered to do anything, really. I have to confess, Gudetama is my favorite Sanrio character: everything is just sooooo much effort. He really can't help but lie back down. I can relate, especially during the hot summer months in Japan.

To evoke this lazy feel, I've concocted a jelly donut design that's cute and easy to achieve. The goal with this recipe is to not work hard at all, so we're buying the jelly donuts and just putting our energy into making the design on top. Luckily, that's as easy as whipping up a quick icing and arranging some lemon curd artfully on top. Try this for yourself on a slow Sunday morning and spend the rest of the day luxuriating, just like Gudetama.

1 HOUR

MAKES **6 DONUTS**

SPECIAL EQUIPMENT: **PASTRY BAG AND ROUND PIPING TIP**

NUT-FREE

SUBSTITUTION TIP: Don't like lemon curd? Make the egg yolks out of melted yellow candy coating wafers instead!

½ cup confectioners' sugar

2 tablespoons whole milk

6 jelly donuts, store-bought or homemade

Lemon curd

Black bar sprinkles

1. Combine the confectioners' sugar and the milk in a bowl and stir until you get a thick paste. Add a spoonful of this mixture to the top of each donut (this is the "egg white") and let the icing fall where it may. Allow the icing to dry fully.

2. Spoon the lemon curd into a pastry bag fitted with a large round piping tip. Pipe various "egg yolk" shapes onto each donut: Make an egg yolk resting on its side by holding the tip horizontally to the donut and making a fat oval of lemon curd. Loosen your hold, drag the pastry bag back, and squeeze briefly again to give him a little booty. Make one lying on its back by simply piping a large oval shape. Or pipe one sitting up by holding the tip perpendicular to the donut and pulling up gently as you squeeze.

3. Using a toothpick and leftover lemon curd, add little egg yolk arms and legs where needed.

4. Using a few straight black sprinkles, give the eggs little faces. The more annoyed they look, the better.

5. Eat that day for the freshest bite of donut!

CHECKERED BATTENBERG CAKE

Tanjiro, the eldest in his family, comes back from selling charcoal early one morning to find his entire family has been killed by a demon. His eldest sister is the only survivor, if you can even call her that. During the attack, she was bitten by the demon and transformed into a monster herself! Tanjiro swears to make his sister human again, so he sets out to become a Demon Slayer and find the demon who transformed his sister.

Tanjiro wears a signature black-and-green-checkered haori, a type of coat normally worn over a kimono. His story has become so popular in Japan that not only can you buy all manner of *Demon Slayer* memorabilia, you can even buy the very *fabric* used in the signature outfits from the show. If fabric stores can print Tanjiro-inspired fabric, I figured I could put the pattern into a cake. Taking inspiration from more traditionally colored Battenberg cakes, I decided to make one in Tanjiro's colors, but you could also make this recipe in his sister's colors—maroon-and-cream check, which is seen on her obi.

OVERNIGHT

SERVES 8

SPECIAL EQUIPMENT:
BATTENBERG CAKE
PAN (OPTIONAL)

SUBSTITUTION TIP:
If you don't want to use modeling chocolate, use fondant instead. Don't like fondant? Go with marzipan, the more traditional choice. And if you're not a fan of ganache, try gluing the cake together with jam instead.

FOR THE MODELING CHOCOLATE
12 ounces chocolate candy coating wafers, such as Candy Melts

¼ cup light corn syrup

FOR THE CAKE
¾ cup (1½ sticks) unsalted butter, at room temperature, plus more for greasing

¾ cup sugar

3 large eggs

1 cup all-purpose flour

½ cup almond flour

2 tablespoons whole milk

1¼ teaspoons baking powder

¼ teaspoon kosher salt

1 teaspoon vanilla extract

Green food coloring

2 tablespoons unsweetened Dutch-process cocoa powder

Black food coloring

FOR THE GANACHE
¼ cup heavy cream

½ cup semisweet chocolate chips

1. Make the modeling chocolate: Place the candy coating wafers in a microwave-safe bowl and microwave in 30-second intervals, stirring after each, until most of the chocolate has melted, then microwave for 10-second stints, stirring after each, until completely melted and smooth.

2. The melted chocolate should feel warm but not hot. If the bowl feels hot to the touch, transfer the chocolate to a new bowl to stop it from scorching from the residual heat. Pour in the corn syrup and stir with a rubber spatula. Scrape slowly and carefully all around the bowl, making sure all the chocolate comes into contact with the corn syrup. Don't overmix—stop as soon as the corn syrup looks mostly incorporated and the mixture has started to cling together rather than to the sides of the bowl. It should look wet and the consistency should be similar to soft-serve ice cream. Pour the mixture into a zip-top plastic bag, squeeze the air out, and seal. Store in a cool, dry space. (The modeling chocolate can be made 1 to 2 weeks ahead and stored in a cool, dry space.)

3. Make the cake: Preheat the oven to 350°F. If you have a proper Battenburg cake pan, grease the sides of the pan with butter and line the bottom of the wells with parchment paper cut to fit. If you don't have a Battenberg cake pan, pull out a long sheet of aluminum foil and fold it in half lengthwise. Fold the edges in, creating a 2-inch folded section in the middle of the foil. Line an 8-inch square baking pan with the foil, leaving the flap in the middle of the pan, pointing upward, so the pan is split into two sections.

4. Using an electric mixer, cream the butter and sugar together in a large bowl until light and fluffy. Add all the eggs at once and beat to incorporate, scraping the sides of the bowl to make sure everything is mixed. Add the all-purpose flour, almond flour, milk, baking powder, and salt and mix until there are no lumps.

5. Pour half the batter into a separate bowl (use a scale to get perfectly even amounts). To one bowl, add the vanilla and green food coloring. Mix thoroughly until the color is evenly distributed, adjust the color as needed, then set aside. Add the cocoa powder to the second bowl of batter and mix to combine, then stir in drops of black food coloring until you're happy with the color.

6. Pour the batters into the prepared pan, one on each side of the divider, making sure the foil remains in the middle if you're not using a Battenberg pan. Bake for 40 minutes, or until a toothpick inserted into the center comes out clean. Allow to cool completely in the pan, then chill in the refrigerator for at least an hour and up to 3 hours.

7. Loosen the black and green cakes from the pan by running a knife around the edges of each. Tip them out onto your work surface and peel away the parchment or foil. Trim off any caramelization from the top and sides of the cakes, then trim the cakes so you have two perfectly even rectangles. Use a ruler to measure how wide they are, then cut both rectangles directly in half so you have two long, skinny rectangles of each color. Refrigerate these to chill while you make the ganache.

8. Make the ganache: Pour the cream into a microwave-safe bowl or measuring cup. Microwave for a minute or so, until it's hot to the touch. Add the chocolate chips and wiggle them around so the cream mostly covers them. Let stand for 5 minutes, then whisk until the chocolate has melted and you have a thick, smooth ganache.

9. Pull the cake strips out of the refrigerator. Spread ganache over the top of both strips of black cake, then set a strip of green cake on top of each. Turn one pair of joined strips so it's lying flat on your work surface and spread a layer of ganache over the top. Place the second pair of joined strips on top, with the black strip of one on the green strip of the other, forming a long rectangle with checkerboard ends. If you have some ragged edges, don't worry—you'll cut those away later on. Coat the top and sides of the cake in a thin layer of ganache and return the cake to the refrigerator to chill until the ganache is firm to the touch.

10. Knead the modeling chocolate in your hands to warm it up and make it pliable. When it's at a workable consistency, shape it into a rectangle and roll it out into a thin rectangle large enough to completely enclose three sides the cake, peeling it off your work surface periodically to make sure it doesn't stick. (Measure the cake to ensure the chocolate is rolled

Continued

to the right length and width. The chocolate rectangle should be an inch or two wider than the cake is long; multiply the width of the cake by 3, then add an inch or two to get the length of the chocolate. If you used an 8-inch square pan, the modeling chocolate should measure at least 9 to 10 inches wide and 17 to 18 inches long.)

11. Remove the cake from the fridge, place it on a cutting board, and roll the modeling chocolate over it. Smooth out the chocolate with your hands, molding it to the cake and using your fingers to make sharp corners. With a sharp knife, cut away the excess chocolate at the bottom of the cake and around the front and back. Keep smoothing and pressing the modeling chocolate against the cake so you're left with clean sides and edges.

12. Trim off the ends of the cake to expose the checkerboard pattern, transfer to a serving dish, and enjoy with a hot cup of tea!

FRUITS BASKET

ZODIAC MOCHI FIGURINES

When Tohru Honda's home (a precariously erected tent) is buried under a landslide, her mysterious classmate Yuki offers her a place to stay in exchange for help around the house. With few other options and no small amount of curiosity about her aloof classmate, Tohru agrees and moves in. What she discovers thereafter is the reason Yuki is so distant: he's cursed! Should a member of the opposite sex embrace him, he turns into a rat, one of the twelve animals of the Chinese zodiac. And he's not the only one who's cursed—so are eleven members of his extended family.

The Chinese zodiac is popular in Japan; you can often find small figures or sets to represent all the animals. The same is true in the anime—there are a lot of zodiac references worked into the show, including one family member's set of zodiac figurines. In homage to that set, I've made this edible version, with mochi and ganache instead of wood and paint. The ganache filling positively melts in your mouth, making these figurines the perfect chewy-chocolaty bite.

3 HOURS

MAKES 12 PIECES

SPECIAL EQUIPMENT: ROUND COOKIE CUTTER, FOOD COLORING MARKER (BLACK)

GLUTEN-FREE, NUT-FREE, VEGAN (DEPENDING ON THE CHOCOLATE OF CHOICE)

FOR THE GANACHE

¼ cup heavy cream

½ cup white chocolate chips

FOR THE MOCHI

1 cup shiratamako (sweet rice flour)

1 cup water

¼ cup granulated sugar

FOR THE COLORANTS

1 capsule activated charcoal (Ox)

2 tablespoons black sesame seeds, ground (Rat)

½ teaspoon mango powder (Tiger)

½ teaspoon matcha (Dragon)

1 freeze-dried strawberry, crushed (Bunny)

3 or 4 drops butterfly pea extract (Snake)

¼ teaspoon vanilla extract (Ram)

½ teaspoon packed dark brown sugar (Boar)

½ teaspoon ground cinnamon (Horse)

¼ teaspoon instant coffee granules (Monkey)

½ teaspoon unsweetened cocoa powder (Dog)

Cornstarch, for dusting

1. Make the ganache: Place the cream in a microwave-safe bowl. Microwave for a minute until it's hot, then add the white chocolate chips. Let stand for 5 minutes, then whisk until the chocolate has melted and you have a thick, glossy sauce. Chill in the refrigerator until the ganache has hardened to a scoopable consistency.

2. Make the mochi: Whisk together the shiratamako, water, and granulated sugar in a bowl to combine. You should have 1½ cups of liquid batter; divide it into twelve 2-tablespoon portions, placing each in a separate small, microwave-safe bowl.

Continued

RECIPE TIP: I find coloring and cooking each mochi individually to be less messy, but you could cook a full batch of plain white mochi, then split it into 12 pieces and tint them by hand. To do so, leave all the mochi batter in one bowl, drape the top with plastic wrap, and microwave for 2 minutes. Stir, then microwave for 2 minutes more and stir again. Microwave in 30-second intervals until it turns transparent. Turn the mochi out onto a cornstarch-dusted surface and sprinkle the top with cornstarch. Split it into 12 pieces and add one colorant to each, kneading it through until the color is uniform. From there, follow steps 4 to 6 as directed.

3. Tint the mochi: Add each colorant to a bowl of mochi, leaving the last white for the rooster, and stir to combine. Place the bowls in the microwave and drape a sheet of plastic wrap over the tops. Microwave on high in 10-second intervals, stirring after each, until the mochi has gone from milky to having a transparent quality. Repeat to cook the remaining mochi (you can do this in batches—I worked with three bowls at a time).

4. Sprinkle your work surface generously with cornstarch. Pull out the chocolate ganache and a teaspoon to scoop it with. Working with one at a time, tip the warm mochi onto the prepared surface. Sprinkle the top generously with cornstarch and pat it gently into a flat, circular shape. Use the top of a cup or a round cutter to trim the mochi into an even round and discard the scraps. Scoop out a teaspoon of ganache and place it into the center of the mochi. Bring the sides of the mochi up to enclose the ganache, pinching the edges together to seal and make a ball. Set aside and repeat with the remaining mochi.

5. Decorate the mochi with a food coloring marker. I made the faces of the animals of the Chinese zodiac just by using online images as a reference. Work with a light hand to avoid bleeding from the marker and brush excess cornstarch away to help the ink stick.

6. Mochi doesn't stay soft for long, so enjoy that day or store in an airtight container overnight and eat the next day.

NOTE: The rooster is white; no colorant necessary.

SUBSTITUTION TIP:
If you don't want to go to the trouble of procuring all the natural colorants, food coloring will also work and is a cheaper alternative that will result in some beautiful colors.

ANIME FACT:
The Chinese zodiac, which differs from the zodiac in Western astrology, was introduced to Japan around the fourth century and remains a mainstay in Japanese pop culture. In Japan, it's called junishi (or twelve branches).

POKÉMON THE SERIES

POCKET MONSTER SWISS ROLL

Pokémon is a show that needs no introduction—for many, it's the first anime they saw! Ash, his friends Brock and Misty, and Pikachu hunt for Pokémon and train to be Pokémon Masters. This is a prolific franchise in Japan; promotional materials for the games and shows are everywhere. What's more, other businesses and corporations frequently do collaborations with Pokémon to promote their own products.

One such recent collaboration was between Pokémon and Tokyo Banana, a popular souvenir snack in Japan, similar to a Twinkie with banana-flavored filling, where popular Pokémon were printed onto the sponge cake. This recipe is a riff on that collaboration: a Swiss roll cake that's soft and pillowy, with a filling that's creamy and perfectly flavored, so the banana comes through without being overwhelming. The pattern on top is simple to make—it'll definitely impress anyone you serve this cake to!

2 HOURS

SERVES 8

SPECIAL EQUIPMENT: **12 X 8-INCH JELLY-ROLL PAN, PASTRY BAGS AND SMALL ROUND PIPING TIPS**

NUT-FREE

RECIPE TIP: If you don't want to get pastry bags and tips, use a plastic bag with one corner snipped off, then use a toothpick to smooth out lines, fix shapes, and clean edges.

FOOD FACT: Despite being called a "Swiss" roll cake, most historians agree that the cake is not actually Swiss in origin. More likely, it originated in Central Europe.

FOR THE DECORATION

1 ounce unsalted butter, at room temperature, plus more for greasing

1 ounce confectioners' sugar

1 ounce egg white

1 ounce all-purpose flour

2 tablespoons unsweetened cocoa powder

Red food coloring

FOR THE SWISS ROLL CAKE

3 large eggs, separated, at room temperature

⅓ cup granulated sugar

1 teaspoon vanilla extract

½ cup cake flour

½ teaspoon baking powder

FOR THE BANANA WHIPPED CREAM FILLING

1 ripe medium banana

¾ cup heavy cream

2 tablespoons confectioners' sugar

1 teaspoon vanilla extract

1. Preheat the oven to 350°F. Make a stencil for your design: Get a piece of paper and cut it so it is as wide as your jelly-roll pan and 3 to 4 inches across. Trace your design on the paper, making the lines thick.

2. Make the decoration: Grease the sides of the jelly-roll pan with butter and place the design in the center of the pan. The longer the jelly-roll pan is, the more you'll have to offset the card so the design ends up on top. If your jelly-roll pan is square, set it in the middle. If the pan is a rectangle, offset it slightly to one side. Line the bottom and sides of the pan with parchment paper, placing it over the design and pressing it into the corners of the pan.

Continued

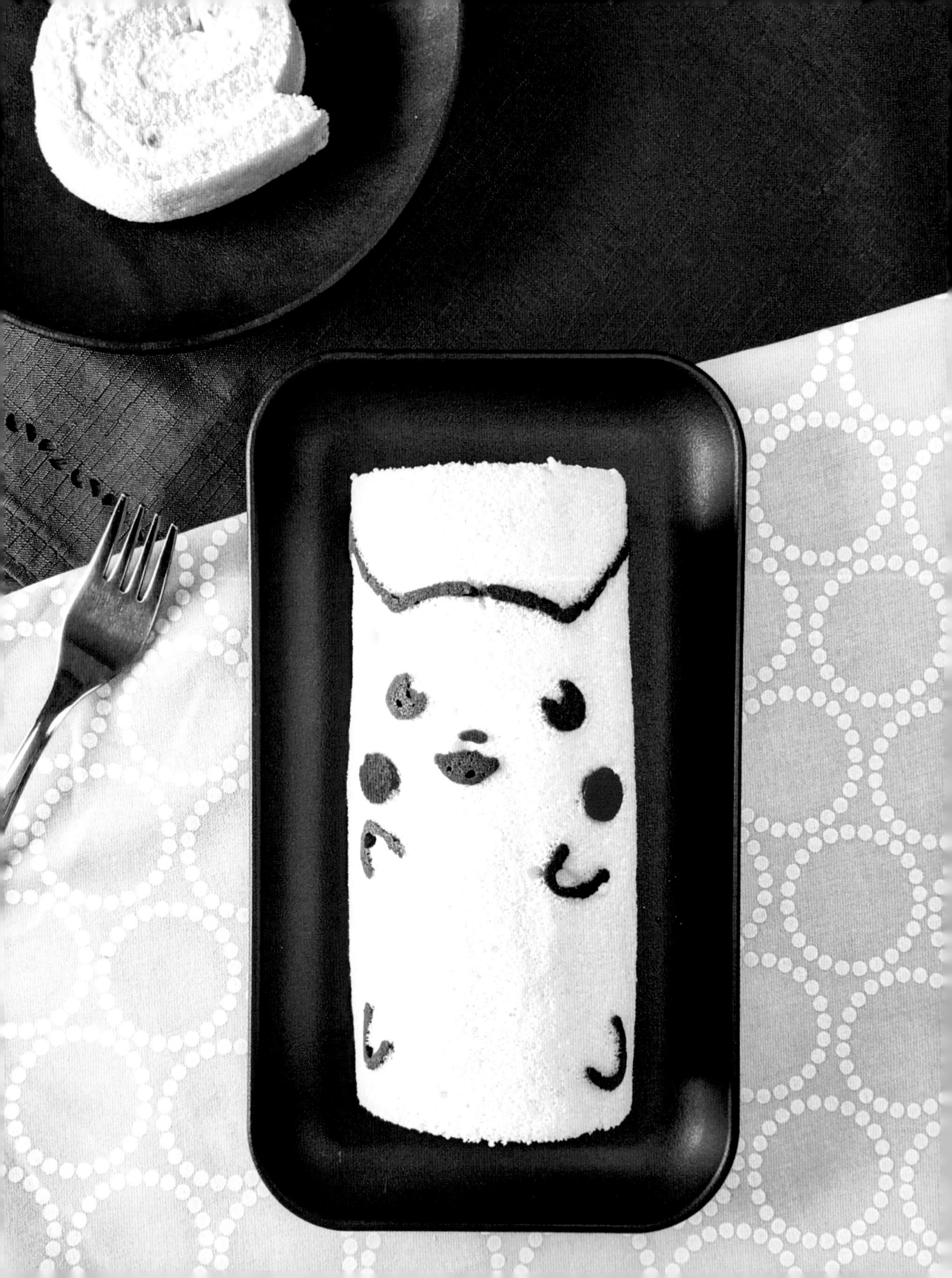

3. Combine the confectioners' sugar, butter, egg white, and flour in a bowl. Whisk until combined and smooth. Transfer 1 tablespoon of the batter to a small bowl and set aside. Add the cocoa powder to the bowl with the remaining batter and stir until it's smooth and there are no chocolate lumps. Add red food coloring to the batter in the small bowl and mix until uniform in color.

4. Transfer the two batters to separate pastry bags fitted with small round piping tips. Pipe the chocolate batter onto the prepared jelly-roll pan, tracing your template for everything but the cheeks. Pipe the red batter onto the template for the cheeks. Chill in the freezer while you make the cake.

5. Make the Swiss roll cake: Put the egg whites and egg yolks into separate bowls and set the egg yolks aside. Using an electric mixer, beat the egg whites until they have started to foam, then add the granulated sugar spoonful by spoonful until it's all incorporated. Keep beating until you've achieved stiff peaks, 5 to 8 minutes, then set aside.

6. Use the mixer to break up the egg yolks and beat in the vanilla. Sift the flour and baking powder over the yolks and mix to combine.

7. Add a scoop of the egg whites to the egg yolk mixture and use the beaters to incorporate until no white remains. Repeat with another scoop or two of egg white. When the white is fully mixed in, pour the lightened yolk mixture into the bowl with the rest of the egg whites. Use a whisk to gently scrape around the bowl and fold the two together—around, down, under, and up—until the white and yellow mixtures are totally combined and no white lumps remain. Stop immediately once this stage has been reached.

8. Remove the jelly-roll pan from the freezer and pour the batter into the pan over the decorations, using a rubber spatula to make sure you get every last drop. Smooth the top of the batter and spread it into the corners of the pan. Tap the pan briskly on the counter a few times to release any air bubbles. Bake for 10 to 12 minutes, until a toothpick inserted into the center comes out clean.

9. Remove the pan from the oven and immediately tip the cake out onto a cutting board. Gently peel off the parchment, then flip the cake back over so the design is on the bottom. Orient the cake vertically, so that one short edge is toward you. With a serrated knife, trim off the short edge of the cake farthest from you (just ½ to 1 inch) so that it tapers into a triangle, rather than ending in a blunt rectangle.

10. While the cake is still warm, drape a clean dish towel over the surface of the cake and begin tightly rolling up the cake and towel together. Orient the cake so the design is on top, drape a second dish towel over the rolled cake to protect the exterior, and allow it to cool completely.

11. Make the banana whipped cream filling: Mash the banana in a small bowl with a fork until mostly smooth and chunk-free. Using an electric mixer, whip the cream in a large bowl until soft peaks form. Add the confectioners' sugar and vanilla and whip until you attain medium peaks. Switch to a whisk, add the mashed banana, and whip by hand until you have firm peaks and the banana is incorporated.

12. Fill the cake: When the cake has completely cooled, unroll it and remove the dish towel, making sure the design is on the bottom. Spread the whipped cream in a smooth, even layer over the surface of the cake. Use a little more filling toward the the short edge that will be rolled into the center of the cake. No need to leave a border, as you will cut away messy edges later anyway. Roll the cake up tightly around the filling, orienting it so the design is on top.

13. Chill the cake for at least an hour and up to a day before cutting. Trim the edges of the cake so they're neat. Serve chilled and enjoy!

FIRE DEMON FRUIT FLAMBÉ

Calcifer is a fire demon who, as a result of a contract made with the great wizard Howl, must heat and move Howl's castle for him. Calcifer doesn't relish this agreement—he's looking for a way out, and he isn't opposed to throwing Howl under the bus to get free. When a girl named Sophie comes to the castle, he's at first abrasive and rude. However, after learning about her own curse, Calcifer quickly *warms* up to her (haha), especially once she cleans his hearth. As Sophie becomes more valuable to the castle and its inhabitants, Calcifer even goes so far as to come to everyone's rescue in a moment of crisis.

To embody his temperamental personality, this fruit flambé is fiery and fun to make, and warm and sweet to eat. Just as Sophie won Calcifer's heart, this dessert is sure to win yours.

30 MINUTES

SERVES 4

GLUTEN-FREE, NUT-FREE

RECIPE TIP: It's important to be safe when (intentionally) setting things on fire in the kitchen. Turn the flame off under the pan when adding the alcohol so it doesn't ignite before you want it to. Never pour the alcohol directly from the bottle, because if it catches fire as you pour, it could carry back into the bottle and cause it to explode! This is a simple recipe, but *work with caution.*

- **¼ cup apple juice**
- **2 tablespoons packed light brown sugar**
- **1 orange, peeled and cut into chunks**
- **3 ounces fresh or frozen raspberries**
- **¼ teaspoon ground cinnamon**
- **¼ cup light rum**
- **Ice cream, for serving**
- **Fresh mint, for garnish**

1. Combine the apple juice and brown sugar in a pot and bring to a simmer over medium heat. Stir to dissolve the sugar, then add the orange, raspberries, and cinnamon. Simmer until the fruit has softened, 2 to 3 minutes.

2. Briefly turn off the heat and add the rum, then turn the heat back on and bring to a simmer again. Using a long-stemmed lighter, ignite the rum, or carefully tip the pan so the mixture flows away from you toward the flame of the burner, just enough so the fumes of the alcohol catch fire. (Please be safe here! For extra info, see my recipe tip.) Allow the alcohol to burn away, then turn off the heat and let the flambé cool slightly. Serve with the ice cream, garnish with fresh mint, and enjoy!

PRINCESS MONONOKE

FOREST SPIRIT MERINGUES

In this cinematic masterpiece, man and nature are pitted against one another. Exiled prince Ashitaka journeys to bring peace between humans and the surrounding landscape systematically destroyed in pursuit of industry. His principal fight is between Lady Eboshi, the whip-smart and strong-willed leader of Iron Town, and Princess Mononoke, a girl raised by a wolf goddess as one of her own.

Ashitaka spends time in both bustling Iron Town and the magical forest, the latter of which is full of gods and spirits. One such spirit are the Kodama, little humanoid figures with big bobble heads. The Kodama run rampant in the forest and guide Ashitaka. While it's unlikely that you'll see these spirits in real life, they're very easy to turn into crunchy, crispy meringues. Meringues can be tricky because they're prone to cracking if you don't bake them right, but once you get the hang of it, they'll bring magic into your kitchen!

1 HOUR, PLUS DRYING OVERNIGHT

MAKES 30 TO 40 MINI MERINGUES

SPECIAL EQUIPMENT: FOOD COLORING MARKER (BLACK), PASTRY BAGS, AND ROUND PIPING TIPS

DAIRY-FREE, GLUTEN-FREE, NUT-FREE

STORAGE TIP: Stored in an airtight container at room temperature, these keep for up to 2 weeks.

2 large egg whites, as fresh as possible, at room temperature

2/3 cup sugar

1 lemon slice

½ teaspoon vanilla extract

1. Make the meringues: Using an electric mixer, beat the egg whites in a clean bowl on low speed for 1 to 2 minutes, until foamy and forming bubble-bath-like peaks. Shift the mixer speed to medium and add the sugar a spoonful at a time, mixing for 20 to 30 seconds after each addition, until all the sugar has been incorporated.

2. Squeeze a few drops of lemon juice into the mix, then beat the egg whites on high for 8 to 10 minutes, until the sugar has dissolved and the egg whites are glossy and moist and form stiff peaks when you lift the beaters. To test this, take a little egg white and rub it between two fingers; if it feels gritty, it's not yet ready. When this stage is reached, whip in the vanilla.

3. Preheat the oven to 500°F. Line a baking sheet with parchment paper. Gather three pastry bags; fit one with a smaller round tip and another with a slightly larger round tip; the third bag will not need a tip.

4. Divide the batter evenly among the pastry bags and set the bag without a tip aside. Using the bag with the smaller round tip, pipe teardrop shapes in a row on the prepared baking sheet for the forest spirit bodies, leaving 1 inch of space between each. With even pressure, push the meringue out to form the rounded edge of the teardrop, then reduce the pressure and gently pull up along the baking sheet, making the point at the end. Repeat until the baking sheet is full, leaving 2 inches between the rows.

5. Using the bag with the bigger piping tip, pipe circles over the pointy end of the teardrop shapes for the forest spirit heads. Have fun here—they all have weird-shaped heads, so the circles shouldn't be perfect. Pipe lima-bean-shaped heads, oblong heads, and heads with little points at the top.

6. Cut the tip of the final pastry bag to make a very fine opening and use it to pipe arms and legs. Gently push the tip into the body where you want the appendage to emerge and use gentle pressure to push the meringue out of the bag, pulling back with your hand.

RECIPE TIP:
Meringue can be tricky to master. Fresh eggs are important—they're more acidic the younger they are, and as they age, they lose that, resulting in unstable meringues that can crack and pit in the oven. Room-temperature eggs are also important—the temperature helps the proteins in the egg break down more easily, which then makes the reformation of the proteins around air bubbles easier. Don't add the sugar too soon or in a big clump—if you do, you run the risk of shocking the proteins in the egg whites and actually preventing them from forming bubbles, or you could knock all the air out of the egg white foam. Finally, make sure the bowl and beaters are clean before whipping the egg whites! Any trace of fat will prevent the egg whites from whipping up.

7. Turn the oven off and place the baking sheet with the meringues on the middle rack. Leave them in the oven overnight—don't open the oven door until the next morning, so as not to release any hot air.

8. The next day, the meringues should easily lift off the baking sheet. They should be hard on the outside and sound hollow when tapped. Use a black food coloring marker to draw eyes and mouths onto each. These serve as excellent "marshmallows" for hot chocolate or green tea.

THAT TIME I GOT REINCARNATED AS A SLIME

SLIME MONSTER MIRROR CAKE

In isekai anime, main characters are taken out of their own worlds and dropped into new ones. In *That Time I Got Reincarnated as a Slime*, Rimuru is reincarnated as a slime monster. He soon learns that he can absorb the powers of whatever he ingests, and when he happens to ingest an entire dragon, he becomes very powerful *very* quickly.

What follows is a quirky adventure as Rimuru champions the monsters of the world and makes a place for them where they don't have to live in fear. Rimuru is a good person who just wants to make life easier for his newfound friends. Everyone loves him and what he does, and he loves them . . . and brandy. As a nod to this, I've made a mirror cake to look like Rimuru, using brandy as a flavorful component of the mousse cake underneath.

24 HOURS, INCLUDING CHILLING OVERNIGHT

SERVES 10

SPECIAL EQUIPMENT: 9-INCH SILICONE CAKE MOLD, INFRARED THERMOMETER, PASTRY BAG AND SMALL ROUND PIPING TIP

NUT-FREE

RECIPE TIPS:
Don't want to make the cake from scratch? Use a boxed mix or a store-bought unfrosted cake. Just avoid anything especially crumbly or delicate.

Why do we use sheet gelatin instead of powdered gelatin? The final shine on the glaze will be clearer and shinier when you use sheet gelatin as opposed to powdered gelatin. You can use 2 tablespoons of powdered gelatin to replace the gelatin in this recipe if you're truly in a pinch, but the results might not be as pretty.

FOR THE CAKE

1¼ cups all-purpose flour

1¼ teaspoon baking powder

¼ teaspoon kosher salt

½ cup (1 stick) unsalted butter, at room temperature

1 cup sugar

½ teaspoon vanilla extract

Grated zest of 1 large lemon

2 large eggs, at room temperature

½ cup whole milk

1 cup blueberry jam

FOR THE WHITE CHOCOLATE MOUSSE

8 ounces white chocolate (over 30 percent cocoa butter)

6 large egg yolks

3 tablespoons sugar

2½ cups plus 2 tablespoons heavy cream

2 tablespoons brandy

FOR THE MIRROR GLAZE

13 ounces white chocolate (over 30 percent cocoa butter), chopped

7 1.7-gram platinum-grade gelatin sheets

¾ cup sugar

½ cup plus 2 tablespoons water

7 ounces sweetened condensed milk

Black food coloring

Blue food coloring

1. Make the cake: Preheat the oven to 350°F. Line the bottom of an 8-inch round baking pan with parchment paper cut to fit.

2. Whisk together the flour, baking powder, and salt to combine, working out any lumps.

3. Using an electric mixer, beat the butter until light and fluffy, 1 to 2 minutes. Pour in the sugar and beat until well combined and light in color. Add the vanilla and lemon zest, then add the eggs one at a time, mixing well after each addition. Make sure to scrape down the sides of the bowl to incorporate everything.

4. Add one-third of the flour mixture and beat until mostly incorporated. Pour in half the milk and mix again. Repeat, alternating the flour with the milk, until all the flour mixture and milk have been added. Make sure to scrape the sides of the bowl as you go.

5. Pour the batter into the prepared pan and bake for 45 to 50 minutes, or until the top is golden brown and a toothpick inserted into the center comes out clean. Allow the cake to cool completely, then run a knife around the edges of the pan to detach the cake from the sides. Turn the cake out of the pan, remove the parchment paper, and set aside to cool completely.

6. Clean the cake pan, then pour in the jam and spread it into an even layer over the bottom of the pan. Place the cooled cake layer back in the pan on top of the jam and freeze for 4 to 5 hours.

7. One hour before the cake is ready to be unmolded, make the white chocolate mousse: Place the chocolate in a large bowl and set aside. Whisk together the egg yolks and sugar in another bowl to combine.

8. Pour 1 cup and 2 tablespoons of the heavy cream into a small pot (chill the remaining cream until needed). Heat the cream over medium heat until steaming but not boiling or simmering. While whisking continuously, carefully spoon 3 tablespoons of the hot cream into the egg mixture and whisk to combine, then repeat with another 3 tablespoons of cream. While whisking, pour the egg mixture into the pot with the remaining cream.

9. Bring the cream mixture to a simmer, whisking continuously, then cook until it coats the back of a spoon; if you drag your finger through the cream on the back of a spoon, you should leave a clear clean line. Immediately remove the pot from the heat and pour the cream mixture over the chocolate. Let stand for 3 to 5 minutes, then whisk until the chocolate has melted completely and the mixture is smooth. Stir in the brandy. Cover the custard with plastic wrap, pressing it directly against the surface to prevent a skin from forming, and refrigerate for 1 to 2 hours.

10. Using an electric mixer, whip the remaining 1½ cups chilled heavy cream in a large bowl until you achieve stiff peaks. Refrigerate to chill.

11. When the custard is cool, spoon in the whipped cream. Fold the two together until completely incorporated, then set the chocolate mousse aside.

12. Pull the cake from the freezer. Pour the chocolate mousse into a 9-inch round silicone pan and spread it into an even layer. Unmold the frozen cake and jam by prying it out with a spatula. Place the cake layer onto the mousse, jam side down, and press until the top of the cake is level with the top of the mousse. Clean up the edges and then freeze the mousse cake overnight.

13. The next day, make the mirror glaze: Put the chocolate in a large bowl and set aside. Place the gelatin sheets in a bowl of water, making sure they are fully submerged. Set aside to bloom for about 5 minutes, until it has absorbed some of the water.

14. Combine the sugar, water, and condensed milk in a pan. Heat over medium heat until the mixture is hot to the touch.

15. Squeeze out any excess water from the gelatin sheets, add them to the milk mixture, and stir until the gelatin is fully melted and incorporated into the milk.

Continued

SUBSTITUTION TIP:
Seems like too much work? Just make the brandied white chocolate mousse and serve with fresh blueberries for a simpler *Slime*-inspired dessert.

FOOD FACT:
Out of all the recipes in this book, this may be one of the most novel. Though mirror glazes have been made for many years, the first mirror glaze cake to be made with this method was created by a Russian baker named Olga Noskova, whose creations first became popular in 2016.

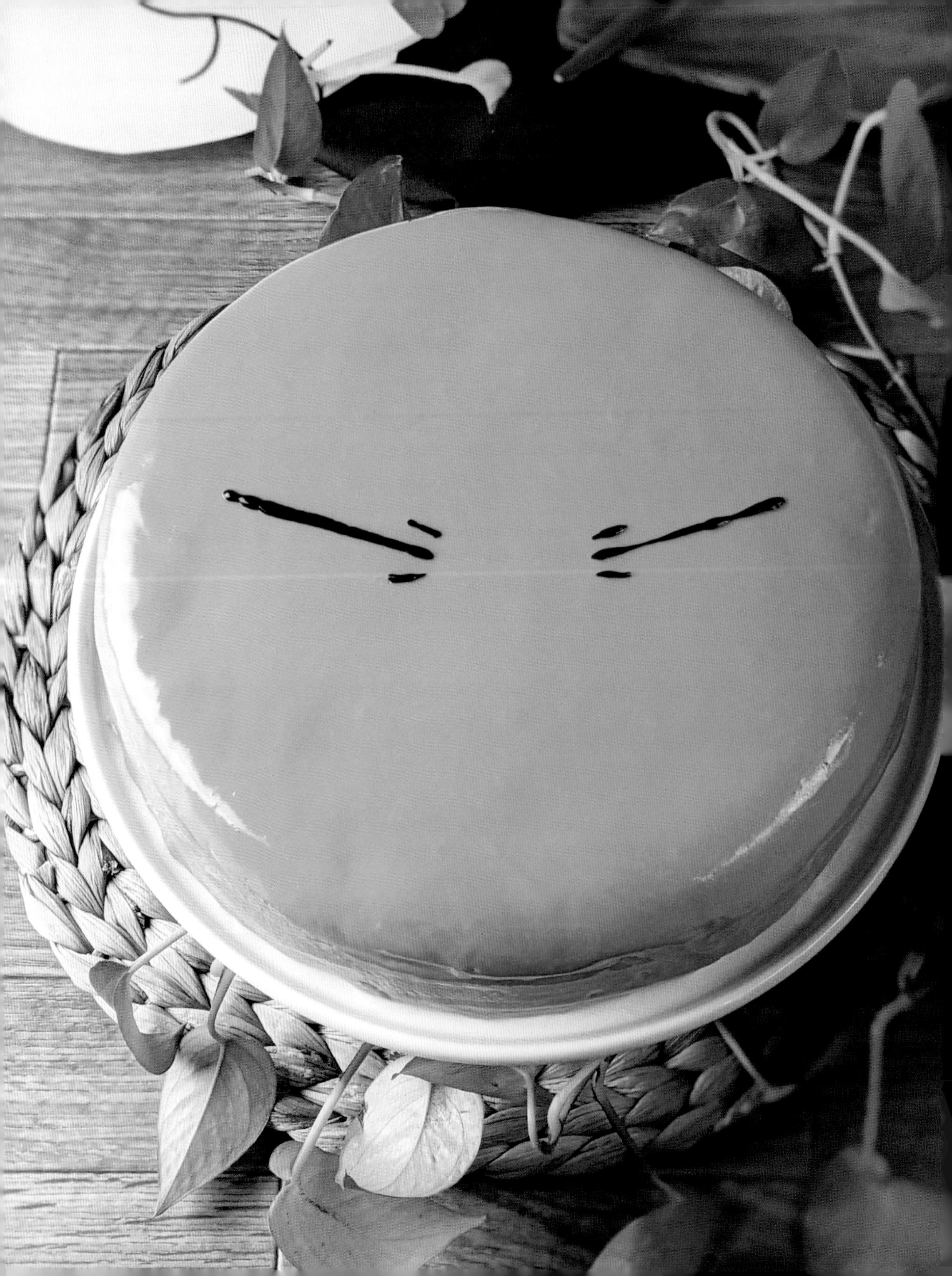

16. Tip the hot milk mixture out over the white chocolate. Let stand for 3 to 5 minutes, until the chocolate has softened and partially melted, then whisk until the chocolate has melted completely and the glaze is well combined.

17. Transfer 2 tablespoons of the glaze to a small bowl bowl and tint with black food coloring. To the rest of the glaze, add as much blue food coloring as you'd like, mixing it in thoroughly. Rimuru is pale blue, so start lightly. I found the white chocolate I used left the blue looking a little green, but a half drop of red food coloring helped correct this. Strain the blue glaze through a fine-mesh sieve to remove air bubbles, then set aside.

18. Set a wire rack over a baking sheet or a large sheet of aluminum foil to catch any drips of glaze. Flip a bowl upside down and place it on the rack. Unmold the frozen cake and place it on a cake board that fits neatly underneath the cake with no exposed edges, then set the cake and cake board on top of the bowl.

19. If the blue glaze has cooled too much to pour (it should be around 95°F), reheat it in the microwave in 30-second bursts, stirring after each, until it reaches around 100°F. Quickly and cleanly pour the glaze over the top of the cake. Pour the glaze into the center of the cake and spiral outward so the glaze spills over the sides, making sure to get smooth coverage over the sides of the cake. The glaze will begin to set on contact, so don't dawdle! Smooth away the drips along the bottom of the cake.

20. Transfer the black glaze to a pastry bag fitted with a small round tip. Pipe out two lines for the eyes that gently slope upward, then make the eye crease by adding a short line above and below the inner edge of the longer eye line for each eye.

21. Place the cake on a serving dish and refrigerate for an hour to allow the glaze to fully set before serving. Cut into slices and enjoy!

SOOT BALL BRIGADEIROS

Appearing in both *Spirited Away* and *Totoro*, these little sprites can be found in dusty spots around your house. In *Spirited Away*, the soots live with the Boiler Man, Kamaji, who keeps the bathhouse he works in running.

Chihiro is initially frightened by the spirits. But Kamaji urges her to feed them their favorite treat—konpeito, or star candies—and Chihiro warms up to the little creatures as the soots rejoice. Kamaji keeps the sprites busy: without a job to do, they turn back to soot. Our brigadeiros won't turn to soot, but they *will* disappear quickly once you make them, so consider doubling the recipe.

1 HOUR

MAKES 12 BRIGADEIROS

SPECIAL EQUIPMENT: FOOD COLORING MARKER (BLACK)

GLUTEN-FREE, NUT-FREE

7 ounces sweetened condensed milk

2 tablespoons unsweetened Dutch-process cocoa powder

1 tablespoon unsalted butter

Black food coloring

Black sprinkles

Candy eyes, or white chocolate chips and a black food coloring marker

Konpeito (Japanese sugar candy), for decoration (optional)

1. Combine the condensed milk, cocoa powder, butter, and about ½ teaspoon black food coloring in a pot on the stovetop. Cook over medium-high heat, stirring continuously to avoid burning, until the mixture has thickened, 3 to 5 minutes. Pour the condensed milk mixture onto a plate and allow to cool to room temperature.

2. Pour the sprinkles into a bowl. Use a spoon to grab a gob of the condensed milk mixture, then roll it into a ball between your hands. Roll this ball in the black sprinkles to coat, then set aside. Repeat with the rest of the condensed milk mixture.

3. If you're using candy eyes, press them into the balls close together. If you're making eyes, press two white chocolate chips into the brigadeiro and finish by adding a pupil to each with a food coloring marker. If you've purchased konpeito, place them around the soot sprites.

4. Eat within a week and enjoy!

RECIPE TIP:
The black food coloring in the brigadeiro is simply to help them look a little darker under the sprinkles, but if you'd prefer to omit it, you can.

FOOD FACT:
Brigadeiros are Brazilian in origin, which might seem like a random choice for an anime cookbook. However, Brazil features one of the largest communities of Japanese descendants in the world outside of Japan!

MINI KITTY TARTS

Hello Kitty, also affectionately known as Kitty-chan, is one of the most iconic Japanese characters. Her image has spread to anime, manga, games, theme parks, and more. Beloved for her cute appearance, she's meant to be a friend for the people—there to support you no matter what.

To depict this beloved and trendy kitty, I opted for a Japanese treat with matching characteristics: the Hokkaido cheese tart. This treat is a mild, creamy cheese tart encased in a crunchy outer shell. These have become very popular in Japan and for good reason—they're addictive. Plus, the white cheese filling is the perfect backdrop for Hello Kitty's face.

3 TO 4 HOURS

MAKES EIGHT 2-INCH TARTS

SPECIAL EQUIPMENT: EIGHT 2-INCH EGG TART MOLDS, INFRARED THERMOMETER, PASTRY BAG

NUT-FREE

RECIPE TIPS:
Don't feel like making tart shells? You can find them online or in baking stores.

Don't want to decorate the tarts? Refrain from smoothing the cheese filling out and instead simply brush the tops with egg wash (whisk an egg with a tablespoon of water) before they go in the oven to give them an attractive browned appearance when they come out.

FOR THE TART SHELL

1½ cups all-purpose flour, plus more for dusting, if needed

Pinch of kosher salt

½ cup (1 stick) unsalted butter, at room temperature

¾ cup confectioners' sugar

1 large egg

1 teaspoon vanilla extract

FOR THE CHEESE FILLING

5 ounces cream cheese

2 ounces mascarpone cheese

¼ cup grated Parmesan cheese

⅓ cup whole milk

2 tablespoons unsalted butter

⅓ cup confectioners' sugar

1½ tablespoons cornstarch

1 large egg, at room temperature

1 tablespoon fresh lemon juice

¼ teaspoon vanilla extract

Pinch of kosher salt

FOR THE DECORATION

Black, red, and yellow fondant, or an assortment of black and yellow sprinkles

A red chewy candy or fondant, for the bow

1. Make the tart shells: Whisk together the flour and salt in a small bowl to combine. Be sure to remove any lumps.

2. Combine the butter and sugar in a large bowl and beat with an electric mixer until smooth and light. Scrape down the sides of the bowl with a rubber spatula, then add the egg and vanilla. Mix again to incorporate, scraping down the sides as you go. Add the flour all at once and mix on low speed until just combined.

3. Turn the dough out onto a sheet of plastic wrap and press it into a disc shape. Wrap the dough in the plastic wrap and refrigerate for at least an hour and up to 3 days.

Continued

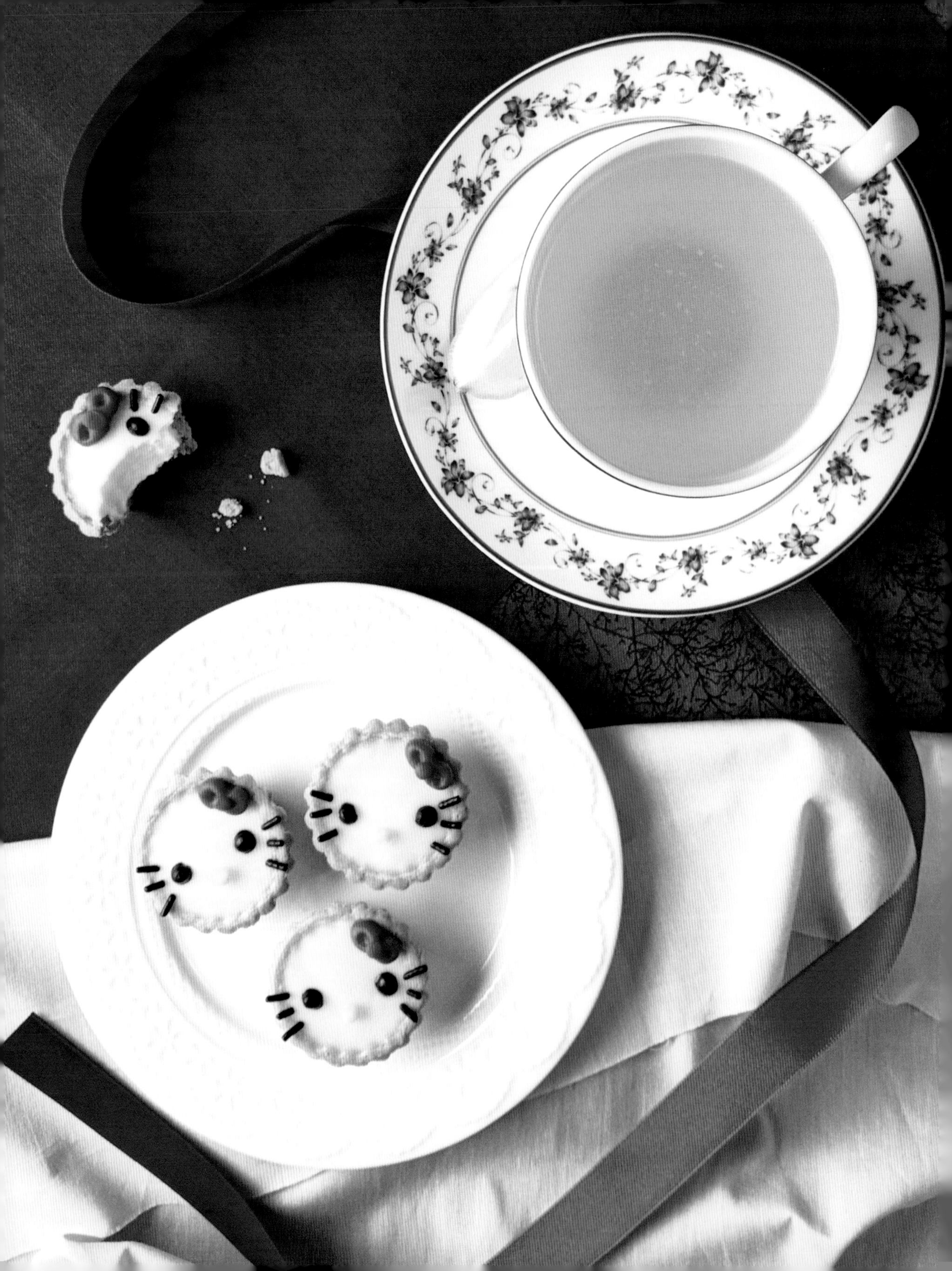

4. Make the cheese filling: Fill a pot with 3 inches of water and bring to a boil over high heat. Combine the cream cheese, mascarpone, Parmesan, milk, and butter in a tempered glass or metal bowl. Place the bowl over the pot to make a bain-marie (make sure the bottom of the bowl does not touch the water), reduce the heat to medium-high, and allow the cheeses to melt, stirring occasionally. While you wait, whisk together the confectioners' sugar and cornstarch in a small bowl. Prepare the other filling ingredients while you wait for the cheese to melt.

5. When the cheese has melted, add the confectioners' sugar and cornstarch a little at a time, whisking to bring everything together, then cook, whisking continuously, until the mixture has thickened to a pudding-like consistency. Add the egg and lemon juice and whisk briskly to incorporate, then cook, stirring the cheese as it thickens, until it reaches 150°F. Remove the bowl from the pot and whisk in the vanilla, then taste and add salt if needed. Strain the mixture through a fine-mesh sieve into a bowl to remove lingering lumps. Cover with plastic wrap, pressing it directly against the surface of the cheese mixture to prevent a skin from forming, and refrigerate until cool, at least an hour.

6. Preheat the oven to 350°F.

7. Roll out the tart dough between two sheets of parchment paper to a thickness of ⅛ inch, dusting with flour as necessary to stop sticking. Cut rounds of dough that are about ½ inch bigger than the tart molds. Press the dough into each mold and prick the bottoms with a fork to prevent bubbling. Place the tart shells on a baking sheet so they're easy to maneuver into and out of the oven. Bake for 10 minutes, or until the tart shell is golden brown all over. Remove from the oven and allow to cool before filling. Raise the oven temperature to 450°F.

8. Transfer the cheese mixture to a pastry bag. Cut the tip of the bag, then pipe a generous amount of filling into each tart shell. Use a small palette knife (or the back of a butter knife) to smooth and flatten the tops. Bake for 6 minutes, then remove and allow to cool completely.

9. Decorate the tarts: I used fondant, but sprinkles can work. Use two large round black sprinkles for the eyes, a small yellow sprinkle for the nose, and black sprinkles for the whiskers. For the bow, use red fondant or a moldable red candy: Roll it into a pill shape and use the pointy end of a chopstick to press a dot into the candy at either end, then use the pointy end of two chopsticks to pinch in the middle of the bow. Finally, roll a little ball of red fondant or candy into a circle and place it over the pinched middle of the bow. Serve and enjoy.

FREE! IWATOBI SWIM CLUB

FROSTED ANIMAL COOKIES

Gifted swimmer Haruka reunites with his childhood rival, Rin, inspiring Haruka to start swimming again. Haruka gets two friends from the team he was on as a child to form a new swim team, but there's still one problem: in order to be an official school club, they need at least four members. Enter Rei—a man who idolizes athletic feats of beauty. Initially, he thought swimming to be inelegant, but after watching Haruka, he's persuaded to try the butterfly stroke.

As the boys work together, their friendship and their skills grow. Each character has an animal that represents them: Haruka is a dolphin, Nagisa is a penguin, Makoto is a killer whale, and Rei is a butterfly. Rin, of course, is a shark. These are all cute animals that are perfect in sugar cookie form. Frosting cookies is a relaxing afternoon activity. While the boys battle it out at the pool, you can sit back and go to town decorating these cookies.

3 TO 4 HOURS

MAKES 15 COOKIES

SPECIAL EQUIPMENT: **COOKIE CUTTERS OR TEMPLATES, PASTRY BAGS AND PIPING TIPS**

NUT-FREE

FOR THE ANIMAL COOKIES

2 cups all-purpose flour

½ teaspoon kosher salt

½ teaspoon baking powder

½ teaspoon ground cardamom

½ cup (1 stick) unsalted butter, at room temperature

¾ cup granulated sugar

¼ cup corn syrup or honey

Grated zest of 1 orange

1 teaspoon vanilla extract

1 large egg, at room temperature

1 to 2 teaspoons whole milk, as needed

FOR THE ROYAL ICING

8 cups confectioners' sugar

½ cup plus 2 tablespoons meringue powder

1 teaspoon kosher salt

2 teaspoons vanilla extract

¾ cup water

Black, blue, pink, orange, yellow, and purple food coloring

3 to 4 tablespoons unsweetened cocoa powder

1. Make the animal cookies: Combine the flour, salt, baking powder, and cardamom in a bowl. Whisk to combine and to knock any lumps of flour out of existence.

2. Put the butter in a separate bowl and beat with an electric mixer until light and fluffy. Add the granulated sugar and beat to incorporate, then pour in the corn syrup and beat until you have a butter-sugar paste. Add the orange zest, vanilla, and egg and beat to incorporate.

3. Pour in the flour mixture all at once and mix until you have a slightly sticky paste. If you find the dough is too dry, add the milk 1 teaspoon at a time. Turn the dough out onto a sheet of plastic wrap and form it into a disc. Wrap the dough in the plastic wrap, then chill it in the refrigerator for an hour.

Continued

DECORATING TIPS:
When using a pastry bag, make sure you twist the top shut to stop the icing from escaping, and when you squeeze, use firm, even pressure. To stop icing from coming out of the tip, especially when it's runny, simply tilt the tip upward. Or, if you're actively piping the icing out, ease off on squeezing the bag that the flow of icing slows and elevate the tip as quickly as possible. If you're nervous about getting the design right, try tracing it out on the cookie with a food coloring marker to make adding the icing even easier.

Scared your cookies will come out looking wonky? Consider drawing the lines and details of the animal onto the unfrosted cookie with a food coloring marker and going over them with the icing.

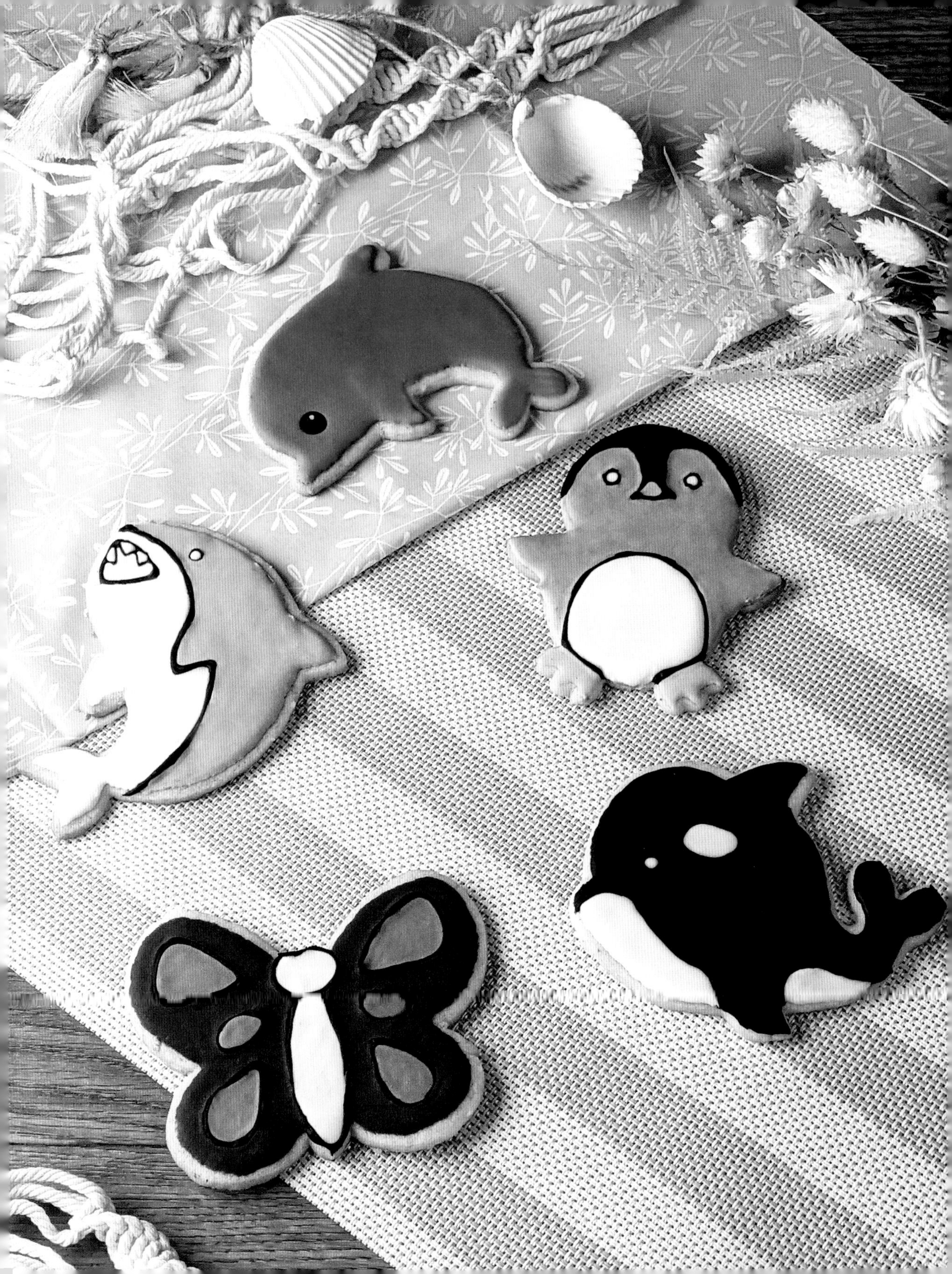

4. In the meantime, print and cut out cookie templates, or make your own.

5. Halve the dough and set one half aside. Cut a sheet of parchment paper big enough to line a baking sheet. Lightly flour your work surface and the surface of the dough, then roll the dough into a sheet that's roughly ¼-inch thick, moving the dough around to prevent it from sticking as you work. Shift the dough onto the parchment and use cookie cutters or templates to cut out cookies. If you're using templates, trace around the edge of the template with the tip of a knife. Remove the excess dough, leaving the cookies on the parchment, and slide the parchment onto a baking sheet. Chill the cookies in the refrigerator for 30 minutes and up to 3 hours. Repeat with the remaining dough.

6. Preheat the oven to 350°F.

7. Bake the cookies for 10 to 12 minutes, until the bottoms are golden brown. Allow the cookies to cool completely on the baking sheet, then transfer them to a wire rack. Repeat with the remaining dough.

8. Make the royal icing: Using a hand or stand mixer, combine the confectioners' sugar, meringue powder, and salt in a large bowl. Pour in the vanilla, then add the water 1 tablespoon at a time, mixing it through until you get a thick paste.

9. Split the icing into eight small bowls. First, portion off a third of the royal icing into the biggest bowl for the black icing. Then add two heaping tablespoons of icing each to three separate smaller bowls for the yellow, orange, and pink colors. Split the rest of the icing evenly among four medium bowls. Then add the food coloring: leave one bowl plain white, but mix a few drops of food coloring into the other bowls to achieve your desired shades of gray, blue, and purple frostings. The purple frosting is a little special; start by making the icing a light purple, and then after you've used some of it for the lighter spots on the butterfly, darken the remaining icing for the rest of the wings. For the black icing, first mix in cocoa powder to darken the frosting naturally, then add black dye to achieve a true black.

10. Decorate the cookies: Transfer the black icing to a pastry bag fitted with a small round tip. Outline each animal's features in black, including the outlines of the entire animal and the inner details. Where two inner edges meet—for example, the inner white and gray edges of the shark—use one black line to create the border between color sections.

11. Once your outlines are done, thin all the remaining icings with water until similar in consistency to chocolate syrup. Pipe frosting in the right color into the blank spaces on each cookie. Go slow and steady—it's easy to plop a bunch of icing down, but can be messy to clean up if you make a mistake. Use a toothpick to help even out the icing and nudge it into corners.

12. Refrigerate for at least 3 to 4 hours, but preferably overnight, to set the icing completely. Store in an airtight container for up to a week.

Here are the color breakdowns for each animal:

Dolphin: blue and black

Orca: black and white

Shark: gray, white, and pink

Penguin: black, gray, white, and orange

Butterfly: Light purple, dark purple, black, and yellow

PANNA COTTA GOLDFISH CUPS

Ponyo is a magic little fish who wants to be human. After straying from her father's submarine, she meets a boy named Sōsuke who's overjoyed when she uses her father's magic to turn herself human. Sōsuke eagerly introduces Ponyo to his mom. Unbeknownst to them, Ponyo's use of her father's magic has created a chaotic imbalance in the world, and unless the balance is corrected, devastation will reign!

As Sōsuke and Ponyo set out on a journey to restore balance, they encounter a world that's been transformed. The ocean has risen to their very doorstep, and the island's landscape has changed drastically. This doesn't diminish their excitement—they set out with all the good cheer of well-fed children, ready to take on the world. To capture this fun, childish feeling, this dessert references your favorite childhood snack with cute details that look striking and taste great.

3 TO 4 HOURS

MAKES 6 CUPS

SPECIAL EQUIPMENT:
6 MATCHING GLASS CUPS, GOLDFISH COOKIE CUTTERS

GLUTEN-FREE, NUT-FREE

RECIPE TIP:
It's important to be patient. Wait till everything is cool or room temperature at the least, or you run the risk of melting already-set elements.

FOR THE GOLDFISH CUTOUTS

2½ teaspoons unflavored powdered gelatin

½ cup orange Jell-O mix

1⅓ cups water

FOR THE PANNA COTTA & JELL-O

2½ teaspoons unflavored powdered gelatin

3 tablespoons room-temperature water

1½ cups half-and-half

⅓ cup sugar

Pinch of kosher salt

1 teaspoon vanilla extract

1½ cups heavy cream

½ cup blue Jell-O mix

1. Make the goldfish cutouts: Whisk together the gelatin and orange Jell-O mix in a bowl. Bring the water to a boil in a small pot, then turn off the heat and whisk in the Jell-O mixture, stirring until the gelatin has completely dissolved.

2. Line a baking sheet with parchment paper. Spread spoonfuls of the orange Jell-O liquid out into ⅛-inch layer, then add the Jell-O to the refrigerator to chill. (You'll have extra orange Jell-O, which you can pour into a separate container and enjoy later.)

3. Make the panna cotta: Pour the water into a small bowl and sprinkle the gelatin over the top. Stir the gelatin into the water and allow to bloom for 3 to 5 minutes, until the gelatin has absorbed all the water.

4. Combine the half-and-half, sugar, vanilla, and salt in a pot and set it over low heat. Don't bring this to a simmer—just heat it so that it steams. Turn off the heat and add the bloomed

Continued

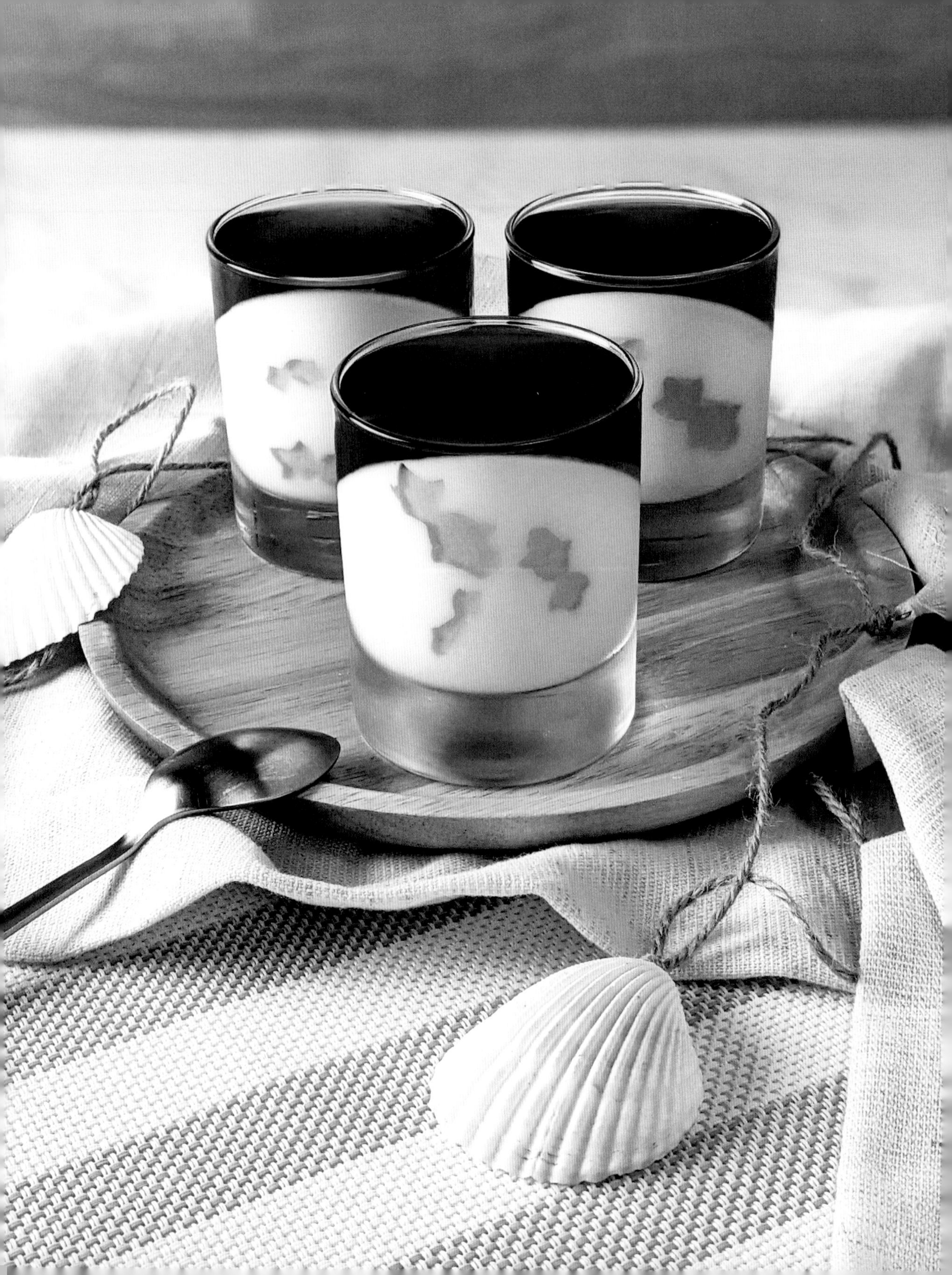

gelatin. Whisk until the gelatin completely melts into the milk mixture, then add the heavy cream. Refrigerate the custard, stirring every 10 minutes, until it's cool to the touch.

5. Arrange six glass cups on your work surface. Cut out the Jell-O fish (you can choose the size and number you want), then gently peel away the excess Jell-O. Lift one fish with a small, flexible spatula, then gently press the fish inside one of the cups, wherever you like. Gently tap the fish down to the inside of the glass, making sure the edges are sealed against the cup and that there are no air bubbles. Repeat for all the cups.

6. Set the cups at an angle inside the wells of a cupcake pan to hold them steady. When the custard is cool to the touch but still liquid, pour it into the cups around the fish in a small arc. Use a spoon to break the fall of the custard so it isn't pouring directly onto the fish. Pour the custard until the fish are covered, then carefully transfer the filled cups to the refrigerator to chill until the panna cotta has set, 3 to 4 hours.

7. Make the blue Jell-O according to the package instructions, then allow the Jell-O liquid to cool to room temperature.

8. Take the cups out of the cupcake pan and set them on your work surface. Fill the rest of the cup with the room-temperature blue Jell-O. Refrigerate the cups until the blue Jell-O has set, then serve chilled.

SILVER SPOON

PIGGY ICE CREAM MOCHI

When Yuugo Hachiken gets the opportunity to apply to a new high school, he decides to move as far away from home as possible. He picks a school where he assumes the workload will be lighter—Ooezo Agricultural High School in Hokkaido. Of course, nothing is ever as easy as it seems, and Yuugo quickly finds that this school is much different from how he assumed it'd be. For starters, he's assigned a pig to raise. Then he learns that this pig will eventually be slaughtered and processed for meat and other products. For a city kid like Yuugo, this comes as a shock. He has to grapple with the fact that he can't save every animal at the school from imminent death, and names his pig Pork Bowl as a reminder of what it'll one day become.

Luckily for us, we don't have to endure the work and chores Yuugo does, but we can still eat Pork Bowl (figuratively, of course). For this recipe, we'll combine mochi, ice cream, and candy to make adorable little ice cream mochi piglets, made in memory of Yuugo's Pork Bowl.

3 TO 4 HOURS

MAKES 12 PIECES

SPECIAL EQUIPMENT: ½-OUNCE COOKIE SCOOP, FOOD COLORING MARKER (BLACK)

GLUTEN-FREE, NUT-FREE

Ice cream of your choice (I went with strawberry to match the pink theme)

¾ cup shiratamako (sweet rice flour)

¾ cup sugar

¼ cup water

Pink food coloring

Cornstarch, for dusting

8 to 10 pink Starburst candies, for decorating

1. Let the ice cream soften slightly, then scoop 12 cookie-scoop-size balls of ice cream (about 1 tablespoon each). Place these scoops on a chilled plate or put them each in their own cupcake liner to keep them separate. Freeze the scoops until hard.

2. Whisk together the shiratamako and sugar in a microwave-safe bowl to combine, then add the water and 2 drops of food coloring. Whisk until you have a uniform liquid. Drape the top of the bowl with plastic wrap and microwave on high for 1 minute. Dampen a rubber spatula, then stir the mochi with it. Cover and microwave on high for 1 minute more, then stir. Finally, microwave in 30-second bursts, stirring after each, until the mochi takes on a translucent quality.

3. Dust a sheet of parchment paper with cornstarch. Turn the mochi out onto the parchment and sprinkle the top with more cornstarch. Allow the mochi to cool until you can handle it, then roll it into a thin sheet. Use cornstarch as needed to help prevent sticking. Slide the parchment onto a baking sheet, then chill the mochi in the refrigerator for 15 minutes.

4. Use a 2-inch round cutter to cut out 12 mochi rounds. Remove one ball of ice cream from the freezer, leaving the others until you need them, and place it in the center of a mochi round. Bring two opposite sides of the mochi up and over the ice cream, then pinch them together firmly to seal. Repeat with the other opposing edges. Keep pulling and pinching to tighten the mochi around the ice cream to enclose it and seal it in the mochi. Smooth the mochi with your fingers if the round has become a little misshapen and smooth the top to have a slightly flat surface. Place the finished mochi in the freezer and repeat to fill the remaining mochi.

DECORATING TIP: If you want more of a 3D effect with the ears and for them to pop off the mochi, you'll have to glue the candy to the mochi with a little chocolate or something that hardens solid when frozen.

STORAGE TIP: These will keep in an zip-top storage bag in the freezer for 2 to 3 weeks.

5. Unwrap the Starbursts, set them on a microwave-safe plate, and microwave for 5 seconds. Testing carefully to make sure they're not going to burn you (please be careful—these can hurt if you microwave them too long), squish all the candies together and knead them into a pliable ball. Thinly roll out the candy on parchment paper. Cut out 12 ovals for the snouts and 24 little triangle ears. I used cookie cutters for this, but you could easily use a boba straw pinched into an oval for the nose. Use a toothpick to poke two holes in each snout.

6. When the mochi are frozen solid, quickly add the noses and ears. We aren't using anything to glue the candy to the mochi, so just lay the ears on the top edges of the mochi and the snout near the middle. Draw eyes on the mochi with a food coloring marker and enjoy.

YURI!!! ON ICE

CHOCO-BERRY KAKIGORI

Kakigori is a popular summer treat in Japan. The soft, fluffy cousin of the hard-crusted snow cone, kakigori is made of shaved ice topped with a syrup, sweetened condensed milk, fruit, and dessert bites. It also frequently appears in anime, so what would an anime cookbook be without a kakigori recipe? And what better anime is there to pair with shaved ice than *Yuri!!! on Ice*, a show about competitive male figure skating?

Yuri, a figure skater who's faced defeat one too many times, takes a break from his career to question his decision to compete. In a stroke of luck, a routine he performs for fun is brought to the attention of his figure skating idol, Viktor, who agrees to coach him. Viktor's dog, Makkachin, is a frequent companion to the idol and a welcome addition to the team as Yuri scoops up win after win on his journey to the Grand Prix Final.

I took inspiration from the show's colors and theming in the syrup and chocolate decor and the little chocolate Makkachin is an easy and cute decoration to add on top. Whatever you choose, enjoy this on a warm summer's day. While Yuri's run on the ice gets hot and steamy, this icy treat will cool you right off!

3 TO 4 HOURS

MAKES 1 BOWL

SPECIAL EQUIPMENT: **INFRARED THERMOMETER, FOOD-SAFE PAINTBRUSH (OR PASTRY BRUSH), SHAVED ICE MACHINE, SNOWFLAKE MOLD**

GLUTEN-FREE, NUT-FREE, VEGAN (DEPENDING ON THE CHOCOLATE OF CHOICE)

FOR THE DECORATIONS

2 ounces white chocolate, chopped

1 ounce milk chocolate, chopped

Black circle sprinkles

1 ounce milk chocolate square

Pearl luster dust

5 to 7 blueberries

3 to 4 raspberries

FOR THE SHAVED ICE

2 to 3 cups ice

3 to 4 tablespoons blue shaved ice syrup

2 to 3 tablespoons condensed milk

1. Prepare the toppings: Set aside a few chunks of the white chocolate and place the rest in a microwave-safe bowl. Microwave in 30-second bursts, stirring after each, until the chocolate is melted.

2. Stir the melted chocolate until the temperature falls to 95°F, then add the reserved chocolate pieces and stir until the chocolate cools to 87°F. Tip the melted white chocolate onto a snowflake mold. Scrape any excess chocolate off the top of the mold and allow to set, about 15 minutes.

3. Repeat step 1, melting the chopped milk chocolate and reserving a few pieces of that for tempering. When it hits 95°F, add the reserved chocolate pieces and stir until the melted chocolate cools to 87°F. Transfer the chocolate to a small plastic bag and snip off a small corner. Pipe a poodle face (a half circle for the head, two little circles for the nose and mouth, and two long ears) onto parchment paper or a silicone baking mat. Use a toothpick to even out the chocolate distribution as needed, then add sprinkles for the eyes and mouth. Shave the remaining un-chopped milk chocolate with a zester over the top of the puppy. Using the toothpick, gently clear off the eyes and nose. Allow to set completely, about 15 minutes.

RECIPE TIP:
If you don't want to futz around with tempering chocolate, simply melt candy coating wafers to get the same effect. Just follow the package instructions to melt the chocolate properly.

FOOD FACT:
Like many older Japanese sweets, kakigori was once a treat reserved for the elite due to the ephemeral nature of its main ingredient. The ice was harvested in winter and stored until summer, when it was shaved by hand and topped with sweet syrups.

4. Pop the white chocolate snowflakes out of the mold and use a dry, clean paintbrush to apply luster dust to the snowflakes to give them a shine. Do the same for the berries you've selected for the bowl.

5. Shave a bowl of ice, then anoint it with the blue shaved ice syrup and a little condensed milk. Decorate with the snowflakes, the berries, and the little doggy. Enjoy immediately!

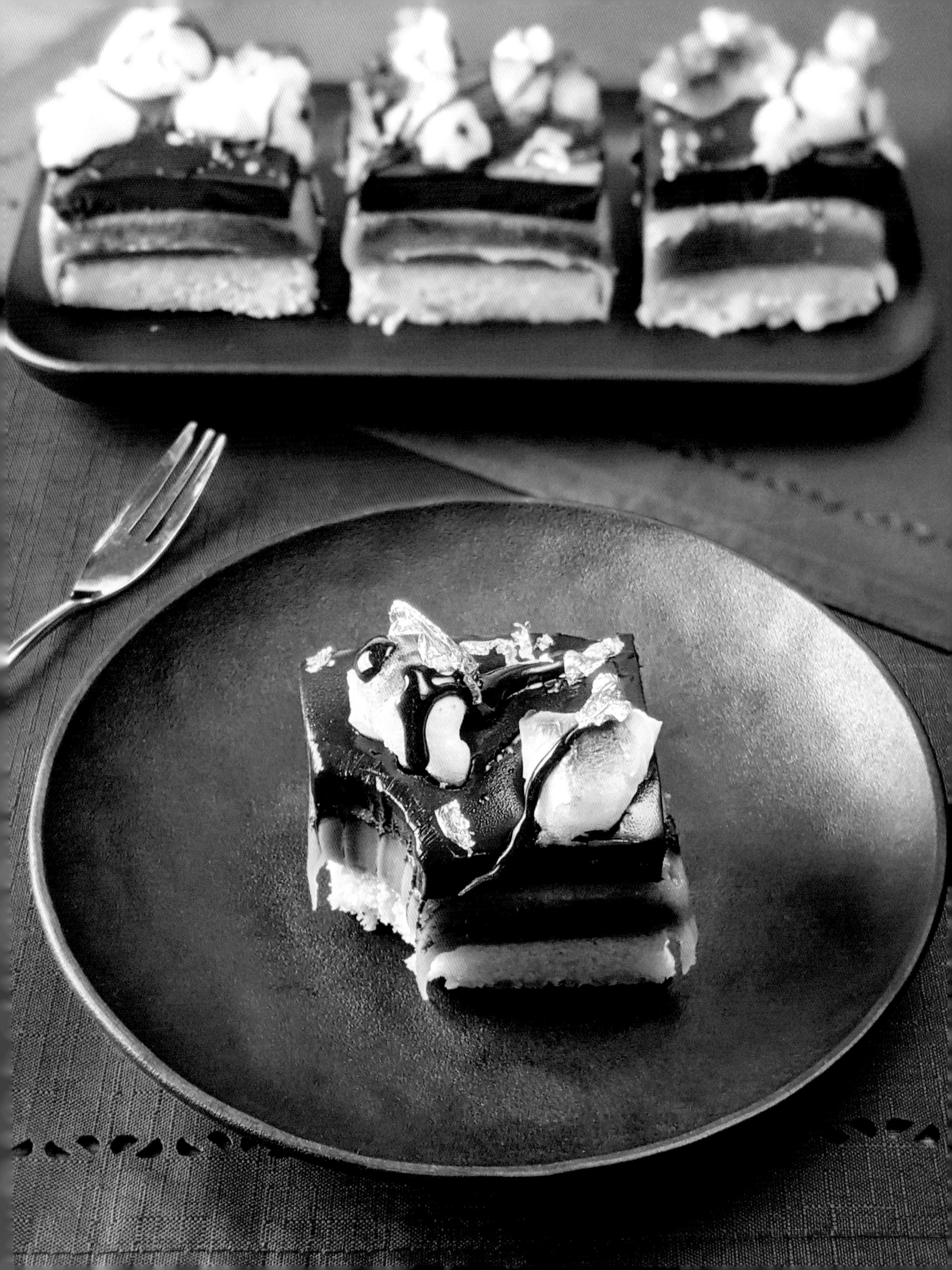

MILLIONAIRE'S SHORTBREAD

When Edamura looks for a job so he can financially support his sick mother, he lands at a company that engages in fraudulent activities. This leads to him going to jail for his involvement! Unable to find honest work after his release, he becomes a full-time con artist, joining a team of professionals to scam some of the richest people in the world. In the anime, we watch as Edamura engages in his first risky con—selling a new "drug" (which is actually candy) to a Los Angeles tycoon. The question is: Will he become a millionaire?

This dessert will make *you* feel like a millionaire. With its decadent layers of shortbread, caramel, and ganache, this dessert is indulgence itself. I've added puffed rice cakes for crunch, a kuromitsu drizzle for complexity, and real gold leaf for the blinged-out sensation. The result is the perfect marriage of Western and Japanese flavors, and it's mouth-wateringly delicious.

3 TO 4 HOURS

SERVES 10

SPECIAL EQUIPMENT: INFRARED THERMOMETER, FOOD-SAFE PAINTBRUSH (OR PASTRY BRUSH)

NUT-FREE

RECIPE TIP:
Can't find kirimochi? Try marshmallows instead for a similar visual effect, or a puffed-rice cereal for a sort-of-similar-tasting substitute.

FOR THE SHORTBREAD BASE
1 cup (2 sticks) unsalted butter, at room temperature

⅓ cup granulated sugar

⅓ cup packed dark brown sugar

1 large egg yolk

¾ teaspoon vanilla extract

½ teaspoon kosher salt

2¼ cups all-purpose flour

FOR THE MORINAGA MILK CARAMEL LAYER
2 cups packed light brown sugar

1 cup (2 sticks) unsalted butter

1 cup kuromitsu (black sugar syrup)

2 tablespoons corn syrup

14 ounces sweetened condensed milk

1 teaspoon kosher salt

1 teaspoon vanilla extract

FOR THE CHOCOLATE GANACHE LAYER
2 cups chopped dark chocolate

½ cup heavy cream

Pinch of kosher salt

FOR THE TOPPINGS
4 blocks of kirimochi (Japanese rice cake)

½ cup kuromitsu (black sugar syrup)

Edible gold leaf

1. Preheat the oven to 350°F. Line the bottom of an 8-inch square baking pan with parchment paper cut to fit.

2. Make the shortbread base: Using an electric mixer, beat the butter in a bowl on high speed until light and fluffy. Add both sugars and beat until combined. Add the egg yolk, vanilla, and salt and beat until smooth.

Continued

3. Pour in the flour all at once and mix until you have a thick dough. Tip the dough into the prepared pan and press it into a even layer with a rubber spatula. To make it perfectly flat, place a square of parchment over the top of the dough and use your hands to smooth its surface, then peel off the square of parchment. Bake for 40 minutes, or until golden brown. Allow to cool completely.

4. Make the Morinaga milk caramel layer: Combine the brown sugar, butter, kuromitsu, and corn syrup in a heavy-bottomed pot. Bring to a boil over medium heat, stirring continuously, and cook until the butter melts and the ingredients are incorporated. Reduce the heat to low and stir in the condensed milk. Sprinkle in the salt, then stir until completely combined. Allow the caramel to bubble away until it reaches 235°F to 240°F, then remove the pot from the heat and stir in the vanilla. Pour the caramel over the cooled shortbread and allow to set and cool, about 1 hour.

5. Make the chocolate ganache layer: Put the chocolate in a bowl. Pour the heavy cream into a microwave-safe bowl and microwave until hot to the touch, about 1 minute. Pour the cream over the chocolate so that as much of the chocolate is submerged as possible. Let stand for 2 to 3 minutes, then stir until the chocolate has melted and the ganache is smooth. If there are any remaining lumps of chocolate, microwave the ganache in 15-second bursts, stirring well after each, until melted. Stir in the salt, then allow the ganache to cool and thicken for 5 minutes. Pour the ganache over the cooled caramel layer, then set aside.

6. Make the toppings: Preheat the broiler. Line a baking sheet with aluminum foil.

7. Cut the kirimochi into small cubes spread them over the prepared baking sheet. Toast them under the broiler for 2 to 3 minutes, until puffed and browned on top. Allow them to cool slightly, then sprinkle them over the top of the ganache, pressing them down gently to help them stick. Chill in the refrigerator for 30 minutes.

8. Bring the kuromitsu to a simmer in a small pot and bring it to a simmer over medium heat. Simmer until the syrup has reduced by half so it's thick and looks like molasses, 3 to 5 minutes. Remove from the heat and allow to cool slightly, then drizzle the kuromitsu over the kirimochi layer.

9. To serve, run a knife around the edges of the pan to loosen the layers from the sides. Tip the whole thing out onto a cutting board and remove the parchment. Cut into bars and use a clean paintbrush to lift pieces of gold leaf off the protective paper and float them artfully over the bars, touching it to any spot that looks like it needs a hint of gold.

THE RISING OF THE SHIELD HERO

MELTY CHOCOLATE BOMB

Naofumi wasn't expecting to be summoned to a parallel reality, and he certainly wasn't expecting to be declared one of the Cardinal Heroes! He's given a Legendary Shield and sent out to protect his new kingdom, but then his only companion robs him and falsely accuses him of committing a crime. Unable to return to his original world and stuck with his Legendary Shield and a bad reputation, Naofumi has no choice but to protect himself from his newfound enemies.

Of course, not everyone hates him. Naofumi slowly grows a coterie of friends who assist him on his journey. One of these friends, Melty Q. Melromarc, is a noble and next in line for the throne. While Melty is young, she's talented and fun-loving. What I love best about her is her name. Happily, it translates well into dessert! I wanted to make the most over-the-top dessert possible to match Melty's ruffly clothes and elaborate hair. This gooey chocolate bomb is both melty and magical, because as you pour chocolate over the top, a secret is revealed. . . .

1 HOUR

MAKES 1 BOMB

SPECIAL EQUIPMENT:
INFRARED THERMOMETER, SILICONE SPHERE MOLD

GLUTEN-FREE, NUT-FREE

RECIPE TIP:
Tempering chocolate seems like so much effort, but it's worth it. If you don't, the chocolate will never fully set and you won't get the effect you want.

FOR THE MODELING CHOCOLATE (OPTIONAL)

12 ounces chocolate candy coating wafers, such as Candy Melts

¼ cup light corn syrup

FOR THE CHOCOLATE BOMB

2 ounces good-quality milk chocolate, chopped

¾ cup heavy cream

4 ounces dark chocolate, chopped

Blueberries

Treat of choice (brownie, cake, or cheesecake [pictured])

Strawberry jam

1. Make the modeling chocolate (if using): Place the candy coating wafers in a microwave-safe bowl and microwave in 30-second intervals, stirring after each, until most of the chocolate has melted, then microwave for 10-second stints, stirring after each, until completely melted and smooth. The melted chocolate should be warm but not hot. If the bowl feels hot to the touch, transfer to chocolate to a new bowl to stop it from scorching from the residual heat.

2. Pour in the corn syrup and stir with a rubber spatula. Scrape carefully all around the bowl, making sure all the chocolate [illegible] in contact with the corn syrup. Don't overmix—stop as soon as the corn syrup looks mostly incorporated and the mixture has started to cling together rather than to the sides of the bowl. It should look wet and the consistency should be similar to soft-serve ice cream. Pour the mixture into a zip-top plastic bag, squeeze the air out, seal, and store in a cool, dry location overnight to harden.

3. Make the chocolate bomb: Place a sheet of parchment paper on your work surface. Set aside one-quarter of the milk chocolate and place the rest in a microwave-safe bowl. Microwave in 30-second bursts, stirring after each, until the chocolate is melted.

Continued

4. Stir the melted milk chocolate until it cools to 97°F, then add two chunks of the reserved chocolate and stir vigorously to cool the chocolate down to 87°F. If the milk chocolate chunks melt completely into the mix before it reaches 87°F, add more pieces and keep stirring.

5. Tip the melted chocolate into the halves of the sphere mold and roll it around to coat the inside of each, all the way up to the top. Tip the excess chocolate back into the bowl and place the molds upside down on the parchment to set. This will encourage more draining and will thicken the top walls of the mold. When the first layer of chocolate has set, repeat to add a second coat to both halves of the mold and let set. You may need to melt and temper the chocolate again to get it back to a workable consistency and temperature.

6. When the chocolate in the molds has completely set, pop the half spheres out and set them aside in a cool-room-temperature spot.

7. Place the heavy cream in a microwave-safe bowl and microwave until hot to the touch, about 1 minute. Add the dark chocolate and let stand for 5 minutes, then whisk until the chocolate has melted and the mixture is smooth; set the chocolate sauce aside.

8. To make a ribbon bow for decorating the bomb, take a 2-inch square of modeling chocolate and knead it between your fingers until it's soft and pliable. Thinly roll it out on a piece of parchment. Cut a rectanglular strip around 4 inches long and bring the ends together to make a ring. Pinch the middle of the ring together where the seam is so you have two loops on either side of a squished center. Cut another rectangular strip around 2 inches long and gently wrap it around the pinched center, leaving the seam in the back.

9. Cut two 3-inch rectangles from the modeling chocolate for the ribbon ends. Cut a triangle into one end of each ribbon, creating the pointy ends. Set the bow and the ribbon ends aside.

10. Assemble the bomb: Heat a skillet until the surface is warm to the touch, then turn the heat off. Carefully touch the domed top of one chocolate half sphere to the surface of the pan to gently melt the bottom. Stick the dome to a serving plate, using the melted chocolate as glue. Fill the half sphere with blueberries and your treat of choice (I find blueberries keep with Melty's color scheme).

11. Gently touch the flat bottom edge of the second half sphere to the warm pan to melt the edge slightly, then carefully place it on top of the upturned half sphere. Use your finger to carefully smooth away any melted chocolate and fill in the seam around the middle of the sphere.

12. Decorate by placing the bow in front of the sphere, using a toothpick to arrange the ribbon ends artfully. Add extra fruit, a smear of jam for color, and any extras to the plate.

13. When ready to serve, reheat the chocolate sauce to 120°F or warmer. Pour it onto the center of the top of the chocolate sphere until the chocolate breaks and the sauce pours inside. At that point, swirl it around a little to melt more of the ball open. You won't need all the sauce and should have some left over . . . unless you want a *very* chocolaty dessert (which, honestly, isn't a bad decision).

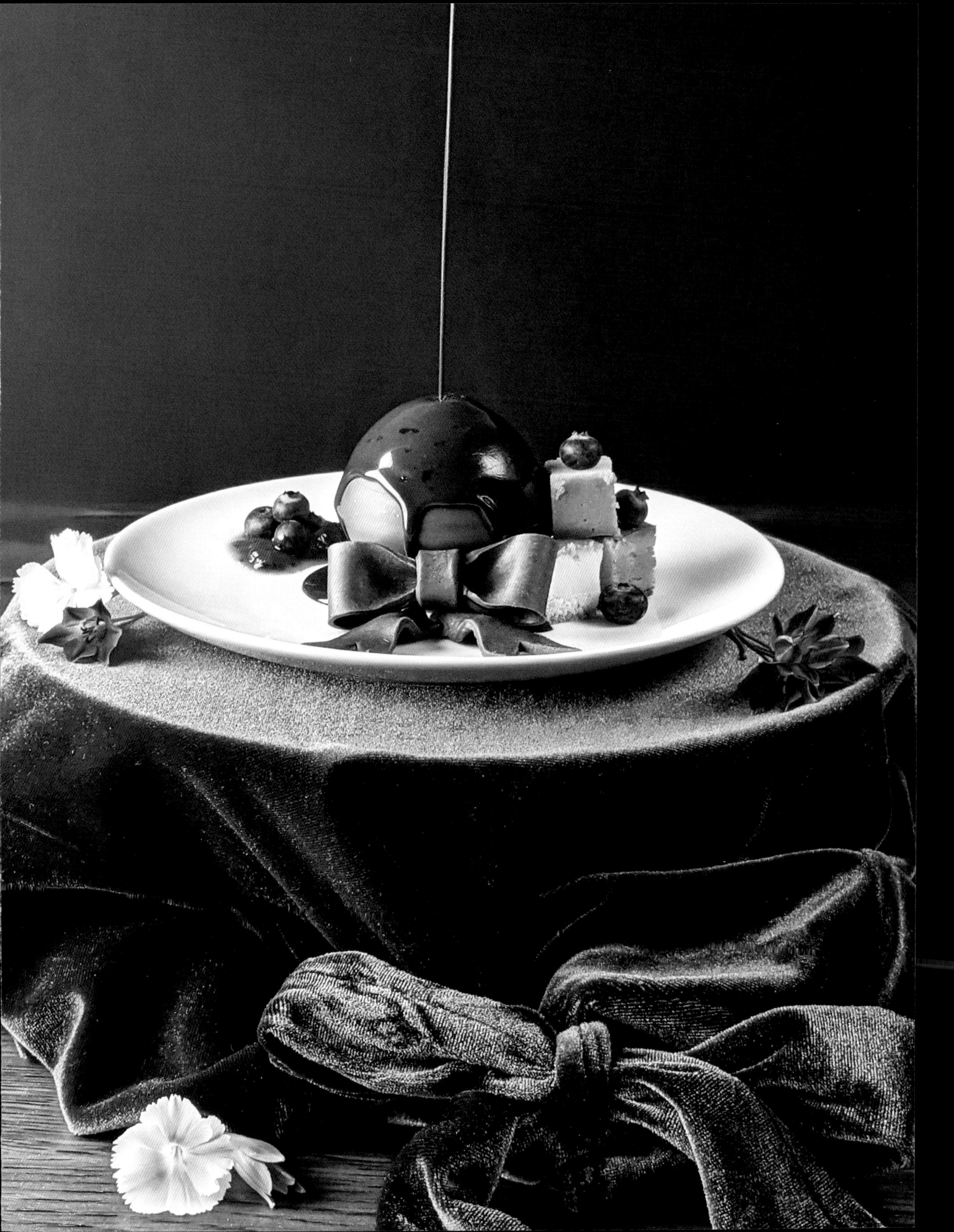

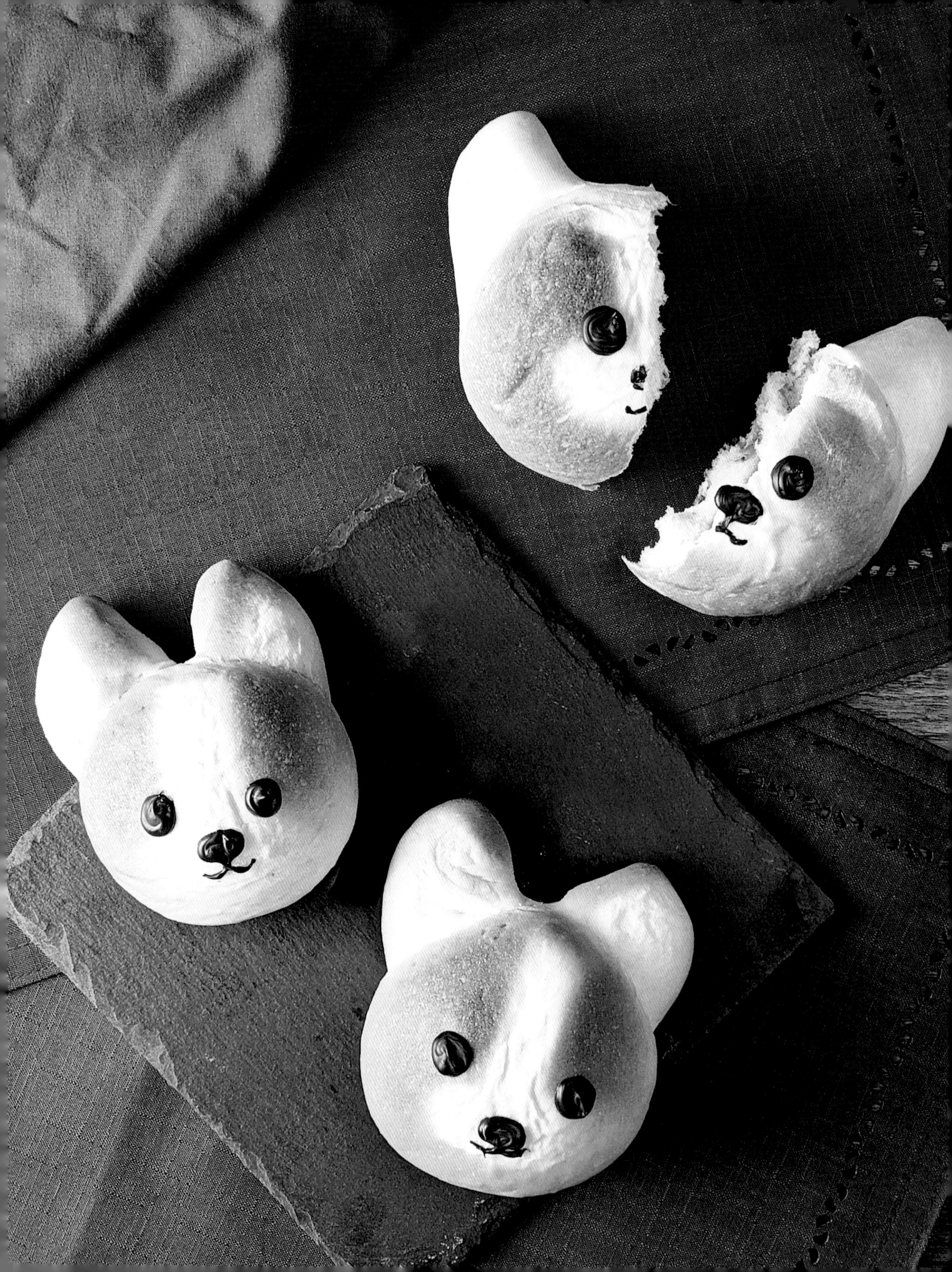

COWBOY BEBOP

CORGI BREAD BUNS

In *Cowboy Bebop*, a great tragedy has befallen Earth and most people have begun living in the solar system. As life has moved to space, so has crime. In order to catch these criminals, the Inter Solar System Police puts out bounties for bounty hunters, or "Cowboys," to collect. The series follows one such bounty hunter, Spike Spiegel, and his crew—Ed, an elite hacker; Faye, a con artist; Jet, a former cop; and Ein, the best corgi in space.

Brought aboard after a bounty gone wrong, Ein is a genius Pembroke Welsh corgi made smarter by a series of science experiments. Ein can perform a number of tasks, such as answering the phone, steering the spaceship, and playing games. These jam-filled bread buns are designed to look like little corgis, and the dough was chosen specifically to be soft, tender, and pillowy, just like a corgi's fur. While these baked "corgis" don't exactly have enhanced brains, they're pretty dang tasty.

3 TO 4 HOURS

MAKES 5 BUNS

NUT-FREE

RECIPE TIP: You can beat an egg yolk and use it to "paint" the darker spots on the corgi faces instead of using the foil. However, this will result in less-pronounced coloring.

FOOD FACT: These buns were inspired by corgi "butt buns" originally conceived by a bakery in Japan—instead of making corgi faces, the bakery makes little corgi bread butts for their hungry customers.

1½ cups bread flour, plus more for dusting

½ cup cake flour

½ cup water

¼ cup sugar

3 tablespoons unsalted butter, at room temperature

3 tablespoons whole milk

1¾ teaspoons instant yeast

1 teaspoon kosher salt

Jam of choice

Handful of semisweet chocolate chips

1. Make the dough: Combine the bread flour, cake flour, water, sugar, butter, milk, yeast, and salt in a bowl. Mix with a spatula to combine until you get a loose dough. Tip the dough out onto a lightly floured counter and knead for 20 minutes; the dough should be sticky, but not so much that it's clinging to everything and needs to be scraped off your hands. (Alternatively, combine the ingredients in the bowl of a stand mixer fitted with the dough hook and mix for 10 minutes.) When the dough is soft and stretchy and passes the windowpane test (see Tip, page 97), it's ready. Place the dough in a clean bowl, add a few drops of water to the inside of the rim, then cover the bowl with plastic wrap. Set somewhere warm until the dough has doubled in size, about 1 hour.

2. Line a baking sheet with parchment paper. Punch the air out of the dough and split it into 5 pieces. Then, split each of those 5 pieces into two smaller balls, one that's a third of the original dough and one that's two-thirds. Working with one at a time, flatten the larger piece of dough into a rough round. Dab 1 tablespoon of the jam into the middle, then bring the edges up around the filling and pinch them together to seal, so you have a round, filled bun—this will be the corgi's head. To form it into a vague triangle (which is the shape of the corgi's face), pinch the dough at one edge of the round together to create sloped sides. The soft point of the triangle should be the lower part of the face. Continue pinching the dough at the back of the bun until you have the desired shape, then place the bun seam side down on the prepared baking sheet. Repeat with the 4 remaining larger pieces of dough.

Continued

3. Shape each smaller piece of dough into a square, then cut it in half diagonally into two triangles for the corgi's ears. Situate these triangles on top of the heads, straight edges inward, sloped edges outward. Use a toothpick to press the dough at the top of the head into the ears.

4. Cover the buns loosely with plastic wrap and set in a warm spot until doubled in size again, around 40 minutes, or until the buns are jiggly when you wiggle the pan.

5. Preheat the oven to 350°F. Cut out pieces of aluminum foil to lay on the buns to help make the color variation. For each head, you need a strip of foil ending in a wide oval (this creates the stripe down the face and the coloring around the nose). For the ears, you need triangles to cover all but the inner edge of the ears.

6. Remove the plastic wrap from the buns and gently position the foil cutouts in the right spots on the corgi faces, then slide the buns into the oven. Bake for 15 minutes, then remove the foil pieces and bake for 5 minutes more. Allow to cool.

7. Put the chocolate chips in a zip-top plastic bag, fill a mug with hot water, and rest the chocolate in the water for 3 to 5 minutes, until melted. Snip the tip off the plastic bag and carefully pipe eyes, noses, and mouths for the corgi faces. Serve and enjoy.

CUTIE HONEY

HONEY HEART TOAST

Honey Kisaragi is a typical high school student: smart, funny . . . and a ROBOT?! She doesn't learn this important fact until *after* her scientist father is kidnapped by the secret organization Panther Claw. She also discovers her father installed a device that allows her to transform matter, which means she can transform herself into a superhero: Cutie Honey. Considered to be one of the earliest magical girl anime, *Cutie Honey* is really unique, especially for the '70s when it first aired.

In honor of Cutie Honey, I made a recipe for honey toast. Honey toast has been a popular snack in Japan for a while. You can fill your honey toast with pretty much anything—there are tons of variations here in Japan—but I went with a red-and-pink heart theme to match Honey's outfit when she transforms. This dessert is best shared with a friend or two—additional points to you if you yell "Honey flash!" during serving.

30 MINUTES

SERVES 1

SPECIAL EQUIPMENT: HEART-SHAPED COOKIE CUTTER

NUT-FREE

4 red Starburst candies

FOR THE GANACHE

¼ cup heavy cream

½ cup semisweet chocolate chips

FOR THE HONEY TOAST

½ loaf unsliced white bread, preferably Japanese shokupan

2 tablespoons honey

1 tablespoon unsalted butter

FOR THE FILLINGS

Handful of cherries, pitted and chopped

Handful of raspberries, chopped

Pocky sticks

Chocolate sauce

Strawberry ice cream

1. Unwrap the Starbursts, place them on a microwave-safe plate, and microwave them for 5 seconds. Test carefully to make sure they're not too hot to handle, then knead the candies together. Thinly roll them out on parchment paper, then use heart cookie cutters to cut out as many hearts as you'd like. Peel away the excess candy, leaving the hearts on the parchment, then set the hearts aside.

2. Make the ganache: Pour the heavy cream into a microwave-safe bowl and microwave until warm, then add the chocolate chips. Let stand for a few minutes, then stir until the chocolate has melted and the mixture becomes a glossy sauce. Place the sauce in the refrigerator to firm

3. Make the honey toast: Preheat the oven to 350°F. Line a baking sheet with parchment paper.

4. Take the half loaf of bread and hollow it out. I like to do this by making cuts into the loaf along the inner walls, leaving a small border of bread to fortify the crust, then scooping out the fluffy white bread from the inside as cleanly as possible and cutting that into cubes.

Continued

RECIPE TIPS:
All toppings and fillings are optional. In keeping with the anime's pink theme, I'd recommend any kind of pink snacks, but it's your decision. Make what you want to eat!

Can't find a block of bread and don't feel like making one? Make individual honey toast slices by toasting bread, brushing it with a combination of melted honey and butter, and decorating each slice with berries, cherries, chocolate sauce, and a mini scoop of ice cream.

FOOD FACT:
Also called "brick toast" or "Shibuya toast," this dessert started out as a popular karaoke snack in the Shibuya area.

5. Combine the honey and butter in a microwave-safe bowl and microwave for 30 seconds. Brush the inside of the bread down with the honey butter, as well as the top rim of the bread. Put the bread cubes in a bowl, drizzle with the remaining honey butter, and toss lightly to coat.

6. Set the hollowed-out bread loaf and the bread cubes on the prepared baking sheet, spreading the cubes out in a single layer, and bake for 10 minutes. Flip the cubes and bake for 5 minutes more, or until everything is toasted and just starting to go golden brown.

7. When the bread is done, allow everything to cool slightly. Decorate the crust of the hollowed-out loaf by pressing the hearts to the front lightly. The stickiness of the candy and the warmth of the bread should work in your favor to attach them, but if you're struggling, glue them on with a little honey or chocolate syrup.

8. Fill the bread with the toasted bread cubes, some cherries and raspberries, and spoonfuls of ganache. Alternate how you layer them so you get a bite of everything each time. Top off with a scoop of ganache, Pocky, more fruit, chocolate sauce, and a few small scoops of ice cream. Serve with extra honey and chocolate sauce.

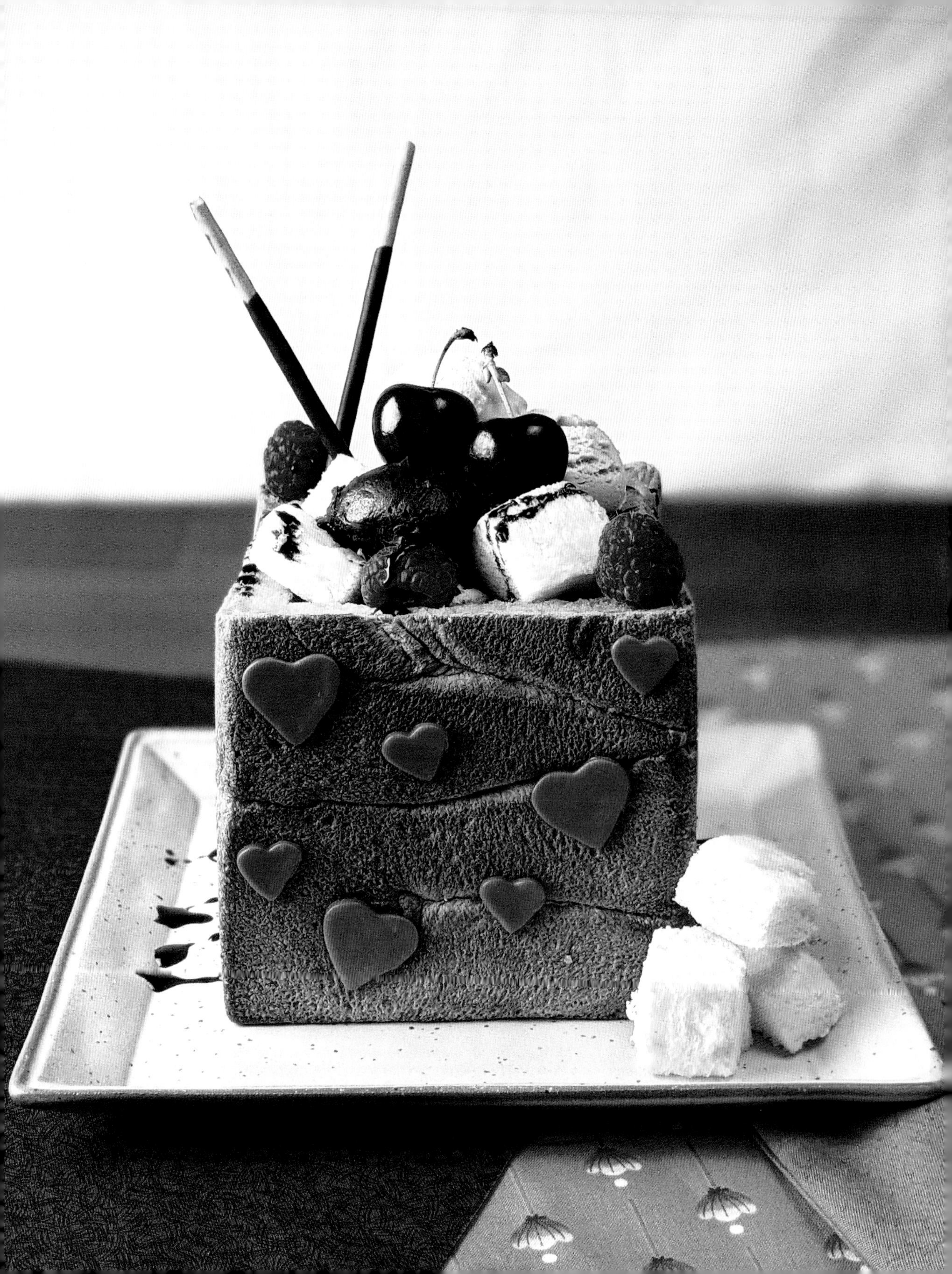

Metric Charts

The recipes that appear in this cookbook use the standard US method for measuring liquid and dry or solid ingredients (teaspoons, tablespoons, and cups). The information on these pages is provided to help cooks outside the United States successfully use these recipes. All equivalents are approximate.

Metric Equivalents for Different Types of Ingredients

A standard cup measure of a dry or solid ingredient will vary in weight depending on the type of ingredient. A standard cup of liquid is the same volume for any type of liquid. Use the following chart when converting standard cup measures to grams (weight) or milliliters (volume).

STANDARD CUP	FINE POWDER (ex. flour)	GRAIN (ex. rice)	GRANULAR (ex. sugar)	LIQUID SOLIDS (ex. butter)	LIQUID (ex. milk)
1	140 g	150 g	190 g	200 g	240 ml
¾	105 g	113 g	143 g	150 g	180 ml
⅔	93 g	100 g	125 g	133 g	160 ml
½	70 g	75 g	95 g	100 g	120 ml
⅓	47 g	50 g	63 g	67 g	80 ml
¼	35 g	38 g	48 g	50 g	60 ml
⅛	18 g	19 g	24 g	25 g	30 ml

Useful Equivalents for Dry Ingredients by Weight

(To convert ounces to grams, multiply the number of ounces by 30.)

OZ	LB	G
1 oz	¹⁄₁₆ lb	30 g
4 oz	¼ lb	120 g
8 oz	½ lb	240 g
12 oz	¾ lb	360 g
16 oz	1 lb	480 g

Useful Equivalents for Length

(To convert inches to centimeters, multiply the number of inches by 2.5.)

IN	FT	YD	CM	M
1 in			2.5 cm	
6 in	½ ft		15 cm	
12 in	1 ft		30 cm	
36 in	3 ft	1 yd	90 cm	
40 in			100 cm	1 m

Useful Equivalents for Liquid Ingredients by Volume

TSP	TBSP	CUPS	FL OZ	ML	L
¼ tsp				1 ml	
½ tsp				2 ml	
1 tsp				5 ml	
3 tsp	1 Tbsp		½ fl oz	15 ml	
	2 Tbsp	⅛ cup	1 fl oz	30 ml	
	4 Tbsp	¼ cup	2 fl oz	60 ml	
	5⅓ Tbsp	⅓ cup	3 fl oz	80 ml	
	8 Tbsp	½ cup	4 fl oz	120 ml	
	10⅔ Tbsp	⅔ cup	5 fl oz	160 ml	
	12 Tbsp	¾ cup	6 fl oz	180 ml	
	16 Tbsp	1 cup	8 fl oz	240 ml	
	1 pt	2 cups	16 fl oz	480 ml	
	1 qt	4 cups	32 fl oz	960 ml	
			33 fl oz	1000 ml	1 L

Useful Equivalents for Cooking/Oven Temperatures

	FAHRENHEIT	CELSIUS	GAS MARK
FREEZE WATER	32°F	0°C	
ROOM TEMPERATURE	68°F	20°C	
BOIL WATER	212°F	100°C	
	325°F	160°C	3
	350°F	180°C	4
	375°F	190°C	5
	400°F	200°C	6
	425°F	220°C	7
	450°F	230°C	8
BROIL		Grill	

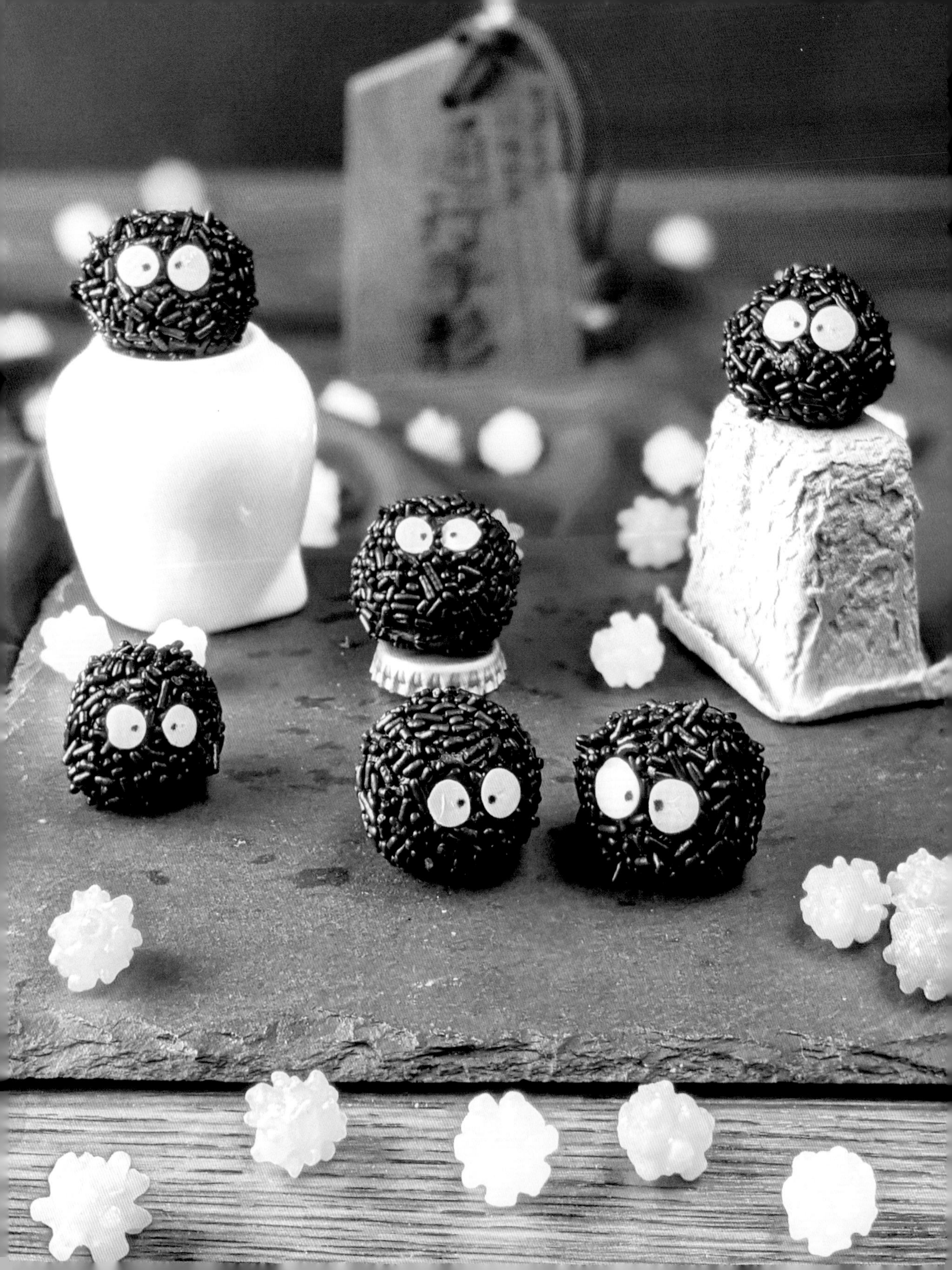

Acknowledgments

First and foremost, a huge thanks to my editor, Tasha Yglesias, who approached me with this project. Tasha, you gave me purpose and a project when I needed one most and helped me sound the best I possibly could. There have been ups and downs with this book, but you've been such a rock through it all. I'm so grateful for the opportunity you and Simon Element gave me to bring my dreams to life. Thank you for your wonderful editing and support.

Big thanks to the support from everyone at Simon Element who helped to shape this cookbook into a real thing of beauty, especially Samantha Lubash and Justin Schwartz—I'm grateful for your expertise and have learned so much.

And I cannot forget to mention the many talented Japanese home cooks and food bloggers who generously share many traditional and modern Japanese recipes and food histories online and in person, in English and in Japanese, so that a foreigner like me with a keen appreciation for Japanese cuisine can learn and take inspiration from them. In particular, the food blog *Just One Cookbook* has been a go-to for brushing up on useful techniques, and my friend Rio helped set me on the right path with Japanese sweets, for which I'm grateful!

I could not have done this without Sarah. For eating my food, giving me photo shoot advice, helping me design character faces, and soooooo much more, from the bottom of my heart, thank you. You are the dearest friend a girl could ask for, and I'm so lucky to have you in my life. When I'm in doubt, your belief in me helps me believe in myself. Also, thanks for saving my life that one time in that Korean restaurant in Tokyo. Really glad I survived thanks to your superior Heimlich skills. Your asking fee wouldn't be enough to cover all you've done for me, even if I could afford it.

All my students who love and support my work are so important to me, but especially Jingu Kim, who helped me with some art for this project. You are so talented—never forget that!

Mom—besides the fact that you taught me how to cook, you also saved my life by sending me some essentials from the States for some of these desserts. This cookbook would not be what it is without you and your care packages (not to mention your sympathetic ear and advice with recipes).

Dad—for always asking the right questions and for encouraging me with your wisdom and positivity. Also, for introducing me to anime (along with KC!). Love you!

Everyone who helped me double-check anime facts and gave me photo reassurance—Natey, Rajan, Rio, Sarah, Lauren, Idy, Lizzy, Bex, Drew, Jack, Hannah S.—thank you for lending me a second set of eyes on this.

For encouraging me to give anime food blogging a try and helping to give me a chance at Crunchyroll way back in 2015—thank you, Miles, for your mentorship! I never thought I'd come this far, but you did. Thanks for always having faith in me. And to Cam, who has worked with me on way too many videos—thanks for always being excited about my ideas.

To everyone who ate my desserts and gave me feedback or praise or advice (or all three!) as I was writing this cookbook: my SMIS lunch gang, my pirate crew—Joe, Kristin, and Hannah S.—and my friends and cooking pals here in Tokyo. You're the best, and your encouragement really kept me going.

Finally, to all my longtime fans and supporters, online and in person—you've pulled me through some hard times in my life with your curiosity and interest in what I'm making online. Thank you always for your support and kind words!

Recipe Index

D

H

I

J

K

L

M

T

U

V

W

Z

Anime Index

A

B

C

F

E

F

G

O

P

Q

R

S

T

About the Author

EMILY BUSHMAN is a self-taught cook and baker who started her blog, *Penguin Snacks*, about food in anime in 2015. Born and raised in Fresno, California, she grew up reading manga and watching anime with her friends, and by the time she was in college she was helping to host full-blown anime conventions. A high school English teacher by day, Emily began her blog as a way to spend more time on her cooking hobby and to keep in touch with her anime roots. The blog has since grown into a career working on video creation for the likes of anime streaming platform Crunchyroll and for beloved franchises like *Naruto, One Piece, Food Wars!: Shokugeki no Soma, Jujutsu Kaisen,* and more. She currently lives, works, and bakes in a small apartment (with an even smaller kitchen) in Tokyo, Japan.